# Contemporary Canadian Women's Fiction

# CONTEMPORARY CANADIAN WOMEN'S FICTION
## REFIGURING IDENTITIES

CORAL ANN HOWELLS

CONTEMPORARY CANADIAN WOMEN'S FICTION
© Coral Ann Howells, 2003.

First published 2003 by
PALGRAVE MACMILLAN™
175 Fifth Avenue, New York, N.Y. 10010 and
Houndmills, Basingstoke, Hampshire, England RG21 6XS.
Companies and representatives throughout the world.

PALGRAVE MACMILLAN is the global academic imprint of the Palgrave Macmillan division of St. Martin's Press, LLC and of Palgrave Macmillan Ltd. Macmillan® is a registered trademark in the United States, United Kingdom and other countries. Palgrave is a registered trademark in the European Union and other countries.

ISBN 0–312–23900–9 hardback

Library of Congress Cataloging-in-Publication Data

Howells, Coral Ann.
    Contemporary Canadian women's fiction : refiguring identities / by Coral Ann Howells.
        p. cm.
    Includes bibliographical references and index.
    ISBN 0–312–23900–9 (alk. paper)
        1. Canadian fiction—Women authors—History and criticism.
    2. Women and literature—Canada—History—20th century.
    3. Canadian fiction—20th century—History and criticism.
    4. Identity (Psychology) in literature. 5. Group identity in literature. I. Title.

    PR91888.H67 2003
    813'.540353—dc21                                        2003048676

A catalogue record for this book is available from the British Library.

Design by Newgen Imaging Systems (P) Ltd., Chennai, India.

First edition: August, 2003
10  9  8  7  6  5  4  3  2  1

Printed in the United States of America.

For Robin, Phoebe, and Miranda, as always

# TABLE OF CONTENTS

# ACKNOWLEDGMENTS

In writing a book like this, which moves across different cultures in its attempt to represent the multiple traditions embodied in contemporary Canadian identities and English-Canadian fiction, I have been very lucky in the help I have received from so many people. Since 1997 when I began to think about this project in earnest, my ideas have evolved not only through the numerous seminars, lectures, and conference papers I have given, but also through the comments both encouraging and challenging that I have received. I am particularly grateful to the following persons for inviting me to speak on different aspects of my topic at their conferences over the past few years: Pilar Somacarrera at the Universidad Autonoma de Madrid; Danielle Fuller at the University of Birmingham; Maria-Teresa Chialant at the University of Salerno where I also benefited greatly from discussions with Laura di Michele on monstrosity; Conny Steenman-Marcusse at the University of Leiden; Marc Maufort at the Université Libre de Bruxelles, and Ruth Blair at the University of Queensland. The late Catherine Bélanger and her colleagues at the Department of Canadian Heritage in Ottawa have been unfailingly generous in helping me to clarify my understanding of the workings of Canada's Multiculturalism Policy, and I owe them many thanks. I am grateful to the Arts and Humanities Research Board and the University of Reading for funding my research leave award that facilitated the completion of this book and to the Foundation for Canadian Studies in the United Kingdom and my university's Research Board for travel assistance on my research and conference visits.

Many friends and colleagues have generously encouraged and advised me. My special thanks yet again to Paula and Larry Bourne in Toronto and to Linda and Leslie Marshall in Guelph for their hospitality and their kindness in keeping me supplied with books and newspaper clippings throughout this project; to my former student Claire Uchida who now lives in Kagawa for her assistance in understanding the Japanese cultural framework in Kerri Sakamoto's novel; to Peter Jefferys who gave me the benefit of his professional expertise on Alzheimer's

Disease; to my colleagues on the editorial board of the *International Journal of Canadian Studies* and especially to Editor in Chief Robert S. Schwartzwald, to Susan Billingham, Faye Hammill, and Heidi MacPherson of the Literature Group of the British Association for Canadian Studies, to Michael Hellyer of Academic Relations at the Canadian High Commission in London, and to Lorna Hawthorne and Rowan Hopkins for their website research on the sasquatch. I would like thank the students in the postgraduate seminar on Canadian women's writing at the Universidad Autonoma de Madrid in 2001, and (closer to home) to thank my colleagues at the University of Reading, especially Madeleine Davies, and students on my Canadian Women's Fiction classes, particularly Sarah Parrish and Cherry Williams in the class of 2001–2002 who helped to clarify my ideas in the final stages of revision for this book. I am also extremely grateful to Jan Cox of the School of English and American Literature at the University of Reading for her excellent help in preparing my typescript, and to my editors at Palgrave/St. Martin's for all their assistance. Finally, my best thanks as always to my husband Robin and my daughters Phoebe and Miranda.

To keep the record straight, earlier partial versions of the following chapters have appeared in print: parts of chapter 2 as "Margaret Atwood's Discourse of Nation and National Identity in the 1990s" in *The Rhetoric of Canadian Writing*, edited by Conny Steenman-Marcusse (Amsterdam and New York: Rodopi, 2002), 199–216; part of chapter 6 as "Globalization and Its Discontents: 'The Age of Lead' and *The Electrical Field*" in *College English* (Union Christian College, Alwaye, Kerala) 3.4 (1999): 11–14; parts of chapter 8 as "Towards a Recognition of Being: Tomson Highway's *Kiss of the Fur Queen* and Eden Robinson's *Monkey Beach*" in *Revista Canaria de Estudios Ingleses* 43 (November 2001): 145–59; the title of chapter 3 I have borrowed from my essay published in *British Journal of Canadian Studies* 14.1 (1999). Thanks are due to the original publishers for permission to reprint in part those materials here.

# INTRODUCTION

This book is designed to chart significant changes that have taken place in Canada's literary profile since the early 1990s, as it is figured through women's fiction written in English. As a reader and critic working outside Canada, I have been impressed by two remarkable phenomena during this period. One is the increasingly familiar presence of Canadian women's fiction on international publishers' lists together with the high visibility of Canadian women writers as winners of international literary prizes, and the other is the substantially growing number of novels by women from diverse ethnic and racial backgrounds, who make the traditional image of "white" Canada look rather outdated. Clearly, the concept of Canadianness has changed, and it is in response to these changes that I want to explore how women's voices contribute to some of the issues within Canadian debates about identity. I shall consider how some significant contemporary novels written by women from a variety of ethnocultural perspectives refigure the nation and questions of national identity, opening up spaces for a revised rhetoric of Canadianness. Of course national affiliation is only one component of identity construction, and indeed it may not always be the most crucial in comparison with other identificatory markers like race and ethnicity, gender and sexuality, or education and social class. I shall pay attention to the ways that individual writers represent these intertwined affiliations, as their fictions offer different answers to the questions: Who am I? and Where do I belong?

Though multiculturalism as coded into the *Canadian Multiculturalism Act* of 1988 has been a major factor for making Canadians and non-Canadians think again about what being Canadian means, this is not a book that focuses primarily on ethnic and minority fiction.[1] What I offer is an analysis of a representative range of nine women's novels and one short-story collection in English, all published since the mid-1990s, through which to explore the complexities of identity construction, investigating continuities and differences of emphasis from one text to another. This is an anglophone perspective, which leaves out the different inflections of francophone Quebec women's experience.[2] Beginning with Margaret Atwood, Alice Munro, and Carol Shields, who are the most widely read Canadian women writers outside Canada, I shall go on to present a constellation of younger writers whose novels have gained wide international visibility: Ann-Marie MacDonald, Kerri Sakamoto, Shani Mootoo, Gail Anderson Dargatz, and Eden Robinson.

Multiculturalism, feminism, and nationalism in the postcolonial context are the key concepts debated in this study, though those topics are given very different inflections in this deliberately diverse selection of texts. The emphasis will often fall on women's counter-narratives to discourses of patriarchal authority in the home, the importance of maternal inheritance, and women's revisions of traditional narrative genres, which they reshape for their own purposes. All these writers are engaged in writing and rewriting history across generations and frequently across countries and cultures, all of them uncover secrets hidden in the past, so that storytelling becomes an agent of confession or exorcism and possibly of regeneration. Arguably these novels are symptomatic of a larger process beyond their domestic plots, representing a nation in the process of unearthing deliberately forgotten secrets and scandals, as they share in the enterprise of telling stories that recognize the differences concealed within constructions of identity in contemporary multicultural Canada. What is more, all of them register that "slippage in the bedrock" of Anglo-Canadian myths of identity, which Margaret Atwood signaled at the beginning of the 1990s with her ambiguously titled short-story collection *Wilderness Tips* (1991).

When it comes to questions of refiguring identity, inevitably different novelists follow different agendas, depending on a range of factors. There is always the gender issue that conditions women's relation to culture and history, but there are often powerful issues of ethnicity and race, sexuality, immigrancy, expatriatism, or indigeneity, through which identities are constructed and reconstructed. All these writers raise the question of how much of anyone's identity is authentic and dependent on inheritance, and how much it is performative, subject to circumstances, and so redefinable in different contexts. As the black British critic Stuart Hall says: "Identities are the names we give to the different ways we are positioned by, and position ourselves within, the narratives of the past"—and I would add, within narratives of the present as well.[3]

Where are the women's voices in my book coming from, in these stories from across Canada east to west? Specificities of location are important, for though biographical data is sometimes regarded as reductive or as the kind of marginal information provided in publishers' blurbs and author interviews, its significance is not entirely extratextual. Many of these texts explore representations of cultural and racial difference together with "the extreme difficulty of having to negotiate everything through race, gender and ethnicity,"[4] so that it forms a significant element not only in the creative process but also in the reader's responses to the texts. Moreover, it would seem wise to dispel misconceptions about Canada's national self-image as one of uniformity and cohesiveness, just as one would wish to avoid the scandal of generalizing visible minority writers as "others." The writer's signature is on the text if only we can learn to read it, for as Atwood remarked of her historical novel *Alias Grace*, "We have to write out of who and when and where we are, whether we like it or not, and disguise it how we may."[5] So, some brief biographical information about these writers is given here, beginning with Margaret Atwood, Canada's most famous novelist. An Anglo-Canadian and a descendant of Empire Loyalists who fled the United States for Nova Scotia, she was born in Ottawa and has lived in Toronto for many years. As an international literary star she travels extensively on publicity tours for every new novel and to give readings and lectures. Alice Munro, a descendant of nineteenth-century Scottish settlers to rural Southwestern Ontario, was brought up in that area and still lives part of the year in a small town there and the rest of the time in British Columbia. Her local connections were publicly celebrated on her seventy-first birthday in the summer of 2002 by the opening of the Alice Munro Literary Park in her hometown of Wingham. Carol Shields, born and brought up in Oak Park, Illinois, moved to Canada in the late 1950s after her marriage to a Canadian whom she had met on a student exchange in Exeter, England; after living in Winnipeg for many years, she now lives in British Columbia. Ann-Marie MacDonald, who lives in Toronto, was born on a Royal Canadian Air Force base in Germany, the daughter of parents from Cape Breton Island, Nova Scotia; her father's family is Scottish and her mother's Lebanese. Kerri Sakamoto is Sansei, a third-generation Japanese Canadian, the child of parents who were interned in Canada during World War II; she grew up in Toronto and then spent seven years in New York before returning to Toronto, where she now lives. Shani Mootoo, born in Ireland and raised in Trinidad, immigrated to Canada at the age of nineteen; she now lives in Vancouver. Gail Anderson-Dargatz was born in rural British Columbia, the descendant of a white pioneering family in the Rockies, who having farmed with her husband in Alberta now lives on Vancouver Island. Eden Robinson is an Aboriginal writer belonging to the Haisla nation who grew up on the Kiamaat Reserve on the northwest coast of British Columbia; a graduate from the famous creative writing program at the University of British Columbia, she now lives in Vancouver. While it may be useful to know these bare essentials, it is also evident that such facts do not tell us much about the subjective identities of these writers nor about the identities of their fictional characters. (What relative significance, for example, would each of them attribute to sociological factors such as race, age, sexuality, education, family background, to locality, to dislocations and relocations in the construction of their identities?) Their fictions are in no sense autobiographical texts, though the "composite genealogies of the self," to use Smaro Kamboureli's excellent phrase,[6] inevitably shape the positions from which these novelists write. One further comment would seem to be in order here, this time from a European critic speaking about refiguring identities in a broadly North American context: "Positions are needed in order to claim that they are not stable; some idea of identity or literary tradition is needed in order to begin to work cross-culturally."[7]

A sketch of chapter arrangements will indicate the context for my narrative and cultural analysis of the variety of positions from which these selected storytellers renegotiate questions of identity. Chapter 1 outlines the parameters, where I discuss the changing discourses of nationhood, heritage, and identity in Canada over the past two decades. My main interest is in how English-Canadian literary and cultural traditions have shown obvious signs of becoming destabilized during the 1990s, in what might now be seen as a necessary process of refiguring multicultural Canada in a very different mode from the cultural nationalism of the 1960s and 1970s. Increasingly, creative writers, literary critics, and cultural theorists have been debating what Homi Bhabha has called "the disjunctive forms of representation that signify a people, a nation, or a national culture."[8] True, there *has* been a slippage in the bedrock, as I shall show through my examination of a number of key texts of Anglo-Canadian literary and cultural criticism from the early 1990s, which signal crucial stages in the process of refiguring what Canadianness means. It was Barbara Godard in her interrogative essay "Canadian? Literary? Theory?" (1992) who trenchantly formulated the challenge: "What 'Canadian' means in literary terms is a question that needs to be addressed if only to rephrase it as a problem in the meaning of 'national' as it operates in literary discourse."[9] Since then, that question has been repeatedly addressed by critics and indeed it is possible just by looking at the titles of some of these studies to gain a sense not only of the shifts of emphasis in the debate but also to perceive how emotionally charged the issues around nationality and identity can become. W.H. New's *Land Sliding: Imagining Space, Presence, and Power in Canadian Writing* (1997) and Jonathan Kertzer's *Worrying the Nation: Imagining a National Literature in English Canada* (1998) are cases in point. Kertzer's book appeared in the same year as Arun Mukherjee's *Postcolonialism: My Living* (1998), a collection of essays that is a turning point in the radical interrogation of the Canadian literary canon. By 2000 those accumulating signs of slippage began to look like a landslide, as the balance tipped from Anglo-Canadian critics' anxieties about accommodating "other" voices toward a sharp focus on the writing of those others, through new studies by diasporic critics like Smaro Kamboureli and Himani Bannerji. The landslide has continued, with Helen Hoy's *How Should I Read These? Native Women Writers in Canada* (2001) and Robert Wright's *Hip and Trivial: Youth Culture, Book Publishing, and the Greying of Canadian Nationalism* (2001). Wright's answer to the question Godard asked ten years ago is this: "In a postmodern, globalized world of seemingly infinite choice, the idea of *the national* as the defining element in Canadian Lit appears to have had its day."[10]

So it is all the more surprising to find Wright quoting the following accolade from Russell Smith, one of Toronto's new urban novelists: "But I would also say that one of the hippest writers in Canada, who knows a great deal about contemporary urban life, modern sexual relations, trends and mass culture, and who always writes in a humorously satiric way, is Margaret Atwood" (p. 153). Is that so surprising really? What "hip" writer was it who warned that the national icon of Canadian wilderness landscape was becoming outdated back in the early 1990s? Who wrote a prose poem in 1992 in which the following complaint is heard: "Forest? Forest is *passé*, I mean, I've had it with all this wilderness stuff. It's not a right image of our society today. Let's have some *urban* for a change"?[11] That voice is Margaret Atwood's, and it is with Atwood's ongoing inquiry into Canadian discourses of nationalism and identity that I begin my narrative analyses in chapter 2, where I discuss her two recent novels *Alias Grace* and *The Blind Assassin*. Whether she looks into nineteenth-century colonial history or the history of English Canada in the twentieth century, Atwood suggests that history is "not as we learned it in school."[12] Addressing official Canadian history through the voices of the marginalized—women, working-class underprivileged immigrants from Ireland or Eastern Europe, criminals or suspect criminals (and these categories are, needless to say, not exclusive), Atwood's fiction unearths secrets and scandals that have been carefully hidden away and forgotten. Arguably both these novels might be read as sociohistorical projects masquerading as women's fictive autobiographies. Alice Munro is also concerned with the secrets of history, though hers unlike Atwood's are private histories and their resonance sounds in the subjective lives of her protagonists, where identities are reinvented and narratives of the past are reshaped to reveal hidden meanings long after the events have happened. In chapter 3, I discuss what I have called Munro's "intimate dislocations" of identity in her most recent short-story collection, which explores secret spaces within her familiar home territory of smalltown Ontario and the fracture lines that split open to reveal secret alternative histories within the life stories of her female protagonists. Chapter 4 discusses Carol Shields's radical critique of essentialist concepts of identity in *The Stone Diaries* and *Larry's Party*, for Shields uses fictive biography and autobiography to question the very notion of identity and its representations. Writing about the "accidental lives" of decentered subjects in narratives that move easily across the borders from Canada to the United States and back again, she refuses to believe in either gender or nationality as foundational fictions for the self. Instead she adopts a postmodern performative concept of identity as shifting, relational, and subject to endless refigurings, in hybridized fictional forms that "break open the phantom set of rules about how stories should be shaped."[13] In fact, Shields is more interested in constructions of gender than in national identities, about which she ironized as early as her first novel *Small Ceremonies* back in 1976 where a popular Canadian male prairie novelist turns out to be an American draft dodger from Maple Bluffs, Iowa, who took up residence in Saskatchewan.

Ann-Marie MacDonald's *Fall on Your Knees*, which I discuss in chapter 5, is a neo-Gothic Maritime novel where issues of identity are enormously complicated by mixed race relationships, transnational affiliations, and transgressive sexualities that are hidden away in the "locked box of our inheritance" or erased from the family tree. In this family saga patriarchal obsessions with genealogy are continually subverted by the stories of rebellious daughters, and the novel ends far from Nova Scotia in New York City where "the ocean finally gives up her dead" in true Maritime literary fashion. Stories of origin are exposed as myths of origin through women's storytelling and set out on a revised version of the family tree where identities are refigured and missing links are restored. MacDonald's novel resists myths of racial purity in a narrative that reveals how identities within the spaces of the family and the nation become hybridized over time as part of the ongoing process of social history. By contrast, Kerri Sakamoto's *The Electrical Field* in chapter 6 takes as its subject the traumatized identities of the generation of Japanese Canadians who suffered internment during World War II. As historical fiction set in the 1970s long before the Redress Settlement of the late 1980s, this novel is dominated by images of paralysis and betrayal as the psychological legacy of that experience. Sakamoto's alienated protagonists have no sense of being Canadian as they cling to a Japanese cultural identity from which they are already displaced by their Canadian birth. Looking back, Sakamoto sees such haunted identities as forms of entrapment, and her novel reads like an exorcism as the narrator struggles to break through the uncanny shadows of the past.

Unlike the other texts I discuss, Shani Mootoo's *Cereus Blooms at Night* in chapter 7 does not have a Canadian frame of geographical or historical reference at all but is set on a fictive Caribbean island. As a novel by an immigrant writer about the history of another country (and there are many examples in recent fiction published in Canada, by Dionne Brand, Shauna Singh Baldwin, Michael Ondaatje, and Rohinton Mistry, to name but a few) it raises interesting questions about the way in which definitions of Canadian identity and traditions of Canadian literature are currently under revision. Certainly it is a warning against the assumption that being Canadian means being Canadian born, white, and heterosexual, just as it exemplifies a national identity that can accommodate multiple cultural affiliations. In her fiction as in her poetry, which I shall also discuss briefly, Mootoo writes about liminal identities positioned on the margins or between worlds. Such issues relate not only to the immigrant condition but also to sexual and racial politics and the legacy of colonialism, figured here in a narrative that shifts between reality, fantasy, and dream in the mode of magic realism.

Of course the condition of liminality and culturally hybridized identities are not exclusive to immigrant fictions, as my discussion in chapters 8 and 9 of two Canadian wilderness novels will show. Both these novels set in rural British Columbia are borderline fictions that represent the ambiguous positions of their adolescent female narrators, one white and one Native, each of whom is situated on the edge of the other's culture. For the white protagonist in *The Cure for Death by Lightning* the wilderness is a dangerous place haunted by the legendary Native Trickster Coyote, who becomes the means of figuring her own traumatic sexual fears, while Robinson's Haisla protagonist in *Monkey Beach* has an entirely different imaginative apprehension of the natural world focused through the elusive figure of the sasquatch, wild man of the woods.

Both narratives are pervaded by anxiety, but whereas the focus of the white girl's story is on avoidance and escape, Robinson's narrator is searching for something that is lost in the wilderness landscape as her story becomes a quest to retrieve her Aboriginal identity through dismembered almost forgotten traditions. These two novels speak out of different cultural heritages—one in a revision of traditional pioneer women's wilderness narratives as it speculates on the possibility of a racially mixed Canadian inheritance recognizing the presence of Aboriginal people and Native spiritual values missing from white society, and the other deriving from traditions of Native oral storytelling in a fictional form that is inevitably hybridized by white education in English and Western print culture. Though both Dargatz's and Robinson's narrators strive to move beyond the divisive heritage of colonialism in their redefinitions of postcolonial feminine identities, their narratives offer two very different cultural lenses for understanding the relation between human beings and the wilderness environment in contemporary Canada.

Such heterogeneous representations of identity in these contemporary fictions would seem to throw the reader back to Godard's questions of how to define "Canadian" in literary discourse. Yet they also provide a sketch for the future where multiculturalism, itself an evolving concept, looks like the transformation mechanism through which the terms for social relations and national identity will be reinterpreted. As well as policies and ideologies however, any society needs models through which to imagine redefinitions and possible futures, and this is where the role of fiction is so important. Believing as I do that fiction shows how individuals and communities articulate their identities through their cultural self-awareness, I am arguing for the significance of women writers as the unofficial negotiators of change and for women's fiction as an index of crises and shifts in Canada's evolving narrative of nationhood.

# CHAPTER 1
## REFIGURING IDENTITIES

Since Laura is no longer who you thought she was, you're no longer who you think you are, either. That can be a shock, but it can also be a relief . . . You're free to reinvent yourself at will.

(Margaret Atwood, *The Blind Assassin*)[1]

She loves her daughter-in-law, would you believe? And her five grandchildren who are only each perfect. They speak French at home, English at school and Yiddish with every second shopkeeper. Real Canadians.

(Ann-Marie Macdonald, *Fall on Your Knees*)[2]

But being "just Canadian" is a privilege only white people enjoy in this country . . . I doubt that I will ever become "just Canadian," whatever that means.

(Arun Mukherjee, "The 'Race Consciousness' of a South Asian")[3]

I begin my study of contemporary English Canadian literary traditions and questions of cultural and national identity as they are being refigured through women's fiction since the mid-1990s with this assemblage of three different women's perspectives on identity construction. They would seem to be emblematic of the multivoiced narrative of Canadianness at the present time, where all the speakers appear to be looking in different directions. Margaret Atwood speaks out of a white Anglo-Canadian context in a radical questioning of traditional narratives of origin and heritage; Ann-Marie MacDonald's old German Jewish immigrant to Nova Scotia contemplates the multiple identities so easily assumed by her grandchildren who live in Montreal where her son is married to a Roman Catholic Quebecoise; Arun Mukherjee speaks as a South Asian academic who came to Canada in the early 1970s about her experiences as a non-white woman in a smilingly racist society where a national identity is so elusive that it is not recognizable to someone living there. Yet these different perspectives converge at a very significant point, for they all challenge traditional nationalist approaches to the definition of what "being Canadian" means. All of them signal an urgent need to interrogate cultural conventions around private and public formulations of identity at the same time as they represent the formidable individual complexities within the multicultural nation-space of contemporary Canada. English Canadians would seem to be experiencing a pluralized present moment when myths of nationhood and the rhetoric of national identity are under reconstruction. How this situation arose, what the key stages have been in a gradually accelerating revisionary process, and what contribution cultural criticism and women's literary texts are making to this process of reimagining Canadianness, are the major topics that I address in this book.

From my perspective as an interested outsider, what makes Canada so distinctive in its representations of postcolonial nationhood is its official commitment to the ideology of multiculturalism. Canada was the first country in the world to introduce an official Multiculturalism Policy back in 1971 under Prime Minister Pierre Trudeau, and this was codified into the *Canadian Multiculturalism Act* of 1988, the first clause of which is as follows:

> It is hereby declared to be the policy of the Government of Canada to (a) recognize and promote the understanding that multiculturalism reflects the cultural and racial diversity of Canadian society and acknowledges the freedom of all members of Canadian society to preserve, enhance and share their cultural heritage.[4]

"Multicultural Canada" represents a radical revision of the country's colonial image as a dominantly white English- and French-speaking nation, and not surprisingly multiculturalism as concept and social policy has generated much vigorous debate and savage critique—not only from right-wing white traditionalists but also from Quebec and Aboriginal people as well as from ethnic and racial minorities.[5] (It is also worth remembering the warning given by an American academic: "If multiculturalism simply means a belief in the autonomy and integrity of distinct cultures, then it can be put to the service of very different political agendas.")[6] During the past ten years it has been a fascinating spectacle to witness Canada's discourse of national identity being rewritten as creative writers, cultural theorists, historians, and literary critics have responded to a revised official rhetoric of nationhood. In this same period the profile of English-Canadian literary production has changed remarkably, featuring an increasing number of writers from diverse ethnic and racial backgrounds, both immigrant and indigenous, whose voices challenge the traditional definitions of what being Canadian means and what constitutes Canadian literature. In 1995, Arun Mukherjee commented on what she saw as the continuing dominance of white cultural nationalism in the English-Canadian literary canon, which promoted "the settler-colonial view of Canada" and "environmentalist explanations of a Canadian identity," arguing that although those views had been frequently challenged, "they have not been replaced yet by more inclusive theories of Canada and Canadian literature . . . we do not hear any concerted responses to what Aboriginals and racial minority writers tell us about Canada and Canadian literature."[7] Ironically, Mukherjee was making this complaint at the very point in time when I locate the beginnings of a shift and the introduction of new cultural coordinates into the mapping of Canadian literary traditions, as fictions by ethnic and racial minority writers come increasingly into visibility. Certainly Mukherjee is right when she asserts that prior to the 1990s there were only a handful of racial minority writers in the Canadian literary canon; the Japanese Canadian Joy Kogawa and Michael Ondaatje (born in Sri Lanka, educated in Britain and an immigrant to Canada in 1962) are among the few well-known names before that time.[8] However, the revisionary impulse has become a full-scale project for redefinition, and I would argue that the policies relating to multiculturalism have been a major force in transforming Canada's discourse of nationhood and identity.

Though my major concern is with contemporary women's fiction, I should like to begin by glancing back at the history of Canada's nation building, emblematized by its official motto, *A mari usque ad mare* ("From sea to sea"), a proud claim to national unity across the vastness of the North American continent. That motto, which codes in the strong spatial elements in Canada's national rhetoric, was incorporated in the coat of arms in 1921, though it was apparently formulated back in the days before the Dominion of Canada even came into existence in 1867, when the term "Dominion" (instead of "Kingdom") was decided upon and derived as tradition has it from Psalm 72:8, when David prayed that Solomon "shall have dominion also from sea to sea, and from the river unto the ends of the earth."[9] It looks very like the expression of a nation builder's fantasy of transcontinental unity, or as Canadian critic Gerald Lynch recently described it, "a kind of geo-political fictional linkage of abiding bonds and creative gaps as opposed to the continuous totalizing story written *E Pluribus Unum*."[10] The historical struggles to achieve national unity and the current pressures internal and external on maintaining Canada as a unified nation constitute the public political context within which my narrative is situated.[11] However, the focus of this study is set at an oblique angle to official history, being concerned with what resonance these wider political questions have in relation to cultural and literary discourse and to women's fiction in particular.

Returning to the spatial metaphor, I shall adopt (and adapt) Homi Bhabha's dynamic concept of the "nation-space" where any discourse of nation:

> investigates the nation-space in the *process* of the articulation of elements: where meanings may be partial because they are *in medias res*; and history may be half-made because it is in the process of being made; and the image of cultural authority may be ambivalent because it is caught, uncertainly, in the act of "composing" its powerful image.[12]

That concept of a textual space where competing voices insistently articulate differences has its close parallel in the sociocultural space of Canada, though as a theoretical formulation it inevitably glosses over the day-to-day experiences of Canada's individual inhabitants with their own subjectivities and cultural histories. How do we encounter the nation as it is being written/rewritten by literary critics and cultural historians since the early 1990s? To chart a direction through the wide diversity of opinions on this topic, I have chosen to look at a selection of texts that register crisis points in the recent refiguring of English Canadian literary tradition. These contribute a range of responses to those wider political processes and ideological shifts that have characterized postcolonial Canadian society. Of course "where to start is the problem, because nothing begins when it begins and nothing's over when it's over, and everything needs a preface; a preface, a postscript, a chart of simultaneous events. History is a construct."[13] Bearing that in mind, I shall plunge in at a specific point, marked perhaps arbitrarily by Atwood's warning in *Wilderness Tips* (1991) about that "slippage in the bedrock" of Anglo-Canadian myths of national identity, built on the historical base of a white settler society and strengthened by the vigorous propagandizing of Canadian cultural nationalism of the 1960s and 1970s. However, since then many changes have intervened on both national and international levels, and by the 1990s that national narrative once again showed signs of needing to be revised in order to accommodate the "fractious politics" and demographic realities of an increasingly urbanized multicultural society, which is also one of the rich G7 nations in the globalized community.[14]

In 1992 Barbara Godard's essay "Canadian? Literary? Theory?"[15] began the interrogation in earnest with her radical analysis of the theoretical underpinnings of Canadian Literature, which had become institutionalized as an academic discipline in the late 1960s and 1970s as the product of a newly emergent cultural nationalism. In her highly theoretical essay Godard makes some devastatingly practical points about the critical fictions on which a national literature is based:

> The terms "Canadian literature" or "theory" are not embodied in the texts or authors themselves but are invested by institutionalized reading practices and their narratives of legitimation . . . Without some form of nationalism, the textual system of the Literary would not overlap with the textual system of the Canadian. (p. 9)

In other words, a political imperative overdetermines what constitutes a national literature, dictating what is included and what is excluded. Of particular importance to my argument are Godard's comments on the ways in which feminist critics were already problematizing fictions of national identity by introducing questions of gender and racial difference that "expose the conflictual social relations underlying the articulation of the codes of nationalism, gender, race operative in the constructions of a Canadian literary discourse" (p. 20). Those uncomfortable questions set out in Godard's groundbreaking essay have continued to resonate in Canadian literary debates ever since, though with different emphases depending on what any particular critic believes is most crucially at stake.

Frank Davey's *Post-National Arguments: The Politics of the Anglo-Canadian Novel since 1967* (1993)[16] takes the cultural debate into the territory of Canadian fiction in his analysis of sixteen novels, which include Japanese Canadian Joy Kogawa's *Obasan* (1981) and Aboriginal writer Jeannette Armstrong's *Slash* (1985). Davey makes the disturbing claim (or disturbing for those who seek an assertive Canadian identity in its fiction) that he fails to discern strong signs of nationalist commitment, arguing that these have been displaced by signs of individual estrangement and internationalism where the nation does not figure as a significant presence between the "local" and the "global." He reaches the sobering and somewhat polemical conclusion that any sense of a collective national consciousness has vanished from Canadian fiction of the 1970s and 1980s, and that instead it announces "the arrival of the post-national state—a state invisible to its own citizens, indistinguishable from its fellows, maintained by invisible political forces, and significant mainly through its position within the grid of world-class postcard cities" (p. 266). The book ends as a lament for a lost sense of community. We may ask whether the situation looks any different when viewed from a transatlantic perspective. Lynette Hunter, writing as an academic in Britain in *Outsider Notes* (1996),[17] analyses what she calls the "personal and public negotiations" by which writers resist the very nation-state ideology that has supported publishing and writing in Canada between the 1960s and the early 1990s. Balancing an evaluation of the positive effects of Canadian nationalism on Canadian literary culture against its "corporate ethos," which demands a more conformist public rhetoric and the necessary forgetting of the artificial structures of nationalist ideology, Hunter concentrates on women, Native writers, and racial minority writers who represent the disempowered in society. Unlike Davey's focus on the post-national state however, Hunter sees the relationship of literature to nation differently, where many newly visible writers have been attempting to restructure nationalist rhetoric, in order to "build new ground for the articulation of different voices that redefine the modes of personal and public/political action" (p. 271).

That recognition of the need to redefine national discourse within the increasingly pluralized space of contemporary Canada characterizes two of the best literary analyses to have appeared recently: W.H. New's *Land Sliding: Imagining Space, Presence and Power in Canadian Writing* (1997) and Jonathan Kertzer's *Worrying the Nation: Imagining a National Literature in English Canada* (1998).[18] Both these critics are writing in response to a crisis that is more than rhetorical and literary in its implications. Beginning with a definition of "landslide" as a "reconfiguring of land formations, particularly of unstable material," New investigates the connections between images of the land and changing discourses of nationhood throughout Canada's history, from settlement narratives to contemporary representations of landscape. His investigation includes feminist writing, Aboriginal writing, and immigrant writing, all of them voices that disrupt traditions of white colonial authority coded into a territorial representation of Canadian identity. With a title that echoes Atwood's *Wilderness Tips* with its sense of slippage and sliding as symptomatic of English-Canadian anxieties within a changing cultural landscape, New engages with the most traditional metaphors for a collective Canadian identity ("Canadians have always thought of themselves in connection with the land," p. 17), in order to scrutinize the cultural assumptions encoded in notions of land ownership, dispossession, and marginality in a "complex interplay between place, power and the English language" (p. 20). Kertzer's *Worrying the Nation*, or more accurately, worrying about the relation between English Canadian literary traditions and discourses of nationhood in contemporary Canada, voices similar anxieties to *Land Sliding*. Interestingly these critics take up a speculative position in the ongoing debate about what "Canadian" means, as indicated by their subtitles where the word "imagining" occurs somewhat surprisingly in both. For Kertzer, the connections between "National + Literary + History" (p. 17) look much shakier in the present context than they have done at any point since the late nineteenth century and his anxiety borders at times on the apocalyptic: "What happens to a national literature when the very idea of the nation is set in doubt" (p. 5)? He appeals to history, only to find that "there have always been challenges to nationalist ideology, first made in the name of regionalism, modernism, or cosmopolitanism, now made in the name of feminism, ethnicity, postmodernism or post-colonialism" (p. 22). As Atwood would remind us, "Nothing has happened, really, that hasn't happened before."[19] The discourse of nationhood is probably always an unstable ideological project and constantly in need of revision, but the concept of nation remains inescapable: "The nation is both a historical reality and a discursive need" (p. 166). Kertzer earnestly engages with recent feminist, ethnic, and Aboriginal fictions to illustrate the alternative narratives that need to be taken into account in any redefinition of an English-Canadian literary tradition, believing that it is only through literary representation that the national discourse will be regenerated. Though he cannot yet see the shape of things to come, he offers an astute analysis of the complexities that need to be taken into account in order to refigure a tradition responsive to contemporary Canada's version of multicultural nationhood.

Of course the debates about Canadian identity, Canadian literature, and nationalist discourse together with their sociological implications have never been one-sided, and in fact both New and Kertzer are writing in the context of the vigorous charges of a new racism within multiculturalism spelled out by Indo-Caribbean Canadian writer Neil Bissoondath's *Selling Illusions* (1994).[20] In the same year as Kertzer's book appeared, the voice of another racial minority critic, Arun Mukherjee, entered this ongoing conversation with *Postcolonialism: My Living* (1998).[21] Her outspoken criticism of Canadian nationalist agendas as exclusionary and racist shifts the emphasis away from the dominantly white English-Canadian literary canon and mediatory efforts to accommodate "other" voices within it. Mukherjee presents a different identification, focusing instead on those marginalized others, pointing out that Aboriginal and racial minority writing, which is already circulating within the Canadian literary tradition, argues the need for a radical change where "Canadian minority writers challenge all the official Canadian narratives" (p. 90). For Mukherjee as academic, writer, and teacher, the reality of multiculturalism in Canada is most readily apprehended through minority writing in English, where the writers are positioned in between cultures and languages: "Ethnic minority texts inform their readers, through the presence of other languages, as well as a whole repertoire of cultural signs, about the multicultural and multilingual nature of Canadian society" (p. 102).

Signs of this paradigm shift are evident in two books published in 2000 by immigrant critics from other minorities, with Smaro Kamboureli's *Scandalous Bodies: Diasporic Literature in English Canada* and Himani Bannerji's *The Dark Side of the Nation: Essays on Multiculturalism, Nationalism and Gender*,[22] both of which argue for a transformative multiculturalism where ethnic and racial minorities are recognized not as "others" but as "active, generative participants at the very core of a shared, conflictual history" (Kamboureli, 162). Kamboureli's literary analyses are founded on a vigorous critique of what she calls the "sedative politics" of Canadian multiculturalism policies, which she accuses of "managing" ethnic difference without making a difference to dominantly white Canadian power structures. Far from not acknowledging the cultural and ethnic pluralities of Canadian society, Kamboureli contends that the policy of multiculturalism has systematized this recognition into a process that disadvantages people from ethnic minorities and especially people of color by magnifying differences in what has become another gesture of othering. Like Mukherjee's, her analysis exposes the traditional interests in the implementation of multiculturalism, which she sees as sustaining a dominant white culture and a historical legacy of racial and ethnic discrimination. Kamboureli establishes the literary grounds for the "fictionalizing of the diasporic subject as imaged by the state" (p. 107) most persuasively in her historical analysis of the ethnic anthologies published in Canada in increasing numbers since the mid-1970s. Through her illustration of the multivoiced narratives produced by diasporic subjects, Kamboureli focuses on "the incommensurability of identity," where identities are always in process and always in excess of official categories of identification. On the other hand, Bannerji is not concerned so much with literary issues but with a political and cultural analysis of the representation of visible minority women from her own position as a South Asian Marxist feminist critic, though I include it here as a key text in the refiguring process in order to emphasize the interdisciplinary interests at stake in the debate about narratives of nation in Canada. When Bannerji asks who has the power to define Canadian culture, she is asking the same question that all my selected writers are addressing in their fictions. She too is passionate in her criticism of the way "diversity" has been interpreted within multiculturalism, arguing that it is never a neutral term but a form of cultural classification that disadvantages nonwhite Canadians: "This is its paradox—that the concept of diversity simultaneously allows for an emptying out of actual social relations and suggests a concreteness of cultural description, and through this process obscures any understanding of difference as a construction of power" (p. 36). In "Geography Lessons: On Being an Insider/Outsider to the Canadian Nation" (pp. 63–86) Bannerji deconstructs the Canadian "we" used in official discourse, revealing the nation-space to be an extremely contested site, though on the evidence of contemporary fiction I believe that the process of dismantling the historical legacies of a white settler culture is far more advanced that Bannerji is prepared to recognize.

And so the debate goes on, though several books published in 2001—one on Aboriginal writing, one on the reading habits of young Canadians, and one collection of historical fictions—would indicate that the terms have already shifted significantly. Helen Hoy's *How Should I Read These? Native Women Writers in Canada* and Robert Wright's *Hip and Trivial: Youth Culture, Book Publishing and the Greying of Canadian Nationalism* both take the refiguring process in new directions, with Hoy looking at indigenous narrative traditions marginalized within Canada and Wright looking beyond Canada's margins in a postmodern globalized context.[23] Hoy's interrogative stance as a white critic reading and teaching Native women's writing is particularly significant for the way in which she shifts the boundaries between inside and outside, engaging as a white outsider with contemporary Native fictions written in English, where she asks questions and directives *of* these texts rather than imposing white conventions of reading upon them.[24] These readings are really explorations in reading across cultural gaps, offering a model for a more flexible conversation about differences as a way of reshaping Canadian literary traditions. Hoy is interested in the same questions of race, identity, and national discourse as the other critics I have discussed, but from the perspective of Aboriginal experiences of cultural othering that relates to a colonial history of indigenous dispossession, different from the immigrant experiences addressed by multiculturalism. However, many of the issues of racial inequality and stereotyping are similar, and she too is wary of any pluralist celebrations of diversity, which occlude the "everyday racism" that Bannerji so vehemently criticizes. Through her textual analyses Hoy also prises apart easy assumptions about national allegiance, for to which nation does a First Nations writer feel she belongs? A "national identity" may well mean primarily an Aboriginal identity like Haisla or Ojibway or Cree for women whose identity constructions have centered on their racialization as Aboriginals, though their fictions when read through Hoy's sympathetic critical perspective are exercises in cross-cultural negotiation. If Hoy is skeptical of any quest for a "Canadian National Mythos" (which she describes as possibly "wrongheaded," p. 14), Robert Wright would seem to abandon such a myth altogether, at least as far as a literary tradition is concerned. His study of the reading habits of Canadian adolescents in the 1990s argues that the values of Anglo-Canadian nationalism of the 1960s and 1970s, which were so empowering as a new postcolonial and anti-American, agenda are now outdated: "The children of NAFTA and of globalization have little of the nationalist fervour with which so many of their forbears were imprinted" (p. 215).[25] His research suggests that the books they choose to read are not selected according to any nationalist cultural agenda. None of this is really surprising, for who would assume that American or British or Australian or Indian teenagers would read books, watch videos and films according to any nationalist agenda? However, Wright's concluding comment is thought provoking: "In a postmodern globalized world of infinite choice, the idea of *the national* as the defining element in Canadian Lit appears to have had its day" (p. 218). The borders between national and international have become permeable in contemporary Canadian writing, and when Wright talks about an ideological dissolution he is merely documenting the changes that have already occurred in the refiguring of Canada's literary traditions, and where the vocabulary of identity has shifted from "national" as a primary marker to other identity markers (such as race, ethnicity, gender) or even "multiple identities."[26] Yet the idea of the nation has not disappeared; also in 2001 *Story of a Nation: Defining Moments in Our History* was published, a collection of archival photographs and short stories by twelve Canadian writers (including Atwood, Roch Carrier, Dionne Brand, and Thomas King), which attempts to encode a vision of Canada's collective history in a twenty-first century project of nation (re)building.[27] More accurately, it should be called *Stories of a Nation*, for the defining moments of history turn out to be notoriously indefinable and far from momentary when they are reconstructed by fiction writers from a diverse range of age, gender, race, and political perspectives. What this handsome volume does demonstrate is both the continuing need to figure out new definitions of Canadianness and also the extent to which nationalist ideology, like literary traditions and historical fictions, are nothing more than "an experiment in the making of meaning" (p. 4).

It is impossible to assign any single cause to account for the radical changes that have taken place in constructions of Canadian identities both personal and national over the past thirty years. In many ways what has happened in Canada is symptomatic of the demographic and ideological shifts that have characterized late modern postindustrial Western societies. However, at the risk of sounding simplistic, I would argue that the 1988 Multiculturalism Act could be taken as a focus for the refiguring process that Canada is undergoing, where the concept of multiculturalism has officially endorsed and given a name to the social realities of what Homi Bhabha has memorably described as "the irredeemably plural nation-space." In his foreword to the *Tenth Anniversary Annual Report on the Operation of the Canadian Multiculturalism Act*, Prime Minister Jean Chretien announced: "Multiculturalism is the Canadian Way. . . Multiculturalism distinguishes Canada, as a country that not only cares equally about *all* its citizens but also believes that preserving uniqueness of each holds the promise of a better future for all of us."[28] Certainly as an ideology for a progressive and inclusive democratic society multiculturalism addresses ethnic and racial difference, though whether it has yet effected the social transformations envisaged in that vocabulary of rights is still, as we have seen, a matter of intense debate. There are many Canadian citizens who definitely do not see themselves as included in the Prime Minister's phrase "all of us." Thinking of the Multiculturalism Act, I am reminded of the way Native writer Thomas King described the Indian Act; he called it "an endlessly argumentative moment" in Canada's history, "a moment that had some real fluidity to it, a moment that had some real problems with interpretation,"[29] and certainly the Multiculturalism Act has the same contentious resonances. Yet it is through the process of contestation that the social and educational policies of multiculturalism are being reinterpreted, and there is ample evidence in the annual reports from the Department of Heritage that the policies themselves are endlessly subject to revision. It seems to me, looking on from outside, that the Act offers the possibility for a more honest recognition of difference and the multiple affiliations within postmodern constructions of identity that characterize Canadian society. (The Multiculturalism Act refers to immigrants and not to Aboriginal peoples, though interestingly the Department of Canadian Heritage increasingly groups together "Aboriginal people and visible minorities" when discussing issues of representation of the multicultural and multiracial nature of Canadian society.) Canada is now one of the most racially diverse societies in the world, a consequence of the liberalization of immigration policies in the 1960s away from racial and ethnic discrimination, which has shifted the relative proportion of European to non-European immigrants: "While European-born immigrants represented 90 percent of those who arrived before 1961, they accounted for only 25 percent of those arriving between 1981 and 1991."[30] The *Annual Report on the Canadian Multiculturalism Act, 2000–2001* confirms that over the past decade the pattern of ethnocultural diversity has accelerated, and the demographic predictions suggest that in another generation a single racial group will no longer represent a majority of Canada's population.[31]

Any definition of contemporary Canadian identity (who "we" are) needs to take account of the rhetoric and the reality of multiculturalism and the gaps between the two, just as it needs to take a retrospective look at Canadian history and at the other histories that many of its citizens have brought with them. It also needs to take account of contemporary formulations of identity construction, which have moved away from essentialist notions of authenticity and origins to an emphasis on identities as contextual, shifting, doubled or split, and possibly multiple. Stuart Hall's description of this postmodern concept of identities "always in process" seems to be an extremely helpful contribution to identity debates in Canada: "Perhaps instead of thinking of identity as an already accomplished fact . . . we should think, instead, of identity as a 'production' which is never complete, always in process, and always constituted within, not outside, representation."[32] Hall is speaking about Afro-Caribbean diasporic identities in Britain at the beginning of the 1990s and the emergence of Caribbean cinema (hence his imagery of theatrical performance and production), though his comments might be recontextualized to describe a more general phenomenon where identities, individual and collective, are perceived not as fixed but as responsive to circumstance and constructed across a shifting range of categories. Hall's gloss on the above quotation makes the connections between private narratives of identity and the public negotiations involved in a changing national self-image like Canada's:

> Cultural identities come from somewhere, have histories. But like everything which is historical, they undergo constant transformation. Far from being eternally fixed in some essentialized past, they are subject to the continuous "play" of history, culture and power . . . identities are the names we give to the different ways we are positioned by, and position ourselves within, the narratives of the past. (p. 394)

The words "transformation" and "power" are crucial here, for in any intercultural/interracial dialogue between established interests and minority interests, shifts in power are a major part of what is being negotiated. As an American critic defined the vision of multiculturalism (with an explicit emphasis on race): "The greatest contribution of multiculturalism in the fullest sense will be the change that it could bring about within the dominant group, thereby making the conversation of the races less one-sided."[33]

How might novels and stories by women help to shift the terms on which Canadian identity is being reimagined? If identity is constructed within representation, then fictions that offer alternative representations might be seen as a series of different lenses through which identities are perceived as shifting, multiple, and irredeemably plural. All of these fictions lead away from any grand narrative of an abstract nation-space into subjective spaces constructed as the experiential realities of individual lives. These novels look closely at the heterogeneous identities within contemporary Canada, while at the same time they all look back into the past of their characters' personal memories and communal histories, negotiating space for different ways of defining the concepts of identity, history, and nation.

The pervasive impression in these texts is one of destabilization, where it is no longer possible to write narratives that appeal uncritically to traditional frames of reference like the official narratives of Canadian history or constructions of identity based on origin and heritage. Canadian history (like any other nation's history) is full of hidden histories—secrets, falsehoods, and deliberate forgettings—among which are the different histories told by the "other" residents in Canada, like the history of colonization and its consequences told by Aboriginal writers or the Japanese Canadians' version of a history of racism that reached its crisis point in World War II with the internment and dispersal of Japanese Canadians after Pearl Harbor. Such histories remain as sites of otherness within the discourse of Canadian nationhood. Then there are the histories of more recent immigrants, so that frames of historical reference have multiplied at the same time as the master narratives of Anglo-Canadian history have been challenged and discredited. Canada seems to have become an unhomely place to a great many of its inhabitants. As Bhabha points out with subtle complexity:

> The "locality" of national culture is neither unified nor unitary in relation to itself, nor must it be seen simply as "other" in relation to what is outside or beyond it . . . The "other" is never outside or beyond us; it emerges forcefully, within cultural discourse, when we *think* we speak most intimately and indigenously "between ourselves."[34]

Looking more closely at the position of immigrant writers within the contemporary multicultural scene, what difference are they making to Canadian literature as it is being written in the present? Is their writing a supplement to Canadian literature as it has traditionally been understood? Yes it is in the sense of coming later, but it is also supplementary in the Derridean sense that the "supplement" disturbs the dominant narrative by drawing attention to what was lacking or repressed or incomplete. So the supplement necessitates a refiguring of the whole design of tradition, where borders shift between centers and margins and where writers might be positioned "in between" or across boundaries in a more mobile figuration of Canadian literature that recognizes the diverse range of ways of being and writing Canadian.

It is not so much a question of accommodating new voices as recognizing the shifts that have already taken place within Canadian fiction, and those dislocations are very evident not only in the historical novels that I shall be examining but also in the revision of the smalltown fictional genre or the regional novel, in writing about the wilderness, and in the border crossings between countries, cultures, races, and genders, which feature in so many of these contemporary women's texts. There is a new emphasis in the historical novels of Margaret Atwood and Ann-Marie MacDonald on the instabilities and falsehoods within English-Canadian national myths where history begins to look like a Gothic tale full of secrets and lies out of which new figurations of identity struggle to emerge. Hidden histories within intimate relationships unsettle the ordinary surfaces of smalltown life in Alice Munro's stories or else they erupt into murderous violence in Kerry Sakamoto's novel. Carol Shields on the other hand takes apart the classic genre of the fictive biography to register the disparities between literary constructions of identity and the vagaries of subjective life that seem to resist any representation in language, and her fiction finds an unexpected parallel in Shani Mootoo's double biographical narrative about the liminal identities of her Caribbean subjects whose fragmented stories can only be told through a disjunctive mixture of realism and fantasy that blurs into magic realism. Even the most traditional Canadian forms of pioneer fiction and wilderness narrative are refigured, in Gail Anderson Dargatz's autobiographical fiction of a white girl growing up between white and Aboriginal cultures in British Columbia, where the act of writing becomes a form of cross-cultural negotiation. That liminal positioning between races and cultures is further elaborated by Eden Robinson who writes from a Haisla perspective where her teenage female narrator is always "seeing in double exposure" as she seeks to reclaim her Aboriginal identity through historical territory that is cultural and linguistic as well as geographical and where so much is blurred and almost lost.

What this selection of women's writing demonstrates most clearly is that there is no going back to the narratives and rhetorical codes of Canadian nationalism of the 1960s and 1970s, nor are there any homogeneous answers to the construction of identities in multicultural Canada. Instead, these novels speak out of a contested terrain where many different voices struggle to find new directions for the renegotiation of discourses of identity and nationhood. Having these fictions published and reading them may contribute toward revising the rhetoric of multiculturalism so that the ideal of "multicultural Canada" might be opened out in the twenty-first century not only as social policy but as lived reality and meaningful self-image at home and internationally.

# CHAPTER 2

## "DON'T EVER ASK FOR THE TRUE STORY": MARGARET ATWOOD, *ALIAS GRACE*, AND *THE BLIND ASSASSIN*

> How do we know we are who we think we are, or thought we were . . .
> a hundred years ago? These are the questions . . . that arise in connection
> with Canadian history, or indeed with any other kind of history.
> (*In Search of Alias Grace*)[1]

I begin this chapter on Margaret Atwood's two historical novels *Alias Grace* (1996) and *The Blind Assassin* (2000) with her radical questioning of the terms on which identities, individual and collective, are constructed. Addressing a Canadian audience in Ottawa shortly after the publication of *Alias Grace*, Atwood evokes the collective "we" but only in order to break open any comfortable assumptions about national identity based on a sense of history and origins. She draws attention to the relationship between present and past, not by focusing on connections but by pointing to the inbetween space between Now and Then, casting doubts on historical certainties and challenging any notion of an authentic national identity that derives from the legitimating narratives of history, hinting at instabilities and gaps within collective and subjective memory: "We live in a period in which memory of all kinds, including the sort of large memory we call history, is being called into question" (*In Search*, p. 7). Though Atwood widens her frame of reference here by alluding to a general context of postmodernist skepticism, her questions directly address uncertainties generated by the cultural and ideological shifts that have altered the terms of the debate about Canadian identity and heritage during the 1990s. If, as I have argued in chapter 1, multiculturalism has been a major force in transforming Canada's discourse of nationhood, opening up the nation-space to accommodate the heterogeneous histories of its citizens, so in her recent historical novels Atwood has been engaged in a somewhat similar project, opening up English Canada's colonial history and its heritage myths. She argues from history itself the need to refigure Canadian identities, not only in the present for the future, but retrospectively as well. In *Alias Grace* she turns back to nineteenth-century English-Canadian colonial history to tell the story of a double murder and of a heroine whose guilt or innocence is still open to speculation, and in *The Blind Assassin* (the very title of which hints at skullduggery) she exposes a tissue of social hypocrisy and private scandal woven around some of the key events in twentieth-century Canadian history.

Why, we may wonder, does Atwood choose to tell what might be regarded as counter-narratives to the official versions of history? Her answer is that at the end of the twentieth century and now into the new millennium she is investigating questions of Canadian heritage and identity:

> Our inheritance. Ah yes—the mysterious sealed box...But what was inside it? Many things we were not told about in school, and this is where the interest in historical writing comes in. For it's the very things that are *not* mentioned that inspire the most curiosity in us. *Why* are they not mentioned? The lure of the Canadian past, for the writers of my generation, has been partly the lure of the unmentionable—the mysterious, the buried, the forgotten, the discarded, the taboo. (*In Search*, p. 19)

When viewed from this perspective, Canadian history begins to look very like the haunted text of a Gothic novel, full of secrets and obsessed with what is buried or hidden or unspeakable, and where the plot is "a narrative of disclosure and reparation" for "the weight of the past...may be escaped only when its secrets are brought to light through the process of discovering connections between past and present."[2] When we remember that Atwood herself has always been a Gothic writer (from her early poems *Procedures for Underground* and her 1970s wilderness Gothic novel *Surfacing* through poetry collections like *Murder in the Dark* and *Good Bones* to her 1995 novel *The Robber Bride* whose title derives from a Grimms fairy tale), it should come as no surprise to find her recasting Canadian history in the Gothic genre as a series of resurrections of the dead. As her main narrator in *The Blind Assassin* asserts: "Nothing is more difficult than to understand the dead, I've found; but nothing is more dangerous than to ignore them."[3] By not ignoring the muffled voices from the past Atwood reconstructs her multivoiced novels, blurring the boundaries between history and fiction, and providing what Homi Bhabha has described as "a perspective on the disjunctive forms of representation that signify a people, a nation, or a national culture."[4] Paradoxically this procedure brings the nation's past into closer alignment with the nation's present, for Atwood insists on seeing the colonial legacy within postcolonial Canada. Her novels show that Anglo-Canadian society a hundred years ago—or fifty years ago—was no less troubled and divided than today, and beset by the same conflicts around class and gender issues, suspicion and resentment of immigrants from ethnic minorities, and warring political factions: "You want squalor, lies, corruption? Hell, we've got 'em homegrown, and not only that, we always have had, and there's where the past comes in" (*In Search*, p. 24). The past comes in like an uncanny Other lurking behind the present, assiduously forgotten, carefully hidden or locked up—but then, as Atwood says in a different context, "Sometimes this comes to the surface, sometimes that, sometimes nothing. Nothing goes away."[5]

The different context that refers to Atwood's comments on memory processes within the individual psyche might serve to remind us of possible parallels between stories of a nation's history and the life stories of individuals, a point made by the American historiographer Hayden White:

> It is frequently forgotten or, when remembered, denied, that no given set of events attested by the historical record, constitutes a story manifestly finished and complete. This is as true of the events that constitute the life of an individual as it is of an institution, a nation, or a whole people. We do not live stories, even if we give our lives meaning by retrospectively casting them in the form of stories. And so too with nations or whole cultures.[6]

So we find Atwood telling her Gothic tales about Canadian history through the genre of fictive autobiography. Moreover, these are fictive autobiographies told by women: in *Alias Grace* the dominant narrative voice is that of Grace Marks, the Irish servant girl convicted of murder, and in *The Blind Assassin* it is the voice of Iris Chase Griffen, the eighty-two-year-old woman who is the last surviving member of an old Ontario manufacturing dynasty and also the sister of a woman who wrote one notorious cult novel before committing suicide. This is history in the feminine gender, offering an alternative perspective to that of the master narratives of history, which have traditionally been told by men: "If the nation is an imagined community, that imagining is profoundly gendered [in the masculine]."[7] Readers will be familiar with female historians in other Atwood novels: Offred in *The Handmaid's Tale* whose "herstory" chronicles the Republic of Gilead, Tony the medieval military historian in *The Robber Bride* who prides herself on her lectures on warfare: "She likes the faint shock on the faces of her listeners. It's the mix of domestic image and mass bloodshed that does it to them,"[8] or the woman in the poem "The Loneliness of the Military Historian" who realizes that "Despite the propaganda, there are no monsters, / or none that can be finally buried. / Finish one off, and circumstances / and the radio create another."[9] What difference does gender make to the genre of the historical novel? The effect of gender here is comparable with Atwood's use of the Gothic as a dark lens through which to view history from a different angle. Just as the Gothic introduces the uncanny other as a hidden element threatening to disrupt official narratives of the nation's history, so the voices of women story-tellers who have been marginalized from political power but who are also deeply implicated in the social structures of history offer an alternative perspective that undermines any discourse of totalizing authority, revealing what "ought to have remained secret and hidden but [which] has come to light."[10] That is Freud's definition of the uncanny, which in turn locates women as the destabilizing others in narratives of the nation: "The 'locality' of national culture is neither unified nor unitary in relation to itself, nor must it be seen as simply 'other' in relation to what is outside or beyond it . . . The 'other' is never outside or beyond us; it emerges forcefully, within cultural discourse."[11]

It is that concept of otherness within the doubled discourses of national and individual identity that I wish to explore in *Alias Grace* and *The Blind Assassin*. These are texts that transgress generic boundaries in a dazzling variety of ways. *Alias Grace* combines historical documentary, fictive autobiography, Gothic romance, and nineteenth-century melodrama, while in *The Blind Assassin* Atwood appropriates a spectacular range of additional discourses from the Victorian sensation novel, science fiction, modernist female romance, and American detective pulp fiction of the 1930s and 1940s. Such generic hybridization is symptomatic of Atwood's writing of history in a postmodern context, caught in that "paradox of complicity and critique" that Linda Hutcheon describes as characteristic of Atwood's fiction.[12] Indeed, how could it be otherwise? As Atwood has reminded readers: "We have to write out of who and when and where we are, whether we like it or not, and disguise it how we may" (*In Search*, p. 4). Though Atwood's statement about her own position as a writer looks disarmingly straightforward, the positions of her female narrators are far more difficult to pin down. In fact, both Grace Marks and Iris Chase Griffen belong to a long line of Atwood's duplicitous storytellers, stretching from Joan Foster in *Lady Oracle* (1976) to Zenia in *The Robber Bride* (1994) who are all identified as sybils, witches, liars, and supreme plotters. By the end, most of them

have disconcertingly disappeared—into death or back into the text—
and only their voices remain. What better form in which to disguise and
reinvent one's identity than that of the fictive autobiography? Biography
and autobiography, whether factual or fictional, is concerned with the
construction of a subject's identity and his/her representation in the text.
Such "life writing" immediately raises questions about the historical and
social contexts within which identity is constructed, just as it encourages
questions about concepts of the self. Is there an authentic self, or is the
self only a construction with different multiple figurings constructed
through the text? If this is so, then the fictive autobiography becomes a
kind of textual theater where a changing self displays and hides itself
through a series of disguises and a parade of doubles, always eluding
fixed representation. In this case the fictive autobiography, far from
constructing a coherent identity, foregrounds nothing so much as the
problematic construction of female subjectivity in fiction.

With *Alias Grace* Atwood turns back to mid-nineteenth-century
English-Canadian colonial history in her ongoing investigation into
what being Canadian means. The story she tells is of a violent crime
committed in pre-Confederation times, and not a story about wilderness survival and pioneer settlement of the kind that she used previously
in her poetic sequence *The Journals of Susanna Moodie* (1970). Atwood
is still telling stories of pioneer life but this time she is looking at the
violent underside of colonial history, for this is the story of the same
Grace Marks of whom Susanna Moodie had written with such a mixture of fascination and repulsion in her *Life in the Clearings* (1953).
Grace Marks was the sixteen-year-old Irish servant girl who, with her
fellow servant James McDermott, was accused of murdering their employer
Thomas Kinnear and his housekeeper Nancy Montgomery (who was
also his mistress) at Kinnear's farm outside Toronto in 1843. Grace was
not hanged for the murders, though McDermott was. Instead, she
was imprisoned in Kingston Penitentiary and incarcerated for seven years
in Toronto Lunatic Asylum. (Mrs. Moodie viewed her as an inmate in both
these places and Atwood includes extracts from Moodie's account in *Life
in the Clearings* in her novel.) She was finally pardoned in 1872, when
she left Canada and went to live in New York State where possibly she
married and changed her name, and anyway disappeared from official
records. The crucial question remains: Was Grace innocent or was she a
guilty accomplice in the murders? As Atwood has remarked, there is
never any popular doubt about the man's role in such cases, though
opinions over the woman involved are sharply divided. Grace steadfastly
claimed that she could not remember what happened on the day of the

murders, though she admitted she must have been there when they were committed, and to this day her case lies open to speculation. Looking into the tangle of contradictory evidence, we can see that it contains all the classic ingredients of Victorian Gothic melodrama: unspeakable secrets, murder, sex, and violence, and a heroine who may have been criminally insane or a split personality or a hysteric or maybe even innocent. The fascination of a character like Grace is intimately bound up with nineteenth-century anxieties about women and their true nature: are they angels in the house or are they lying devils, and which is Grace? Certainly Grace's story fascinated nineteenth-century readers, as Atwood tells us in her afterword to this novel: "The Kinnear-Montgomery murders took place on July 23, 1843, and were extensively reported not only in Canadian newspapers, but in those of the United States and Britain. The details were sensational with their combination of sex, violence, and the deplorable insubordination of the lower classes."[13] Grace's story clearly fascinates Atwood, who has written two earlier versions of it: *The Servant Girl*, a play for CBC television in 1974, and *Grace*, an unpublished play for the theater later in the 1970s.

We could read *Alias Grace* in a feminist context as a woman's fictive autobiography where Grace eludes patriarchal constructions of her identity. In this we would be following Atwood's guidance: "In my fiction, Grace too—whatever else she is—is a storyteller, with strong motives to narrate, but also strong motives to withhold; the only power left to her as a convicted and imprisoned criminal comes from a blend of these two motives" (*In Search*, p. 36). Feminist approaches may produce fascinating readings that highlight the psychological and social dimensions of Grace Marks as a subject. A psychological reading opens up questions of split personality, female madness, and the bizarre episode of the neuro-hypnotism scene later in the novel, and it may include commentary on the significance of quilting as a feminine mode for Grace's storytelling, while a more socially focused criticism might comment on Grace's position as an Irish working-class woman and her relations with the two other servant girls in the story, Mary Whitney and Nancy Montgomery. Of course it must be remembered that Grace is already framed by history as one of society's others, marginalized by her criminality, her sex, and her class. Who is this woman for whom a full biography can never be written and whose identity as the novel's title suggests, remains elusive? Is her identity always hidden behind a series of aliases? Is she always "Grace Marks alias Mary Whitney" as her name was given at her trial? There are two other intriguing definitions of her identity in the novel: there is Grace's own negative definition in her first interview with the American doctor when she says, "I am not a dog" (p. 44), and there is the mysterious statement by her friend Jeremiah the peddler, "You are one of us" (p. 179), which Grace is still wondering about twenty years later. A hundred years later things are no clearer, for as Atwood points out in her afterword: "The true character of the historical Grace Marks remains an enigma" (p. 539).

The novel gives Grace the chance to plead her own case, and it is her voice that dominates the narrative when she tells her story to Simon Jordan, a young American psychiatric doctor who is engaged in the study of nervous diseases and traumatic mental disorders. It is Grace's voice, disembodied and out of context, which startles the reader's attention in the polyphony of voices with which the novel begins. The reader is quite bewildered by the fragmentary pieces of contradictory historical evidence that are offered in the opening pages: newspaper reports of the trial, an extract from Susanna Moodie's *Life in the Clearings*, snatches of poetry from William Morris, Emily Dickinson, Emily Bronte, and a popular ballad, a page from Kingston Penitentiary's Punishment Book 1843, and among all this Grace's Gothic nightmare of Nancy Montgomery's murder:

> Then up ahead I see Nancy, on her knees, with her hair fallen over and the blood running down into her eyes. Around her neck is a white cotton kerchief printed with blue flowers, love-in-a-mist, it's mine . . . and then Nancy smiles, only the mouth, her eyes are hidden by the blood and hair, and then she scatters into patches of colour, a drift of red cloth petals cross the stones. (p. 6)

This shocking image of a female victim whose body is bruised, broken, and bleeding, is reported by Grace as a recurrent nightmare. It makes the reader wonder from the start about Grace's innocence or guilt. Is this the Gothic return of the repressed, where traumatic memory resurfaces in uncanny repetition? Maybe; but Grace's last sentence in this opening section of the first chapter makes us pause, for she adds: "That's what I told Dr Jordan, when we came to that part of the story" (p. 7). Is this a true or a false memory, or is it just another tale that Grace has fabricated to please the young doctor? He is trying to lead her via an early form of the "talking cure" to remembering the events on the day of the murders in order to solve the riddle of her guilt or innocence, possibly with the practical results of securing her release from prison and establishing his own medical reputation. Do nightmares prove anything?

The novel refuses to give a definite answer, for though Grace has a prodigiously good memory and obligingly tells Dr. Jordan a great deal about her childhood, her journey by ship from Belfast to Canada, her time in domestic service, and her life as a prisoner, she cannot be persuaded to remember the violent events of the murders. Is she suffering from traumatic memory loss, as she claims? Simon Jordan becomes increasingly intrigued and suspicious as Grace eludes his carefully structured inquiries, though right from the beginning Grace is presented as a shape-shifting figure. On his first glimpse of Grace, Simon had imagined a frail hysteric, a sort of Pre-Raphaelite virgin, "but then Grace stepped forward, out of the light, and the woman he'd seen the instant before was no longer there. Instead there was a different woman— straighter, taller, more self-possessed" (p. 68). Just as Simon cannot stabilize her image at their first meeting, he does not manage to do so at their subsequent interviews; though she sits with downcast eyes sewing her quilts, Grace continually changes roles from submissive prisoner to speaking subject. Are her eyes cast down in modesty, or is it so that the doctor cannot see the changing expressions on her face as she tells her story? That unstable location is echoed in her narrative, which switches between present and past, between voluble detailed recollection and traumatic memory lapses, so that Simon has the uneasy suspicion that "the very plenitude of her recollections may be a set of distractions, a way of drawing the mind away from some hidden or essential fact, like dainty flowers on a grave" (pp. 215–16). The question is, whose mind is being distracted—Simon's or Grace's own? How consciously duplicitous is she? Is there, as his theories would lead him to believe, a hidden nugget of memory to be dug up, or is Grace genuinely uncertain as to what happened, as her sense of panic and incoherence surrounding the murders might suggest? "When you are in the middle of a story it isn't a story at all, but only a confusion; a dark roaring, a blindness, a wreckage of shattered glass and splintered wood . . . It's only afterwards that it becomes anything like a story at all. When you are telling it, to yourself or to someone else" (pp. 345–46). Grace's project of storytelling and self-figuring would seem to represent a complex negotiation not only between teller and listener (and that includes the reader as well as Simon Jordan), but also possibly within the teller herself.

Grace is a very slippery subject. Is she suffering from a split personality disorder? Is she a hysteric? Both those diagnoses were popular within the context of mid-nineteenth-century psychiatric medicine on which Atwood draws for her constructions of identity here. Her afterword cites some of the textbooks on the unconscious and dreams, on hypnotism, spiritualism, and the occult, which constitute her frame of reference, though Atwood also writes within a post-Freudian frame of reference as well. As she reminds her readers, no writer can escape being contemporary "and *Alias Grace*, though set in the mid-nineteenth century, is of course, a very contemporary novel" (*In Search*, p. 36).[14] Atwood's representation of the split self both corresponds to and refigures Victorian theories of double consciousness, a model of mind shared by the two doctors concerned with Grace's case. Dr. Jordan works via the "association of ideas" method, whereas the mysterious Dr. DuPont works via a direct appeal to the unconscious through hypnotic trances. Both of them are concerned with therapeutic cures designed to reclaim traumatic memories so as to reintegrate and heal the psyche. DuPont cites the medical authority of the Manchester physician James Braid, who developed his new theory of neuro-hypnotism in the 1850s and was an important influence on Jean-Martin Charcot's work with female hysterics at the Salpetriere Hospital in Paris from the 1860s.[15] If Grace's nightmares do not prove anything, neither do her repeated assertions of traumatic memory loss. On the other hand, she may have been telling the truth when she says she does not remember the murders, for she was prone to lapses of consciousness when suffering from shock, and during her time in prison she was sufficiently unstable (and possibly mad) to be confined to a lunatic asylum for seven years. Again the questions arise: Was Grace "an accomplished actress and a most practised liar" as the former doctor at the lunatic asylum and also her defense lawyer believed ("In my opinion, she was guilty as sin," p. 440)? Was she innocent, or was she mad? If Simon tries to make sense of Grace's narrative through his medical theories, so Grace uses those same concepts to construct her own identity, but in ways so strikingly at variance with the master discourse that he is bewildered:

> It may well be that Grace is a true amnesiac. Or simply contrary. Or simply guilty.
> She could of course be insane, with the astonishingly devious plausibility of the experienced maniac. (p. 375)

Grace has experience of lunatic asylums, and possibly of schizophrenia as well: "*Gone mad* is what they say, and sometimes *Run mad*, as if mad is a direction, like west; as if mad is a different house you could step into, or a separate country entirely. But when you go mad you don't go any other place, you stay where you are. And somebody else comes in" (p. 37).

Grace is certainly haunted by ghosts. There is the ghost of Nancy Montgomery (so like Dickens's murdered Nancy in *Oliver Twist* as Grace's lawyer remarks to Dr. Jordan) and also the ghost of her best friend and fellow servant Mary Whitney, whose death from a bungled abortion caused Grace's first amnesiac attack. Grace asserts that on many occasions she heard Mary's voice in her dreams, but whether Mary was saying "Let me out!" or "Let me in!" Grace cannot be sure. Indeed, Mary apparently proves her undying friendship to Grace in what is surely the most bizarre episode in the novel. That is the neuro-hypnotism scene in chapter 48, when Grace—much against the advice of Dr. Jordan—is put under a hypnotic trance by Dr. DuPont and finally speaks out to an audience in the library of the prison governor's wife, but she speaks in a voice that is not her own. As Dr. Jordan notices: "This voice cannot be Grace's; yet in that case, whose voice is it?" (p. 465). In this episode, which mixes fashions for hypnotism, mesmerism, and spiritualism, Grace is taken over by Mary's ghost who speaks through her when Grace's face is covered by a veil. In consequence of this "confession" Grace is exonerated in the opinions of all present, on grounds of diminished responsibility.

How do we read this striking example of double voicing? Is it psycho-spiritual revelation, or is it a theatrical performance? We are offered different interpretations by the men of science and religion. Is it demonic possession, as Reverend Verringer believes? Is it symptomatic of the neurological condition of *dédoublement* or double consciousness, the voice of the split personality, as nineteenth-century medical opinion would diagnose it? However there is a third possibility that Simon Jordan wonders about: "Was Grace really in a trance, or was she play-acting, and laughing up her sleeve? He knows what he saw and heard, but he may have been shown an illusion, which he cannot prove to have been one" (p. 472). Whatever the explanation, this scene offers the spectacle of the self as the site of estrangement and split identity, which has been a consistent theme in Atwood's fiction. Here we see Atwood's Gothic construction of female subjectivity where the conscious self is shadowed, indeed displaced, by its dark twin whose voice from behind the veil comes closest to figuring what is "unspeakable." There are similar doubles in *Lady Oracle, The Handmaid's Tale, Cat's Eye,* and *The Robber Bride.* The breaking out of the voice is very disruptive, for as Eve Sedgwick explains in her brilliant analysis of the Gothic psychology of the double: "The self is massively blocked off from something to which it ought to have access (like its own past or details of family history) so that there are as it were two parallel lives, one on each side of the consciousness divide, and the worst violence, the most uncanny moments occur, as this barrier is broken."[16] The voice under hypnosis marks the moment of transgression when the unconscious speaks out in a kind of scandalous confessional. That is the theory and that is what DuPont encourages his audience to expect, but that is not what happens, because Grace is taken over by Mary Whitney's ghostly voice in an unexpected combination of hypnosis and spiritualist seance. At least, this is what appears to happen—though I believe Simon Jordan was right to think he had been tricked. After all, the mysterious Dr. DuPont was none other than Grace's old friend and protector Jeremiah the peddler, who had once invited her to go away with him on a touring show as a medical clairvoyant: "With your hair down you would have the right look" (p. 311). Jeremiah is a charlatan and a trickster—and he is also a ventriloquist, as Atwood reveals much later, in a letter from Grace to Jeremiah under one of his many disguises addressed to "Signor Geraldo Ponti, care of the Prince of Wales Theatre, Queen Street, Toronto West." In that letter, Grace also acknowledges the trick: "If they found you out, they would think you had tricked them, as what is done on a stage is not as acceptable, as the very same thing done in a library" (p. 492).

Atwood has staged a performance straight out of nineteenth-century melodrama but with a serious purpose, for by her ironic use of hypnotism and spiritualism she manages to demonstrate the collapse of boundaries between self and other in a transgressive speech act. This scene is both like and unlike the stage performance in Nathaniel Hawthorne's *The Blithedale Romance*, for there his Veiled Lady is silent whereas Grace "speaks out" in Mary's voice. This is a rewriting of Hawthorne's mesmerism scene not as female victimization but as feminist social protest, speaking what is unspeakable by Grace herself in everyday life. This testimony from the ghost not only asserts Grace's innocence but it also makes some other revelations—not about the murders but about Victorian sexual hypocrisy and social oppression, and especially about the appalling conditions for servant girls like Grace and Mary who worked in the big houses of respectable wealthy citizens in Toronto. The twist that saves Grace is Mary's assertion of demonic possession, so that instead of the murderess being named as "Grace Marks alias Mary Whitney" as at the trial, she could be renamed as "Mary Whitney alias Grace Marks." Exploiting Grace's claim not to remember, this performance stages a reinterpretation of Grace's *crime passionnelle*, which is neither lust nor jealousy but a woman's anger and indignation. As Mary complains, "No one listened to me. I was not heard" (p. 468). Her voice reminds us of Cathy's ghostly voice in *Wuthering Heights* and also of the dramatic monologues by nineteenth-century women poets like Elizabeth Barrett Browning and Felicia Hemans, where the ventriloquial mode was frequently used to express the feelings of socially marginalized women.

However, it is worth noting that in this crucial scene the voice that animates the performance is still a male voice, speaking for a silenced woman. Grace is after all in a hypnotic trance, or at least pretends to be. Jeremiah's performance allows Grace to keep her secret about the murders and it even silences Dr. Jordan, who cannot write his medical report for fear of being professionally discredited. He abandons Grace though he acknowledges that he has fallen in love with her, and he never writes the letter that might have helped to secure her pardon. He returns to the United States condemned to not knowing, and in strange ways he finds himself figuring as one of Grace's doubles. Ironically, he too suffers from partial amnesia as a result of a head wound in the American Civil War, and his mother reports that he insists on addressing his American fiancée Faith Cartwright as "Grace." This identity confusion is a wonderful example of the way that codes of memory and desire, even when spoken aloud may fuse to conceal the truth and may be easily misinterpreted: "He persists in believing that she is called Grace—an understandable confusion, as Faith is very close to it in concept" (pp. 498–99). Fifteen years later, Grace herself is freed and goes to the States where she marries Jamie Walsh, who had fallen in love with her when they were servants at Mr. Kinnear's and then at her murder trial was the chief witness against her. Now a prosperous farmer in Upper New York State, Jamie is obsessed with being forgiven by Grace, and within the secret space of the marriage bed he insists that she repeat the tales of her former victimization in order to arouse him sexually: "After a few stories of torment and misery he clasps me in his arms . . . and begins to unbutton my nightgown" (p. 531). All her male rescuers share a fascination with the possibility of Grace's sexual transgressions, just as they share the same strangely ambivalent trait of refusing to let Grace speak for herself or of not understanding what she does say. Despite her efforts to resist definitions of her identity imposed on her, Grace cannot escape the controlling discourses of male authority, and she remains "shut up inside that doll of myself, and my true voice could not get out" (p. 344).

Instead of speaking, Grace offers an oblique commentary on her life story through a different medium when she is a married woman and mistress of her own house. Several critics have commented on her skill at quilt making and on the quilt patterns, which are such a distinctive feature of this novel, both visually and in its narrative structure.[17]

MARGARET ATWOOD / 37

Having always had to follow other people's patterns, Grace is at last free to design her own quilt "to suit my own ideas" (p. 459). Needless to say, her Tree of Paradise pattern has some small but significant variations from the traditional one, for her design incorporates "a border of snakes entwined . . . as without a snake or two, the main part of the story would be missing" (pp. 459–60). She also makes hers into a memorial quilt to her two dead friends, Mary Whitney (whose name she borrowed for her alias) and Nancy Montgomery (whom she was accused of murdering and whose clothes she wore in her abortive escape attempt to the States). She pieces fragments of their old clothes together with her own—Mary's petticoat, Nancy's floral dress, her own prison nightgown—"and so we will all be together," perhaps "in Paradise at last" (p. 18), though who can tell? Certainly the story does not tell, though Grace's pattern manages to suggest a rich fund of memory beyond amnesia. As she muses very near the end, "If I wish to commune with the dead, I can do it well enough on my own" (p. 529).

Grace remains an enigma, for though "the dead are in the hands of the living," as Tony the female historian had commented in *The Robber Bride*, there is nothing self-evident about history, any more than Grace's story in its multiple versions: "It is dependent on what she remembers; or is it what she says she remembers, which can be quite a different thing?" (*In Search*, p. 36). We are reminded of Dr. Jordan's comment on Grace's case after the hypnotism scene when he is discussing the strange turn events have taken and raises the modish theory of the unconscious and the mechanics of repression in the human mind: "Perhaps," says Simon, "we are also—preponderantly—what we forget" (p. 471). In one of Grace's frequent silent soliloquies she remarks: "There are some things that should be forgotten by everyone, and never spoken of again" (p. 29). Just because Grace does not remember having committed the murders does not prove that she is innocent, though she may be exonerated on grounds of diminished responsibility.

It is through this crucial concept of forgetting that Atwood makes the border crossing from Grace's personal history to the wider history of Canadian origins and identity, and she makes the connection quite explicit in her lecture on *Alias Grace* as a historical novel: "For history as for the individual, forgetting can be just as convenient as remembering, and remembering what was once forgotten can be distinctly uncomfortable. As a rule, we tend to remember the awful things done to us, and to forget the awful things we did" (*In Search*, pp. 7–8). Atwood is talking about the significance of forgetting in the creation of myths of nationhood:

> It is through this syntax of forgetting—or being obliged to forget—that
> the problematic identification of a national people becomes visible...
> To be obliged to forget—in the construction of the national present—
> is not a question of historical memory; it is the construction of a
> discourse on society that *performs* the problematic totalization of the
> national will.[18]

Ernst Renan, to whose late nineteenth-century essay "What Is a
Nation?" Bhabha refers, puts this more simply: "Forgetting, I would
even go so far as to say historical error, is a crucial factor in the creation
of a nation...Indeed, historical enquiry brings to light deeds of
violence which took place at the origin of all political formations."[19]
Hayden White's argument is very similar when he makes his contemporary historians sound very like Atwood's nineteenth-century psychiatric
doctors:

> Historians seek to refamiliarize us with events that have been forgotten
> through either accident, neglect, or repression. Moreover, the greatest
> historians have always dealt with those events in the histories of their
> cultures that are "traumatic" in nature and the meaning of which is either
> problematical or overdetermined in the significance that they still have
> for current life.[20]

The reliability of individual and collective memory poses problems, and
it seems to me that Atwood's novel is foregrounding the dimensions of
amnesia in Canada's discourse of nationhood (such as forgetting the
treatment of Aboriginal peoples or Japanese Canadians during World
War II) via the personal forgetting of Grace Marks. Interestingly,
Atwood adds Simon Jordan the American to her company of amnesiacs,
for such a nervous condition crosses borders not only of gender but of
nationality as well.

There are other conveniently forgotten historical issues thrown up in
this novel, not least of which is Bhabha's "problematic unity of the
nation," for the main event of the narrative takes place just seven years
after the 1837 Rebellion and the murder trial is caught up in the fallout
from this: "Canada West was still reeling from the effects of the
Rebellion of 1837, and this influenced both Grace's life before
the murders and her treatment at the hands of the press...In 1843—
the year of the murder—editorials were still being written about the
badness or worthiness of William Lyon Mackenzie, and as a rule,
the Tory newspapers that vilified him also vilified Grace...but the

Reform newspapers that praised Mackenzie were also inclined to clemency towards Grace. This split in opinion continued through later writers on the case" (*In Search*, pp. 34–35). It is also likely that Grace's pardon in 1872 is related to Canada's first Prime Minister Sir John A. Macdonald's general amnesty after Confederation (1867), rather than to any special pleading made on her behalf or any strong belief in her innocence, though as Grace herself remarks on the news of her release, this would change her identity in the eyes of the world: "It calls for a different arrangement of the face; but I suppose it will become easier in time" (p. 513).

The novel also reminds us that Canada has always been a society of immigrants, and that Toronto was then as it is now a multicultural city. When Grace arrives there from Northern Ireland, the first thing she notices are the faces of the people (mainly white, it is true, though not exclusively):

> The people appeared to be very mixed as to the kinds to them, with many Scots and some Irish, and of course the English, and many Americans, and a few French; and Red Indians, although they had no feathers; and some Germans; with skins of all hues, which was very new to me; and you never could tell what sort of speech you were going to hear. (p. 143)

*Alias Grace* might be read as Atwood's intervention in debates around multiculturalism and her reply to the backlash against it as a policy in the early 1990s, for she shows that English-Canadian society is no more diversified or violent now than it was a hundred and fifty years ago. Through her historical fiction Atwood is clearing a space for thinking about multiculturalism beyond a national history of ethnic and racial prejudice. Maybe it is not an exaggeration to see Grace's quilts with their pattern of light and dark colors as a metaphor for the cultural and racial mixture of Canada's population; such a reading gives a national resonance to Grace's striking domestic image: "And since that time I have thought, why is it that women have chosen to sew such flags?" (p. 185).

Atwood is scrupulous in her presentation of historical facts, though as she says, "Since there were a lot of gaps, there is a lot of invention. *Alias Grace* is very much a novel rather than a documentary" (*In Search*, p. 35). Interestingly, the two most significant men in Grace's narrative are both Americans, and they are both Atwood's inventions: Dr. Simon Jordan from Massachusetts, and Jeremiah Pontelli (alias Dr. DuPont alias Signor Geraldo Ponti alias Mr. Gerald Bridges), the American-born son of Italian immigrants. Both of them cross the national border regularly, and Grace herself, who had once made an illegal crossing with

MacDermott immediately after the murders, thirty years later makes her home in New York State when she is released from prison. There she marries a Canadian who had gone to the States to work on the railroads and out West; he now owns a farm outside Ithaca where Grace finally becomes mistress of her own house. There are so many border crossings here both legal and illegal, a reminder of the fact that Canada has never been isolated from the United States and that continual border traffic has been a feature in the histories of these two nations. Arguably we could see *Alias Grace* as a late twentieth-century revision of English-Canadian history masquerading as a woman's fictive autobiography, and therefore as Atwood's own elaborate alias for her broad socio-historical project aimed at uncovering scandalous secrets, which may be a necessary stage in refiguring nation and identity.

Whereas *Alias Grace* focuses on the phenomenon of amnesia within the individual and collective psyche and the uncertainties it generates, the emphasis shifts in *The Blind Assassin* to what has been deliberately hidden. What is really in the "mysterious sealed box" containing Canadians' inheritance? Again this is a very Gothic configuration of Canadian history, and *The Blind Assassin* should be read, I believe, as a sequel to *Alias Grace* covering the history of English Canada from the late nineteenth century through the twentieth. Published in the year 2000, it is not only a memorial to the end of an era but it also offers a retrospective view of some of the key events of the past century and of Canada's changing social and political ideologies. The storyteller is an aged member of the Anglo-Canadian establishment, Mrs. Iris Chase Griffen, who was born in the small Ontario town of Port Ticonderoga in 1916 in the middle of World War I, and who finishes writing her life story just before she dies there in her garden in the last year of the century. Her handwritten memoir is left in her will to her absent grand-daughter Sabrina, who is away traveling in India and who does not return to Canada till after her grandmother is dead. Clearly this is a novel concerned with questions of history, identity, and inheritance, told from one woman's point of view in the domestic context of a family saga, for as Atwood remarks when speaking of the novelist's craft:

> I think novelists begin with hints and images and scenes and voices rather than with theories and grand schemes. Individual characters interacting with, and acted upon by, the world that surrounds them are what inter-ests the novel; the details, not the large pattern, although a large pattern does then emerge. (*In Search*, p. 28)

While the large pattern is very important in *The Blind Assassin*, the reader's primary fascination is with Iris and her private narrative. This old woman is haunted by the ghosts of the past, and it is through her duplicitous storytelling that Atwood develops a new mode of fictive autobiography in a multidimensional version that interrogates the boundaries within which subjective identity may be represented. For Iris, writing her life becomes a prolonged negotiation with the dead, and constructing her identity means deconstructing her identity in the recognition that she has always been split, doubled, and defined by her close relationship with her younger sister Laura. That double figuring is complicated by the fact that Iris's memoir provides the frame for two other stories: Laura's modernist love story called *The Blind Assassin*, which was posthumously published after her death in a car crash in 1945, and within that a 1930s pulp science fiction fantasy about a Blind Assassin, written by the male lover of the anonymous woman in Laura's novel. The stories would seem to be quite separate with their three different plots, three different narrators, and all in different genres; only near the end do readers discover the key to the hidden connections as they come to realize that every story happens "in another dimension of space." We discover that all three stories are different versions of Iris's own self-figuring, each acting as a different lens through which her life may be viewed, demonstrating what Paul De Man has described as "the impossibility of closure and totalization . . . of all textual systems made up of tropological substitutions."[21] Iris puts this more simply: "The living bird is not its labelled bones" (p. 484). Her multidimensional narrative shifts the boundaries between subjective and objective reality, as it does between fact and fiction as represented through writing. Iris's uncanny memoir not only raises questions about authenticity (What is the truth? Who is the teller?) but also about the writing process itself, which is figured here as the independent activity of a severed hand endlessly tracing out the lines of the past.

The first thing that strikes the reader however is the novel's title, which could be that of an eighteenth-century Gothic novel or a nineteenth-century melodrama or a 1930s' pulp fiction detective thriller or even a B-grade movie from that period. Somebody gets killed, but the killer cannot see the victim and nobody sees the killer. The second striking feature is the death opening of the novel, narrated by Iris: "Ten days after the war ended, my sister Laura drove a car off a bridge. The bridge was being repaired: she went right through the Danger sign. The car fell a hundred feet into the ravine . . . Nothing much was left of her but charred smithereens" (p. 3). Here is another bruised and broken female body, a curious reminder of the opening of *Alias Grace*. Who is responsible? To that there is no answer, though the mystery seizes the reader's attention. There are no less than three suicides in the first twenty pages—Iris's sister, Iris's husband, and Iris's daughter. Though those deaths are actually spread over thirty years, they are all recorded through newspaper reports right at the beginning. There are other deaths and also a death ending with Iris's obituary, but it is the opening with its uncanny repetitions that arouses our curiosity. Is there any connection between these deaths? Who is the Blind Assassin? Iris did not see any of them; she is only the survivor who tells the story years later when she is quietly living as an old lady in Port Ticonderoga. Yet there is so much left unexplained and so much that is deliberately hidden (Laura's notebooks, a mysterious mutilated photograph, the key to Iris's locked steamer trunk) that we have the uneasy feeling that there is more here than meets the eye and this is another of Atwood's Southern Ontario Gothic mysteries. The reader may be inclined to blame Iris, as she is astutely aware: "Whoever's left alive gets blamed" (p. 577), but unlike Grace Marks Iris is not in prison for murder. As a member of the old Anglo-Canadian establishment and the widow of a prominent Ontario industrialist, she belongs to the social class that is traditionally beyond reproach. The only sentence she awaits is death from old age, and it is against that final silencing that she writes her memoir, dying of a heart attack just as she finishes it.

Why does Iris suddenly decide to begin writing her memoir after all this time? Apparently she has never been a writing woman; it was her younger sister Laura who was the famous novelist. Yet Iris launches into her long narrative on the very day she has to present the Laura Chase Memorial Prize at the local high school in honor of her sister, and Iris wakes up "with a feeling of dread." She introduces herself to the reader with a measure of self-irony, as a frail old lady beset by bodily infirmities who is treated rather like a parcel by the kindly citizens of Port Ticonderoga and propelled through the ceremony until she is allowed to sink into her chair on the platform, "Back into the long shadow cast by Laura. Out of harm's way" (p. 551). But what were Iris's reactions to the speeches on the platform? In fact she was not listening, for beneath the veneer of the public performance she was remembering the scandal of the first publication of Laura's novel when it was she who had to take the consequences for her dead sister's "unmentionable" book. It is this memorial occasion that prompts Iris to start writing her own memoir, breaking open the old wounds of the past and where writing will be, as she dangerously predicts, a kind of bleeding to death. (Is it blood the ghosts want? But I shall return to that question in a moment.) The autobiographical impulse here is an interesting variant on De Man's "specular moment" with its "sudden alignment between past and present selves which opens up multiple possibilities for self-figuration."[22] That theory of biography seemed to account for Elaine Risley's life writing in Cat's Eye,[23] but here the impulse would seem to be exactly the opposite. For Iris, it is a "spectral" rather then a "specular" moment, when she confronts not herself but her memories of the dead Laura. It is a moment that comes close to the uncanny experience of the return of the repressed, leading us back to "what is known of old and long familiar" when "infantile complexes which have been repressed are once more revived by some impression."[24]

That sense of the uncanny is strengthened by Iris's flashbacks to childhood memories on her first morning of writing when she recalls that she and her little sister were like the orphans in a fairy tale, "the two of us, on our thorn-encircled island, waiting for rescue" (p. 53), and also by the fact that at the beginning Iris does not know why she is writing or for whom. It takes her the whole memoir to figure out the answers to these questions. The memoir itself is a very Gothic tale that is part confession, part family history, and part public memorial, like the War Memorials for World War I, which litter the earlier part of this novel. On her daily walks around the town Iris is surrounded by reminders of her family's past greatness—like the Chase Family Monument in the cemetery where her parents and grandparents and Laura's ashes are buried, or the Button Factory built by her grandfather in the 1870s, burnt down during the 1930s, and now refurbished as a tourist attraction, or her grandparents' Gothic mansion with the Tennysonian name of Avilion where she and Laura were brought up and which is now an old people's home. Iris might be said to live "in another dimension of space," where the topography of the present is continually overlaid by a map of the past. Her narrative is filled with ghosts and ghostly voices who figure the secret life of memory, for this is Iris's tour of the underworld, her way of negotiating with the dead:

> What did I want? Nothing much. Just a memorial of some kind. But what is a memorial, when you come right down to it, but a commemoration of wounds endured? Endured, and resented. Without memory, there can be no revenge.
>
> Lest we forget. Remember me. To you from failing hands we throw. Cries of the thirsty ghosts.
>
> Nothing is more difficult than to understand the dead, I've found; but nothing is more dangerous than to ignore them. (p. 621)

Although Iris presents herself in the conventional Edwardian female roles as dutiful daughter, "good sister to Laura," then later as appropriately dressed and frivolous Toronto society wife and mother in a loveless arranged marriage, that self-portrait is continually fissured by odd moments of resentment and by the intrusion of other voices telling fragments of a different story entirely. It is always Laura's voice that is the most disruptive, casting doubts on Iris's version of events, incessantly probing her motives like the secret voice of conscience: "She tends to repeat herself, as the dead have a habit of doing" (p. 600). If that voice speaking from beyond the grave reminds us of Mary Whitney's ghostly voice in *Alias Grace*, it also points to a familiar Atwoodian construction of split female subjectivity, where we recognize Iris and Laura as the latest pair in her long line of doubles.

That relationship between the sisters could constitute a chapter in itself, though here I wish to focus principally on unhiding what has been hidden in Iris's narrative reconstruction. In her memoir we read the history of the girls growing up together—their intense closeness, their insidious rivalries, and also the occasion when they enter into a conspiracy to hide the young Communist agitator Alex Thomas from the police inside their father's house: "He was our guilty secret" (p. 264). Alex remains their guilty secret, but he becomes a secret no longer shared when both the sisters fall in love with him. That love affair is at the broken heart of the novel, the center of the doubling and splitting of identities that has such fatal consequences for both sisters. If we remember Freud's comment that "All these themes [of the Uncanny] are concerned with the phenomenon of the 'double,' which appears in every shape and every degree of development,"[25] then we may begin to understand not only why Iris finds telling her story so painful, but why it is that she says so little about her affair with Alex in her memoir and so much about it in the extracts she gives from Laura's novel, for these two texts shadow each other in a kind of interrupted dialogue throughout. It is significant that in a story about identity and inheritance the only thing Iris tells us about her affair with Alex in her memoir is that her daughter Aimee, born in 1937, is not her husband's daughter but Alex's, and that in Laura's novel the female narrator though also pregnant, never tells her lover and no baby ever appears. The odd points of connection between events in the memoir and the novel teasingly suggest a double identity, which is finally confirmed by the narrative.

Iris's memoir leads inexorably to the memory of Laura's suicide, which occurs when she learns from Iris (who else could it have been?) that Alex has been killed in Holland near the end of World War II.

However it is not Laura's suicide itself but their last meeting the day before that Iris finds most traumatic: "Now I'm coming to the part that still haunts me. Now I should have bitten my tongue, now I should have kept my mouth shut" (p. 595). Hidden at the center of Iris's confession is that profoundly unhomely moment when she has to confront what she has most assiduously repressed: her betrayal of Laura and the recognition that she is responsible for her sister's death. Iris's anguish as she recalls this meeting and its aftermath is exactly paralleled in her feeling of dread on the morning of the prize giving ceremony, where the same image of "being about to step off a cliff" (p. 43) is echoed in the mysterious word "escarpment" (p. 598) at the beginning of the suicide chapter: "Where did that odd word come from?" There are hidden associations here, just as it is characteristic of the uncanny that Iris's recall of her moment of betrayal should read like a replay of childhood memory, leading back to what is old and long familiar. When she tells Laura that Alex has been killed, she sees herself acting from the same spiteful motives as when she pushed the six-year-old Laura off the stone nymph the day after their mother's funeral, while Laura's strange look when Iris reveals that she and Alex had long been lovers is a look that she remembers from the time Laura had jumped into the Louveteau River as a child. Then Iris had rescued her, but now she pushes Laura over the edge. On the day after this meeting the news comes of Laura's accident with which the novel began. Immediately afterwards Iris finds Laura's hidden notebooks, though because of the curious double narrative construction, this discovery has about it the uncanny aura of repetition. (They appear to have been found twice, on pages 4 and 602.) Laura's notebooks contain a coded version of her own life story (Is it her confession?) and the startling revelation of her sexual abuse by Iris's husband, but to Iris's relief there is nothing about a love affair with Alex: "Not Alex Thomas then. Not ever Alex. Alex belonged, for Laura, in another dimension of space" (p. 611). Laura remains the innocent doomed romantic heroine for Iris who now knows "the whole story." But does she? Marina Warner's review of *The Blind Assassin* raises some doubts: "At one point, Laura handtints photographs of the family, coloring Iris blue. Why blue? asks Iris. 'Because you're asleep,' retorts Laura. At this stage in the story we believe Laura. That turns out to be a mistake. Or is it?"[26]

The only piece of external evidence is the black and white photograph of the two sisters with Alex sitting between them, taken at the Button Factory Picnic back on Labor Day 1934, but even that is not available in the original. It only survives in its mutilated form, cut in two by Laura, as the mysterious hidden photograph of "him" and "her" in the prologue and epilogue of Laura's novel: "The photo has been cut; a third of it has been cut off. In the lower left corner there's a hand, scissored off at the wrist, resting on the grass. It's the hand of the other one, the one who is always in the picture whether seen or not. The hand that will set things down" (p. 632). As Iris says, there are two versions of this photo, one of which she has (with herself and Alex) and the other half which belonged to Laura. The uncanny severed hand with a life of its own (but of course there would be two severed hands, each the opposite of the other, in the two photos) is a fitting image for the sisters, each of whom turns out to be the Other Woman. It is also an appropriate emblem for Iris's doubled narrative. When she confesses that it was she and not Laura who wrote *The Blind Assassin* and that she took Laura's name as her pseudonym, Iris insists that they were both responsible. It is in fact a forged signature, but Iris never sees it that way: "Laura was my left hand, and I was hers. We wrote the book together. It's a left-handed book. That's why one of us is always out of sight, whichever way you look at it" (p. 627).

That "collaboration" reminds readers that this is a novel obsessed not only with doubles but also with questions of authorship, and with the slippery relation between fiction and real life. It is full of writers and written texts: Iris constantly reminds us of her painful progress in writing her memoir in all weathers sitting at her kitchen table or outside in her garden, and the anonymous lover hiding from the police in Laura's novel is a hack science fiction writer who tells the fable of the Planet Zycron and the city of Sakiel-Norn to "her" in the course of their affair. There are also Laura's notebooks, which she has left for Iris, just as Iris will bequeath her memoir to her granddaughter. The book is full of references to handwriting as well as to writing hands, moving fingers, left hands, wandering hands, often surrealistically disembodied hands, scrawling graffiti on walls, leaving messages. These strange images of the writing process all cluster around Iris's insistent self-questionings about her motives for writing, whether it be her memoir or further back, *The Blind Assassin* and the science fiction fable. Iris claims that she writes to tell the true story of her family's history, which she has decided to leave as a legacy (locked in her old steamer trunk, together with copies of the first edition of *The Blind Assassin* and Laura's notebooks) to her granddaughter Sabrina: "I offer the truth, I say. I'm the last one who can. It's the only thing in this room that will still be here in the morning" (p. 536). But she also recognizes that hers is the ambiguous gift of an "uninvited black-sheep godmother," and that the truth is never simple, especially when it is already double: "You want the truth, of course. You want me to put two and two together. But two and two doesn't necessarily get you the truth. Two and two equals a voice outside the window. Two and two equals the wind" (p. 484).

This pronouncement is preceded by Iris's admission that what she has written down is subtly "wrong," and it dissolves into her dream of loss and grief when Alex's ghost appears outside her window: "You think you can get rid of things, and people too—leave them behind" (p. 485). Iris edges closer to her deepest motive only as she approaches the end, when with a burst of energy and an invocation to the Furies, she acknowledges that her primary motive all along has been revenge. This is a modern revenge tragedy where the pen is mightier than the sword. Iris takes her double revenge on Laura both in life and after her death by writing the novel and stealing Laura's name as the author, and that novel then becomes a lethal weapon that drove both her husband and her daughter to suicide. Is Iris living under a false identity as an innocent old lady when she is really a murderess? Richard's sister Winifred blames her for his death (p. 348) and Aimee blames her for Laura's death (p. 531), but those two have already been exposed as unreliable witnesses.

Laura's novel raises fascinating questions about authorial identity and authenticity. Of course Richard and Aimee, like the citizens of Port Ticonderoga and Laura's cult followers, have all assumed that *The Blind Assassin* is an autobiographical fiction about her and Alex Thomas, and Iris sharply points out the damaging effects of such misreadings. Moreover, her revelation of authorship discredits this interpretation utterly. (Of course there is always the possibility that it was Iris's malign intention that Laura's novel should be read autobiographically; after all, how could she ever be sure that Laura was not having an affair with Alex too? This is a possibility that Iris never dares to confront directly.) Readers are urged to read novels as fictions, but if this is so, how are we supposed to read Iris's memoir, let alone *her* novel as *The Blind Assassin* turns out to be? To what extent was Iris fictionalizing her own experiences? "I didn't think of what I was doing as writing—just writing down. What I remembered, and also what I imagined, which is also the truth" (p. 626). Perhaps we should remember not only Iris's ambiguous formulation of the truth here, but also what she and Laura learned in school from their tutor Mr. Erskine: "What we really learned from him was how to cheat" (p. 164). Her memoir is a story about complex patterns of treachery that cross the boundaries between generations, genders, and classes as she spins out a black thread of writing in her ambiguous reconstructions of the past.

Iris's memoir is not the only dominant strand in this multivoiced novel, and readers need to take into account "Laura's" novel and the science fiction fantasy, as well as the numerous newspaper reports of national and international events in order to appreciate the breadth and the skepticism of Atwood's vision of twentieth-century Canadian social history. Iris's view of history is very much conditioned by her generation, her gender, and her social class, and while she claims to be telling the truth about scandals within the Anglo-Canadian establishment as she knew it during the 1920s, 1930s, and 1940s, she actually knows very little about what goes on outside her immediate family. (We might feel that she does not even know much about what goes on inside her family either!) Large social events impinge only as they are refracted through her personal circumstances. Like World War I, the Great Depression, and the widespread poverty and industrial unrest of the early 1930s affect Iris only when her father's factory is burned down and the family fortune is lost, while it is through her romance with Alex Thomas, the European-born Communist activist, that Iris learns anything about the Red Scare and the Spanish Civil War or indeed about how the underprivileged members of her society live. From Iris's perspective, class consciousness is just as divisive as race consciousness, and for her the working class is frequently equated with "foreign" and "immigrant," an earlier version of othering in Canada before the multiracial immigration that began in the 1960s. Iris is always an outsider in Alex's world of leftist politics, and he never lets her forget it: "Capitalist's Daughter Aids Bolshevik Murderer" as he jokingly puts it (p. 258). Neither should the reader forget that when the telegram announcing Alex's death near the end of World War II is delivered to her Rosedale home, Iris disowns him, though that gesture is followed by her dream of his ghostly return—transposed into Laura's novel, in a chapter called "The Destruction of Sakiel-Norn"—so that the reader is confused by which sister is doing the writing here. Iris's position is a deeply compromised one and her subversive gestures are entirely personal responses to private betrayals, though no less lethal for that. She manages to destroy her husband's political career and drive him to suicide, while her most damaging blow to the patriarchal system is the illegitimacy of her child, who at the age of thirty-eight commits suicide herself. (Characteristically, Iris makes sure this secret is kept until after she is dead.) Iris allows herself to be a silenced witness, and it is only through the two fragmented texts hidden inside her own that a larger social vision is constructed, "in another dimension of space."

"Laura's" tale of an illicit love affair between a married Toronto socialite and a Communist agitator on the run from the police crosses class boundaries; as Iris confesses, "I wanted a memorial. That was how it began. For Alex, but also for myself" (p. 626). Told in the style of a Raymond Chandler thriller with its wisecracking grittily realist mode, the narrative takes the heroine into Toronto's mean streets with their shabby cafes and seedy lodging houses as she gets in and out of taxis to go to meet her lover. The reader is left with the impression that this is alien territory, which she passes through as quickly as she can, and that all she observes are the interior spaces where their sexual encounters and the science fiction serial take place. We are reminded of Atwood's prose poem "In Love with Raymond Chandler" where she says, "What would matter would be our response to the furniture, and the furniture's response to us."[27] The outside world is blanked out by a private land-scape of desire, and it is only in the juxtaposition of chapter titles like "The Chenille Spread" with newspaper reports of Depression hunger marches and relief efforts, deportations of Communist agitators, and the Army's suppression of strike violence in the mid-1930s that a gap opens up through which social deprivation may be glimpsed.

It is to the science fiction fable about the Planet Zycron and the buried city of Sakiel-Norn that we must turn for explicit social commentary. Told from "his" perspective, that story (written down by Iris) is an allegory of contemporary social history, and given Alex's Marxist ideology, it reads like a satiric attack on the capitalist system and values of the establishment represented by the Chase and Griffen fami-lies. There are provocative correspondences between the sacrificial virgins of Sakiel-Norn who have had their tongues cut out and young society women like Iris who have been married off for money, for exam-ple, as well as the miniaturized and already dead world of Sakiel-Norn itself. Alex would seem to see himself as the Blind Assassin in his story, a kind of hired serial killer wreaking indiscriminate revenge on a corrupt political system, but that plot is disrupted when the Blind Assassin falls in love with the "blue-blooded Snilfard princess." Of course, this is only Iris's recollection of Alex's story. She only ever reads one episode of the Zycron fable, "The Lizard Men of Xenor," in a pulp magazine on a railway bookstall and it says nothing about a secret love affair, but she remembers enough of the generic conventions of his narrative to reconstruct a savage secondhand critique of the corruption and social oppression to which Iris herself remains curiously blind.

This is a strangely duplicitous novel with its ghostly voices, multiple narrators, and overlapping texts that never all tie up, though they are all tied together at the end by Iris in her bundle of papers, which she leaves as Sabrina's inheritance in her old locked steamer trunk in the kitchen.

Several times I have referred to Iris's memoir as her way of negotiating with the dead, and it is to Atwood's recent book, *Negotiating with the Dead: A Writer on Writing* (2002) that I now wish to turn, as the narrative layers around *The Blind Assassin* continue to proliferate.[28] That book developed out of Atwood's Empson Lectures delivered at Cambridge in early 2000, some months before the publication of *The Blind Assassin*, and those lectures shadowily prefigure many of the topics in the new novel. Iris's self-questionings as a writer are the same questions that Atwood is asking here: "*Who are you writing for? Why do you do it? Where does it come from?*" (p. xix). Iris herself is a strange figure and difficult to interpret. Is she the harmless old lady whom the citizens of Ticonderoga see walking the streets, or is she more like Grace Marks, "an accomplished actress and a most practised liar," or as she herself implies the bad fairy or the witch in the gingerbread house? Is she a lonely old woman who sits at home writing out of a sense of "loss and regret and misery and yearning?" (p. 632). "What is the relationship between the two entities we lump under one name, that of 'the writer'?" as Atwood asks in the second chapter of her book, "Duplicity: the jekyll hand, the hyde hand, and the slippery double" (p. 35), where she signals the very motifs that are at the core of identity construction and authorship in *The Blind Assassin*. Iris and Laura are the "slippery doubles" of each other, which engenders the reader's confusion over which sister is telling the story: "this account of Laura's life—of my own life" (p. 627). What began as a metaphor for the writing self becomes a splitting of the self into two, so that Iris is able to describe their authorship as a collaboration: "We wrote the book together" (p. 627). This statement is an amplification of Atwood's reference to the Borges story, "Borges and I," which ends with "I do not not know which of us has written this page" (p. 45). Likewise, Iris's "left-handed book" divides the authorial responsibility at the same time as it represents both herself and Laura as powerless to avoid the writing activity, for Iris sees herself writing as "a bodiless hand, scrawling across a wall" (p. 626), just as she sees evidence of Laura's handwritten messages to her with every piece of graffiti in all the washrooms in Port Ticonderoga.

But why does Iris write and for whom, and why does she have such difficulty in deciding? Again, Atwood offers some suggestive answers in *Negotiating with the Dead*, even before her readers have asked these questions: "*All* writing of the narrative kind, and perhaps all writing, is motivated, deep down, by a fear of and a fascination with mortality— by a desire to make the risky trip down to the Underworld, and to bring something or someone back from the dead" (p. 156). When we consider that the novel is Iris's elegy to Laura and Alex and to her father and mother, her memoir becomes their resurrection, though the cost to her is an outpouring of grief as "the old wound splits open." As she and Atwood know, "The dead make demands . . . and you can't just dismiss either the dead or the demands; you'd be wise to take both of them seriously" (Atwood in *Negotiating*, p. 166), and "Nothing is more difficult than to understand the dead, I've found; but nothing is more dangerous than to ignore them" (Iris in *Blind Assassin*, p. 621). All of which reminds the reader that this novel is also a memorial to the dead, not just a commemoration of loss but also of "wounds endured and resented" by the living, and that writing is perhaps the best revenge Iris can manage when faced with the blind god Eros and the blindfolded goddess Justitia. Iris knows that she too will be dead by the time Sabrina gets the memoir, and that she makes demands too: she wants to be recognized; the novel is her self-justification, and in her writing lies her only chance of survival. Iris's words at the end are very similar to the poet Ovid's words quoted on the last page of *Negotiating with the Dead*: "But still, the fates will leave me my voice, / and by my voice I shall be known" (p. 180).

Faced with this tangle of contradictory evidence out of which private family history and national history must be made, the reader is encouraged to wonder whether the relation between the present and the past might be seen differently if hidden secrets were uncovered. What difference would it make to the terms on which identity might be constructed? Iris answers that question at the end of her story to Sabrina about family inheritance:

> Since Laura is no longer who you thought she was, you're no longer who you think you are, either. That can be a shock, but it can also be a relief . . . Your real grandfather was Alex Thomas, and as to who his own father was, well, the sky's the limit . . . Your legacy from him is the realm of infinite speculation. You're free to reinvent yourself at will. (p. 627)

Iris's final intention is to free her granddaughter from the constraints of legitimating myths of origin by telling her alternative version of family history as a story of illegitimacy, thereby holding out the possibility of escape from predetermining structures of identity. In a sense Iris's story follows the Gothic plot of disclosure and reparation, though like Grace's Tree of Paradise quilt it introduces "a snake or two" as significant variants into conventional patterns. By the time Sabrina reads this Iris will have joined the family ghosts, though she still manages the eerie feat of speaking from beyond the grave through her written words: "But I leave myself in your hands. What choice do I have? By the time you read this last page, that—if anywhere—is the only place I will be" (p. 637).

This "left-handed book" gives Atwood the space to reflect on the historical process of destabilizing traditional English-Canadian stories of national heritage and identity, doing it from within the family, as it were. By the logic of history the novel has to end with Iris's death, for everything she represents has passed, just as predicted at the end of the "Wilderness Tips" story with its strange image of the sinking of the Titanic, echoing Iris's luxurious lifestyle in the 1930s:

> She thinks of a boat—a huge boat, a passenger liner—tilting, descending with all the lights still on, the music still playing, the people talking on, still not aware of the disaster that has already overcome them . . . "Don't you see? It's coming apart, everything's coming apart, you're sinking. You're finished, you're dead!"[29]

*The Blind Assassin* like *Alias Grace* opens up the possibilities for a revised rhetoric of Canadianness, entertaining the prospect of what the Canadian critic Diana Brydon has recently advocated as "a negotiated, not a foundational type of identity,"[30] while acknowledging in a very postmodern fashion that telling history is a way of forging links with a past that is perhaps already "forged." Meanwhile, history with all its "truth and lies, and disguises and revelations" is always available to be reinterpreted in ways that fit the nation's present ideological purposes:

> The past no longer belongs only to those who lived in it; the past belongs to those who claim it, and are willing to explore it, and to infuse it with meaning for those alive today. The past belongs to us, because we are the ones who need it. (*In Search*, p. 39)

# CHAPTER 3

## INTIMATE DISLOCATIONS:
## ALICE MUNRO, *HATESHIP, FRIENDSHIP,*
## *COURTSHIP, LOVESHIP, MARRIAGE*

"On a bridge. This is a floating bridge."
Now she could make it out—the plank roadway just a few inches above the still water. He drew her over to the side and they looked down. There were stars riding on the water. . .
The slight movement of the bridge made her imagine that all the trees and the reed beds were set on saucers of earth and the road was a floating ribbon of earth and underneath it all was water. And the water seemed so still, but it could not really be still because if you tried to keep your eye on one reflected star, you saw how it winked and changed shape and slid from sight. Then it was back again—but maybe not the same one.

("Floating Bridge," 81–82)

Trying to figure out Fiona had always been frustrating. It could be like following a mirage. No—like living in a mirage.

("The Bear Came Over the Mountain," 317)[1]

A female figure in a dark landscape where everything is rocking on water and a man who sees his marriage as a mirage—what is illusory and what is real? And how do such subjective impressions of space relate to questions of identity in Alice Munro's latest short story collection, *Hateship, Friendship, Courtship, Loveship, Marriage*? For over thirty years Munro's stories have mapped the intricate social and emotional geographies of small-town communities in Huron County in southwestern Ontario, where she was born and brought up in the 1930s and 1940s, and to which she returned in the early 1970s after twenty years away in British Columbia. Now she moves regularly between home territory and the west coast, living part of the year in one place and then in the other. Munro's new collection, like *The Love of a Good Woman* (1998), reflects that movement backwards and forwards across the geographical spaces of Canada and across time as well, for there is an increasing emphasis here on elderly people (retired couples, recent widows, old people in nursing homes) with an accompanying sense of individual lives scrolling out over many decades. All this is familiar territory for Munro's readers, and these latest stories resonate with echoes that go back to her first collection, *Dance of the Happy Shades* (1968). As she said in an interview with Peter Gzowski at the time of publication of this book in 2001, "I was afraid people would say 'More of the same, more of the same.' And I felt, well I don't care if they say that, I'm just going to do it."[2] Yet Munro's "revisitings" (to borrow American critic Robert Thacker's word)[3] oddly combine familiarity with strangeness, for like the character in one of her early stories who is asked if he is "back visiting old haunts," she might reply "Not visiting. Haunting."[4] Though there is no suggestion of the supernatural or the psychic here (as there was in *Open Secrets*), there is a very strong sense of added dimensions of vision, both in the collection as a whole and in the characters' own subjective perceptions. The apparent unpredictability of individual lives is shadowed by wider patterns beyond immediate apprehension, intimated through literary allusions, through landscape, or through moments of retrospection and revelation, where what "looked like adventures...was all according to script, if you know what I mean."[5] Every story contains seismic shocks, identities are reinvented and relationships change over time, yet through these fragmented narratives Munro introduces "powerful legendary shapes behind ordinary life" that appear to overlap with the anecdotal present lives of her protagonists, just as they in turn experience moments of slipping sideways between different dimensions of reality.[6] These intimate dislocations point the way back to my opening questions, which could now be reformulated as one question: How much might Munro's explorations of identity be related to her characters' shifting locations within the textual spaces of her stories?

Munro's narratives are always geographically specific and place is frequently a substantial support for her protagonists' sense of identity, as Gerald Lynch argued in his recent study of Canadian short-story cycles, where he commented on Munro's 1978 volume: "*Who Do You Think You Are?* is in fact a supreme example of a contemporary story cycle of character wherein place as small town, Hanratty, is recovered to play a definitive role in the formation of character, and, later, the affirmation of identity."[7] He goes on to suggest that this story cycle illustrates "the traditionally Canadian engagement with the question of individual and national identity in relation to place" (p. 160), and certainly in this most recent collection significant moments of realization and crisis are attached to specific places. Yet it is also true, as Lynch acknowledges, that within the environmental context Munro traces characters' shifts in subjective positioning over time as her stories open out into the spaces of memory and imagination. In *Hateship, Friendship, Courtship, Loveship, Marriage* written more than twenty years after *Who Do You Think You Are?*, there is a proliferation of characters through nine different stories as Munro looks into the complicated processes involved in growing up and growing older when identities appear to change at different times, in different places, in different relationships. Of course "place" is still important even if many of these stories are more concerned with departures than with returns home, though the abstract and malleable concept of "space" would seem better to accommodate the multidimensionality of Munro's representations of identity.

My critical understanding of space owes a great deal to Henri Lefebvre's masterly exposition in *The Production of Space*, where he explores the concept in theoretical and experiential terms, seeking to reconcile human space with physics, metaphysics, and ideology. Within this vast project, he speculates on the relationship between "mental space" (subjective inner space), "physical space" (the space occupied by human bodies and material objects and which would include geographical space), and "social space" (which incorporates social relations both individual and collective as well as social structures like families and towns and cities). It is his discussion about the connections between subjectivity and location that I have found most useful in my attempts to articulate the complexities of identity construction in Munro's latest fictions.[8] Indeed, Lefebvre's question about mapping social spaces might be easily translated into the challenge that Munro's stories pose for her critics: "How many maps, in the descriptive or geographical sense, might be needed to deal exhaustively with a given space, to code and decode all its meanings and contents?" (Lefebvre, p. 85). Lefebvre's depth model of multiple mapping, which effectively deconstructs a place into a series of overlapping spaces, would seem to provide a useful analogy for Munro's narratives, where her stories with their overlapping complexities plot identity not as single and fixed but as a series of alternative histories hidden within individual subjects' life stories. These are "identities always in process," and though Munro asserted recently "You're the same person at nineteen that you are at thirty that you are at sixty that you go on being" and "there is some root in your nature that doesn't change,"[9] her stories suggest a radical ambiguity as to where this core of self might be located when its figurings are always partial and changing. All her characters share the sense that life can be lived simultaneously in two different dimensions or experienced from two perspectives, with the result that her protagonists are not split subjects but pluralized subjects. The critical question is how Munro's stories manage to represent these dislocations and multiplicities within individual identity without her characters becoming estranged from the material spaces of their everyday worlds. As she once remarked, "We are the ones who impose the notion of succession on our lives. Perhaps this is how we avoid confronting what is fantasy and what is reality. That is, if it is ever possible to make a meaningful distinction between the two."[10]

Working with the conventions of realism, Munro begins by mapping her characters' identities through the traditional coordinates of age, gender, and social class, relationship to family and community or to region and place of origin. Though she revises these in multiple ways as connections with realism become more ambiguous, she does not engage directly with identity issues relating to nationality, race, or ethnicity. Such issues remain peripheral to the minds of the small-town Ontario citizens in the majority of her stories, whose attitudes might be summed up by the station master's comment in the first story of *Hateship, Friendship, Courtship, Loveship, Marriage* when a young woman wants her furniture sent by rail to a place out in Saskatchewan named Gdynia:

> "A lot of places out there it's all Czechs or Hungarians or Ukrainians," he said. It came to him as he said this that she might be one of those, but so what, he was only stating a fact.
> "Here it is, all right, it's on the line." (p. 2)

Gdynia may be marked on the railway map, but he will take no responsibility for somewhere so far beyond familiar limits: "Towns out there, they're not like here."

For the station master an unfamiliar name on a map designates a blank space rather than a place, which raises questions around representation. How is a person's identity represented within the textual spaces of Munro's stories, and how much of identity is constructed, as Stuart Hall suggested, "within, not outside, representation?"[11] Of course representation must play a substantial role in the way identities are perceived by the self-conscious subjects themselves as well as by others in a social context, but Munro is interested in hidden dimensions of the self that cannot be directly represented, though they constitute the complex layerings of individual subjectivity. She is fascinated by "the way people fall in and out of love, the way people twist things around, things that are ways that we all contrive our lives, I think . . . to me they seem really extraordinary and things that I want to explore."[12]

Munro's concern is not exclusively with women, though her focus is predominantly on how female characters reexamine and revise their lives for she seeks, as she has always done, to "discover a possible space for the feminine imaginary," always so complicitously involved with and yet other than dominantly masculine discourse.[13] In all these stories relationships between men and women constitute the field in which "the feminine" is defined through varieties of resistance to masculine constructions, as each woman seeks not a room of her own but a space of her own where she can escape the constraints of expectation imposed upon her. Munro is still seeking for new ways of "saying the unsayable" and constructing "probable fictions,"[14] figuring out identities through narratives that reconstruct apparently stable surfaces as multidimensional spaces where characters are aware of slipping in and out of different subjective worlds while their bodies remain grounded in the physical spaces of the everyday.

Those slippages are eloquently suggested in my two opening passages—one from a feminine and one from a masculine perspective— to which I shall return briefly. The episode in "Floating Bridge" is set in a familiar Ontario landscape on the edge of a swamp where Jinny, a middle-aged woman dying of cancer, walks out on the bridge at night with a young man whom she has just met and finds a moment of release from pain and anxiety in that liminal space between the dark water and the reflected stars. There is slippage of a different kind in the mirage effect of the second passage when an elderly husband has a disconcerting flash of insight into his relationship with his wife who is now suffering from Alzheimer's Disease. While the first passage refers to a real landscape where sensory perception shifts into a moment of vision, the second passage is only a figure of speech, a provisional representation for something real, which like any mirage shimmers as an image in empty space.

In the first reflective moment, everything is floating and unstable as reality blurs into a mirror image of itself. The evidence of the senses is not to be trusted and Jinny's experience is one of continual movement with the rocking of the bridge and the vanishing then reappearing stars, while as she looks the real world becomes a floating world and then slides back into dimensions of rationality again. Jinny would like to solve the problem of where she is, not only in relation to physical space (which suddenly appears to be boundless and unfathomable) but also in relation to the "muddle" in her own mind. Is she under immediate threat of death as she had believed, or is she possibly in a period of remission as the doctor has just informed her? Her subjective perceptions of landscape reflect her psychological state as she wonders if the water is as still as it looks, and if the reflected stars are the same or not the same ones she sees at different times. There is a strong temptation to read this stunningly visual passage symbolically as an inbetween space beyond normal life, separated from dry land and floating above the dark waters, or to interpret it through a Freudian model where a "manifest" dream content masks a "latent" content of anxiety, while those reflected stars may remind readers of the "star maps and constellations" in *The Moons of Jupiter* (1982) with their indecipherable patterns visible across the vast distances of the cosmos. It seems to me that all these interpretations are possible, though held as subsidiary meanings within the spaces of the text, where the floating bridge is a real topographical feature of the Sowesto landscape, which at the same time becomes a platform for what Dennis Duffy has described in another "near-visionary" moment as "an account of experience that redefines the nature of experience itself."[15]

A similar redefinition of experience is effected through the "mirage" in the second passage. Though far less elaborate than the first, it also encodes an image detached from reality, this time deconstructing an elderly husband's complacent assumptions about his long married life as he suddenly glimpses how it might be viewed from another perspective altogether, where everything turns strange.[16] As Lefebvre remarks, "Mirage effects can introduce an extraordinary element into an ordinary context" (p. 189) whereby what seemed clear and graspable shifts to become unreachable, delusory. A mirage is nothing but an optical illusion, when an image of something at a great distance or even invisible over the horizon appears in space, owing to the laws of reflection and refraction of light; there is something somewhere but it lies always beyond reach, or as Lefebvre explains it, "The mirage . . . is in some sense that which lies short of—and beyond—each part" (p. 181). It is Grant, the man who married Fiona because "she had the spark of life" ("Bear," p. 275), who suddenly sees his wife and their life together slipping away from him when he has to put her in a nursing home. Indeed, there has been a great deal in this marriage that was not transparent at all: Fiona has never known about Grant's many infidelities and he has never known what she really thought, in a relationship conducted on a bright surface of games and jokes where everything is something like the real thing, though there is always a dimension missing. (The phrase "something like that" is a recurrent emblem in this story.) Ironically, Fiona's dementia seems merely to exaggerate her elusiveness and Grant finds it impossible to believe that anything has really changed. Maybe she is only joking after all? "It would not be unlike her" (p. 291). Visiting her at the nursing home, he continually tries to remake Fiona in her old image, and it is an open question at the end whether enough of the old Fiona remains for him to go on doing this. Under what circumstances does a mirage disappear, leaving only empty space?

This last story in the collection ends appropriately with a "shimmer of signifiers," that evanescent cluster which underlay Jean Baudrillard's definition of seduction,[17] and seduction might be said to characterize not only the thematics of this story but also the appeal of the collection as a whole, which like Fiona's identity is always difficult to pin down. Though the stories are all concerned with different characters, there is a sense of patterning that makes it less like a collection and more like a sequence framed by the first and last stories and where all the others take up the same emotional and thematic resonances introduced in the title story.[18] The first story is named after a schoolgirls' game about romance and marriage that sketches what looks like a traditional sequence in a woman's life, though "hateship" introduces a disruptive element and it soon becomes apparent that the words of the game do not promise a predictable pattern but only a series of possibilities, which may occur in any random order. So it happens in the first story, where a young woman called Johanna suddenly leaves her position as an old man's housekeeper in small-town Ontario and goes out west to Gdynia to meet her "lover" as the result of a romantic correspondence forged by two schoolgirls. Instead of its turning into a disastrous joke, Johanna marries the man and they move to British Columbia where they have a son. However, that marriage happens offstage, and the final emphasis shifts back to one of the schoolgirls, who is suddenly dismayed by the "whole twist of consequence" unleashed by her invented letter narratives. What began as a game swings wide into spaces beyond her control so that she feels like the butt of somebody else's joke. Her sense of limited vision and artful contrivance is related here to the duplicitous powers of storytelling, as it is so many times in this collection—with the stories printed in newspapers or made up by a creative writer ("Family Furnishings"), with a satirical poem found in a dead husband's pajama pocket ("Comfort") or a disturbed young man's dream poem like an impression of "wet leaves" in "Post and Beam," and with the secret letters that a young wife tucks "under the elastic waistband of her under-pants" (p. 267) in "Queenie" to prevent her jealous husband from finding them. The first story also functions as a metafictional commentary where female romantic fantasy is shown up as fabrication (as it is in "Nettles" and "What Is Remembered"), though possibly more signifi-cant is the sense of transgression when the schoolgirls' fantasy script is translated into a real-life narrative that produces a marriage and a child.

That is not the end of the story however, for translation works both ways. When one of the girls hears the astonishing news about Johanna's baby she is doing her Latin homework at the kitchen table, and the words of Horace's Ode, which she is translating, take on a disturbing resonance, like a message from an ancient parallel world addressed directly to her across the centuries. Caught within the frame of an entirely different text, that girl is forced to review her childish prank so that she finds herself more deeply implicated in real-life events than she could ever have imagined. This sudden shift in perspective produces a moment of radical dislocation in mental space for the character and for the reader as well, jolting us into paying a different kind of attention to those "really extraordinary things" within everyday life that so fascinate Munro.

The first story with its emphasis on adolescent girls and young women might be seen as a kind of overture to a collection where all the other stories represent experience through middle-aged or elderly people's lives, so that the sense of arbitrariness and displacement is amplified within the wider temporal frames of retrospective knowledge or prospects of imminent death. In most of these stories loss seems inevitable, though that is alleviated by a surprising amount of laughter—laughing fits, giggles, and smiles of all kinds: silly smiles, absentminded smiles, sly charming smiles, and even a "swish of tender hilarity," while there are lots of games and jokes—word jokes, practical jokes, and other more ambiguous or possibly malicious jokes. As Magdalene Redekop alerted readers in *Mothers and Other Clowns*, jokes have always been an important feature of Munro's storytelling, with their potential to subvert carefully contrived structures of reason and social decorum in outbursts of irrationality, which reveal dimensions of absurdity within the seemingly normal.[19] Most memorable perhaps is Bobby Sherriff's gesture at the end of *Lives of Girls and Women*, which is a marvelous example of the mysterious power of a joke. As Del Jordan reports:

> Then he did the only special thing he ever did for me. With those things in his hands, he rose on his toes like a dancer, like a plump ballerina. This action, accompanied by his delicate smile, appeared to be a joke not shared with me so much as displayed for me, and it seemed also to have a concise meaning, a stylized meaning—to be a letter, or a whole word, in an alphabet I did not know.[20]

Whereas jokes in Munro's stories frequently offer a kind of pleasure in slipping sideways within familiar social spaces, others are much more ambiguous, being presented like Bobby Sherriff's in a coded language

that seems to flaunt its duplicity. The question of jokes and their dis-
locating function will occur frequently in my discussion of particular
stories, though it is also one of the techniques for producing the
phenomenon of double vision or sideways slippage in this collection.
Jokes undermine realism by exposing its limits as a mode of representation, challenging fixed notions of identity by gesturing toward what is
unacknowledged, incomprehensible, or forbidden. Nowhere is this
more apparent than in the last story, where Fiona's identity becomes
fragmented as she succumbs to Alzheimer's Disease. It is the story of a
wife's departure and a husband's bewilderment, but it is so full of jokes
and games that in the end it shimmers like the mirage in my opening
passage. The narrative is always slipping sideways between different
places and periods of time, and the strange sly ending elides divisions
between the present and the past (and possibly the real and the imaginary) as this woman suddenly makes a joke to her husband as she had
always done. But is this just a momentary masquerade, and is her
husband's reassuring response just a repetition of his old marital betrayals?
Perhaps there are continuities in this marriage after all, where a joke is
like a floating bridge rocking on unstable surfaces. The ending may also
be a reminder that there are times when a joke is the only possible vehi-
cle for representing a cluster of emotions too painful or too complicated
to be described in any other way. Such jokes do not lose the mysterious
power that Del perceived in Bobby Sherriff's gesture, though bewilderment may sometimes have a tragic rather than a comic resonance. This
is the case in "Nettles," when a woman's romantic fantasies about an
old childhood friend collapse in the face of his revelation of a terrible
family disaster, revealing secrets lurking under the social surfaces of
normalcy. Childhood memories and the realities of adulthood come
into sharp collision as she remembers that his father was a well digger:

> "Mystery," he said. And again, "Well."
> That was a word that I used to hear fairly often, said in that same tone
> of voice, when I was a child. A bridge between one thing and another, or
> a conclusion, or a way of saying something that couldn't be more fully
> said, or thought.
> "A well is a hole in the ground." That was the joking answer. (p. 183)

Munro's narrative art is so complex that, having sketched the context
for my inquiry, I have selected only four stories from this collection
for detailed analysis: "Hateship, Friendship, Courtship, Loveship,
Marriage," "Floating Bridge," "What Is Remembered," and "The Bear
Came Over the Mountain." Any attempt to analyze the secrets of her

storytelling as it weaves together networks of relationships across space and time is likely to end with something close to a "Well," though it is only through looking closely into the narrative mesh itself that we might hope to trace Munro's explorations of identities in process. That multidimensional concept of identity comes close to the concept of "meaning" in a Munro story as it is described by Carol Shields: "The meaning of a Munro story emerges from this complex patterning rather than from the tidiness of a problem/solution set-up or the troublesome little restraints of beginnings, middles and ends."[21] In turn, both "meaning" and "identity" in Munro bear a strong similarity to the concept of "truth," which Adrienne Rich spelt out in an essay on fiction and lies:

> There is no "the Truth," "a truth"—truth is not one thing, or even a system. It is an increasing complexity. The pattern of the carpet is a surface. When we look closely or when we become weavers, we learn of the tiny multiple threads unseen in the overall pattern, the knots on the underside of the carpet.
> That is why the effort to speak honestly is so important. Lies are usually attempts to make everything simpler—for the liar—than it really is, or ought to be.[22]

The title story, "Hateship, Friendship, Courtship, Loveship, Marriage," provides a programmatic overview of the collection as well as a word of guidance to readers on how to approach these stories. The traditional female destiny sketched out in the title is fulfilled in the narrative in unexpected ways, as a young woman goes out into unknown territory following a fantasy script through which she finds her new identity as a wife and mother. The story begins with the prospect of dislocation set uncompromisingly in a realistic small-town context as the young woman, Johanna, comes to the railway station to inquire about sending a load of furniture out west and also to buy a ticket for herself on the same train. She is represented as unglamorous, bossy, and determined, as unclassifiable as a "plain clothes nun" (p. 5). That is the point of view of the stationmaster who has never heard of Gdynia before, but there is another side to this story that begins to unfold when Johanna enters the feminine space of a ladies' dress shop, an incongruous figure surrounded by the glamor of full-length mirrors, taffeta evening gowns, and velvet trimmings. Though it would seem there is no possible fit between her clumsy body and the trappings of conventional femininity, the saleswoman cleverly finds a simple brown dress that gives Johanna her first glimpse of this new secret world. Appropriately enough at this point Johanna makes her surprising announcement,

"It'll likely be what I get married in" (p. 9), which is all the more astonishing when we discover that her declaration, like her trip out to Saskatchewan with the furniture, is based not on certainty at all but on a romance conducted by letter where no wedding had ever been mentioned.

The story develops with constant shifts in narrative perspective between realism on the one hand and romantic fantasy on the other, though the fantasizing is not Johanna's but that of two schoolgirls, Edith and Sabitha, who forge a correspondence between Johanna and Sabitha's widowed father, Ken Boudreau, who lives out in Gdynia. Johanna does actually write replies to "his" letters, but her letters are never sent and her own voice is obliterated in the girls' malicious game: "So then she falls in lo-ove," as indeed she does. There is a strong counterpoint between Johanna's developing narrative of desire and its realistic under-pinnings, fleshed out by her loving care of Ken Boudreau's furniture from his first marriage, which is stored in her employer's barn and which she cleans and polishes: "It looked glamorous, like satin bedspreads and blond hair" (p. 16). It is this furniture that always has to be taken into account and which provides the link between realism and romance when Johanna goes out west.

Her arrival in Gdynia is like entering a blank space; not only is there nobody to meet her but "there did not appear to be a town." Everything in that bare prairie landscape is so unfamiliar that she first of all mistakes Ken Boudreau's shabby hotel for a derelict family house, and when she does discover the man himself naked in bed, the scene is in no way erotic: "The door of the bedroom at the end of the hall was open, and in there she found Ken Boudreau" (p. 42)—delirious with bronchitis. Johanna begins their relationship by taking command and nursing him back to health. The first thing she tells him is that she has brought his furniture, which was really the last thing he wanted. Boudreau is completely indifferent to this strange woman until he sees her bank account, "which added a sleek upholstery to the name Johanna Parry." Though the scenario is the opposite of romance in every way, ironically Boudreau's words to Johanna when he is recovering echo the words in the forged correspondence earlier, so confirming her belief in his love for her though that letter "exchange" remains a secret part of Johanna's private fantasy life. Boudreau is a shiftless man as his past history reveals, though he has enough self-interest and sense as he lies on Johanna's freshly washed sheets to recognize her strength and devotion "like a net beneath him, heaven-sent, a bounty not to be questioned" (p. 49). Conversely, although she sees that he is weak, "another fine-looking, flighty person in need of care and management" like her beloved former employer Mrs. Willetts, these are qualities that provide Johanna with her chance of emotional fulfillment, "such a warm commotion, such busy love" (p. 51). Munro has deftly turned romance on its head, translating the dynamics of fantasy into real life while subverting the traditional gendered power relationship into celebration of a woman's managerial capacities and a man's gratitude for being rescued. Again, it is the furniture that codes in this link, as Johanna declares that they must sell the hotel and move to British Columbia, taking the furniture with them of course: "We have got all we need to furnish a home" (p. 50), a statement that Boudreau embroiders with thoughts of evergreen forests and ripe apples out in the Okanagan: "*All we need to make a home*" (p. 51).

The rest of Johanna's story of her changed identity as Mrs. Boudreau and mother of an infant son Omar remains untold in a space outside the text, for it happens in a location remote from the interests of small-town Ontario where the letter-writing frame story is set. Johanna's story of escape is one of the narratives embedded here that remains incompletely known, and of which only fragments are given, like pieces of supplementary information that engender radical reinterpretations. Back in Ontario, Edith still lives at home with her parents above their shoe shop, where she suffers from a clever girl's sense of alienation, which readers will remember from Del Jordan in *Lives of Girls and Women*: "And in a way, it seemed only proper that the antics of her former self should not be connected with her present self—let alone with the real self that she expected would take over once she got out of this town and away from all the people who thought they knew her" (p. 52).

Ironically, the news of Johanna's baby's birth is contained in the death notice of Johanna's old employer in the local paper, and it is that missing piece of information that Edith resents most of all. Try as she might to exonerate herself from responsibility for Omar's existence, it reminds her that the past cannot be shut off as completely as she had hoped. Moreover, the Horace quotation in her Latin homework challenges her image of herself as a "godlike arranger of patterns and destinies" (Munro's phrase to describe her own sense of power when as an adolescent she discovered the delights of storytelling),[23] as she is forced to contemplate the consequences of her letter-writing game in a wider frame of reference than she had ever imagined. It is one of those "vertiginous moments" to which Natalie Foy refers "when characters glimpse one of the parallel narratives" that intersect in their lives,[24] causing a tremor of subjective dislocation like a joke from the distant past that subverts any illusion of authority over the future: "You must not ask, it is forbidden for us to know... what fate has in store for me, or for you—" (p. 52).

In "Floating Bridge" the action of the narrative is likewise suspended between past and future though for Jinny Lockyer, the middle-aged protagonist who is dying of cancer, there is no doubt of what fate has in store for her. In the shadow of approaching death the story moves from harsh sunlight to evening and nightfall, though the overall effect is not one of closure as might be expected but of an expanded perspective as Jinny stands on the floating bridge in a liminal space, overcome by "a swish of tender hilarity," contemplating her past and her future with equanimity. The poise of that near-visionary moment holds the structural and thematic complexity of this story in a delicate balance, and in my analysis I shall focus on how the narrative negotiates multiple spaces for representing a distinctively feminine subjectivity through landscape. Though the equivalence between the female body and landscape is a familiar trope in women's writing and one that Munro has used suggestively in other stories like "Oranges and Apples" and "What Do You Want to Know For?"[25] both stories about cancer threats, this revisiting presents no simple identification but a series of physical and emotional dislocations. Jinny moves backwards and forwards between past and present, always shifting between acquiescence and flight until she finds her moment of temporary freedom on the bridge at the end. This is the story of a good woman's resistance to her husband's persistent misconstructions of her identity through their long marriage, where Munro traces a particular kind of feminine anger that has always remained hidden and unsayable except in the disguised form of jokes and one failed escape attempt when Jinny got as far as the bus station and then came home again. That is the point where the story begins, with her departure and then a joke.

In this story, which is full of jokes of various kinds, it is interesting that the first joke, told by Jinny, relates to their marriage and to its threatened break-up, which never happened. As Munro remarked to Peter Gzowski, telling jokes was a popular literary genre in the place where she grew up:

> I don't know if they do that much any more. But it used to be sort of a habit when you went visiting, people one knew well, in Huron County. It meant that you didn't have to introduce conversation where people might not agree—politics and things like that. So you talked about the weather, and then as you relaxed, people began to tell jokes. And I very

seldom had a good joke to tell . . . It's a form of literary composition, but nobody feels it's literary, so anybody can become an expert at it.[26]

Evidently Jinny tells her joke "in company. . . many times," though why she should choose to make such an embarrassing topic into an amusing story for social occasions intrigues Munro's readers if not Jinny's listeners. How do we interpret the meanings coded into Jinny's joke, and why is it there as a flashback at the beginning of the story? This is where Freud's perspective on jokes is helpful for throwing theoretical light on the nature of jokes, or what in his investigations of the subject in *Jokes and Their Relation to the Unconscious* he calls "the problem of jokes."[27] Like Munro, Freud is of the opinion that jokes are a form of social communication designed to give pleasure to tellers and listeners in a licensed transgression of reason or decorum, while making visible hidden connections between words or incidents through shifts of emphasis: "a joke is developed play" (p. 238). Freud discusses verbal jokes and conceptual jokes though not practical jokes, arguing for strong similarities between the techniques of jokes and the dream-work in their processes of condensation and displacement, leading to the indirect representation of repressed materials, all of which are ways of saying the unsayable. Possibly his most revelatory comment in relation to Jinny's joke is the following: "A joke will allow us to exploit something ridiculous in our enemy which we could not, on account of obstacles in the way, bring forward openly or consciously: once again, then, the joke *will evade restrictions and open sources of pleasure that have become inaccessible*" (p. 147).

If all this sounds too far-fetched, it is worth remembering that Jinny's joke originated in a burst of anger and contempt at her husband Neal, a teacher at the Correctional Institute for Young Offenders, because he had joined a group of them in eating a cake she had just made for a meeting at their house, displaying a pattern of disrespect for his wife that the reader will come to see as characteristic of him. Apparently the only reason Jinny did not go ahead with her plan to leave was because of the graffiti messages written on the walls of the bus shelter, which terrified her with the possibility of becoming lonely and marginalized herself: "Would she be compelled to make statements on public walls?" (p. 53). Instead of graffiti, she makes her statement of rebellion against Neal's authority in the form of a joke, being the kind of person, a "Nice Nellie" as one of his friends spitefully calls her, "who finds criticism or aggressiveness difficult so long as they are direct, and possible only along circuitous paths."[28] Nevertheless, that joke foregrounded at the beginning signals a darker subtext to their marriage and provides a context for the puzzling mixed messages and habitual masquerades that constitute the multiple dimensions of Jinny's identity.

This is a story where a woman's hostility and discontent are so close to being inadmissible even to herself that it is quite difficult on a first reading to know what is central and what is marginal. "What is the important thing? What do you want us to pay attention to?"[29] Is Jinny's story of her cancer diagnosis and possible remission at the center of the narrative? Is it her husband's fascination with Helen their new home help, or their trip in the van to pick up Helen's good shoes from her caravan home out in the country? Is it the dynamics of this marriage itself with Jinny's mass of silent rebellious feelings littering her life like a pile of rubbish? Certainly all these strands are interwoven in a narrative whose dislocations suggest that this is a story that, like Jinny's joke, has a secret to hide. Only at the end with the view from the floating bridge do the seemingly random anecdotes fall into a pattern, as if this "barrage of human messages" like the graffiti on the walls of the bus shelter or the piles of letters and newspaper articles waiting to be put on disk in Jinny's front room, all sink to the status of insignificant background noise in the still landscape of the swamp. For most of the story readers find themselves in a position rather like Jinny herself: "The fact was that with so much going on and present events grabbing so much of her attention, she found it hard to take any view at all" (p. 58). Yet when read retrospectively, the apparently random sections and even their arrangement can be seen to take up the resonances of "Hateship, Friendship, Courtship, Loveship, Marriage," though with these varied emotional states deviously interwoven. Finally the reader is able to follow the clues both displayed and concealed in that first joke as the marriage is reconstructed from the disillusioned wife's perspective, though her husband is too busy even to notice. As the jangle of noise dies down, the reader is able to map a series of crisis points through which this woman's identity is represented, as the spaces for her self-figuring keep shifting from one form of domestic entrapment to another until she manages at last to find her glorious moment of escape.

Jinny's predicament might be understood through landscape after all, in the contrast between the freedom she experiences on the floating bridge at night and her evident distress during the heat of the day when she is subjected to her husband's incessantly nervous activity, driving pointlessly around town and then socializing with Helen's foster parents when all she wants to do is to go home. These different places provide a realistic context for Jinny's changing feelings, though it is also possible to read these spatial oppositions in gendered terms through a lens of feminist theory. I am thinking of Helene Cixous's "Sorties" (the very title of which resonates through Jinny's deepest desires), where she lays out a suggestive paradigm of hierarchized relations between man and woman, which outlines the positions between husband and wife in this story:

> Activity / passivity,
> Sun / Moon,
> Day / Night...
> Head / heart...
> Form, convex...
> Matter, concave...
> Always the same metaphor: we follow it, it transports us, in all of its forms, wherever a discourse is organized... The hierarchization subjects the entire conceptual organization to man.[30]

Of course in the story such diagrammatic representation is masked by realistic anecdote, though the pattern is absolutely consistent. Everything is dominated by Neal's activities, his decisions, and his friends, and even their home, which has been converted into an office for his good causes, is a male dominated space where Jinny serves as his secretary. In her bleaker moments she is aware that if circumstances changed, all the papers she is in charge of could easily be thrown out like a pile of useless rubbish. Jinny's resistance surfaces at unexpected moments, like the time when lying in bed she suddenly thinks of Neal's death and is shocked to find that what she feels is "the unspeakable excitement you feel when a galloping disaster promises to release you from all responsibility" (p. 58). Like the first joke, which no doubt she turns against herself in her retellings, so the disaster will be her own death and not his, but this obfuscation cannot hide her sense of the oppressiveness of his presence. This story is full of suppressed feminine rage though Jinny's anger is usually displaced on to other people associated with Neal, like the girl Helen who has for her "a disagreeable power" or like Matt, the grotesquely fat foster father whose purple navel "riding on his belly like a giant pincushion" provokes waves of nausea in Jinny. His shady joke about the pussy willow causes a rare outburst from Jinny, though ironically it has nothing to do with him directly. It is a symptom of her repressed anger against Neal and her doctor, neither of whom shows any sympathy for her condition, giving rise to one of those split moments when the subject inhabits two different worlds at once and the messages get confused. There is no confusion however, about her fierce silent criticism of Neal when she sees him playing his male power games with Helen in the van: "On his face there was an expression of conscious, but helpless, silliness. Signs of an invasion of bliss. Neal's whole body was invaded, he was brimming with silly bliss" (p. 65). This is the man who had not even listened when his wife tried to tell him about the doctor's diagnosis and her possible remission. Of course it is that anger which Jinny carries with her, even when she gains a space of solitude on Matt's farm. Refusing to accompany Neal into the caravan for a beer and a sociable conversation, she wanders off into a cornfield, but even here she is plagued by old resentments and the thought that after her death she will remain misunderstood: "Everyone was wrong... When you died, of course, these wrong opinions were all there was left" (p. 72).

Only at the end when Jinny drives out to the floating bridge with the eighteen-year-old son of Helen's foster parents does she find a precious moment of freedom outside her "old, normal life," and it is a freedom associated with open spaces that might be read in Cixous's gendered terms as feminine. This is one of Munro's secret places hidden within a familiar landscape, reached by driving away from the farm and heading off on a dirt track, where daylight and heat gradually give way to cool darkness and the noises of the day are replaced by the sounds of frogs and lapping water. Jinny's experience is not that of a solitary spectator's rapture at the prospect of sublime landscape; instead it is closer to Aritha van Herk's description of a woman's experience of the prairie: "Landscape beckons escape: escapade."[31] Jinny is not alone, for Ricky the young man drives her out to the swamp and then he leads her on to the bridge, where first of all he shows her the stars reflected in the water and then he kisses her before they walk back the way they came. Though that kiss is an expression of casual intimacy, it is also a moment of intense mutual enjoyment:

> It seemed to her that this was the first time ever that she had participated in a kiss that was an event in itself. The whole story, all by itself. A tender prologue, an efficient pressure, a wholehearted probing and receiving, a lingering thanks, and a drawing away satisfied.
> "Oh," he said. "Oh." (p. 82)

There is a strong inflection of the erotic in Jinny's sense of this fulfillment of her feminine identity, just as there is an odd freakish awareness (for the reader) of a parallel between her experience with Ricky as an enhanced version of Neal's silly infatuation with Helen. Yet it is also Jinny's moment of near-visionary experience, which "redefines the nature of experience itself,"[32] and where for the first time she is able to view Neal's foibles with a "lighthearted sort of compassion." Unlike the rest of the story, the ending is not infused with feminine anger but instead spells emotional liberation where binary oppositions become blurred like the stars reflected in the dark water. It is significant that this is a "floating bridge" where Jinny the older woman is standing with Ricky who is a young man less than half her age, so that neither she nor the reader is allowed to forget that her position is a very unstable one and that her transcendent vision is firmly located in relation to her suffering embodied self. There is no escape possible from the real world except through death, though the final words of the story do grant Jinny a moment of rejoicing with that "swish of tender hilarity, getting the better of all her sores and hollows, for the time given" (p. 83), thus making a joke against death itself.

"What Is Remembered" is also the story of a woman's escape from the dailiness of her marriage, but there is less doubt this time of where the center might be located. It is embedded in the space of female romantic fantasy, though it ends at a point beyond romance as Meriel, now an old woman, remembers her brief secret affair with a bush doctor early in her marriage, telling the story some time after the deaths of both the doctor and her husband. Munro is revisiting old haunts, for throughout her career she has traced the seductive maps of the feminine imaginary, showing how closely a woman's sense of identity is bound up with sexuality and desire that seems to defy age and experience. Meriel's story is situated within a long feminine tradition, marked by Munro from Del Jordan's teenage romance in "Baptizing" (*Lives of Girls and Women*), to adult women's fantasies in "Simon's Luck" (*The Beggar Maid*) and "The Jack Randa Hotel" (*Open Secrets*), a process spelled out most explicitly in "Bardon Bus" (*The Moons of Jupiter*):

> Then I come back again and again to the center of my fantasy, to the moment when you give yourself up, give yourself over, to the assault which is guaranteed to finish off everything you've been before. A stubborn virgin's belief, this belief in perfect mastery; any broken-down wife could tell you there is no such thing.[33]

Nevertheless, those fantasies continue to engross the imaginative lives of older women like Louisa Doud in "Carried Away" (*Open Secrets*) who dreams of a man who died years before and who returns in a hallucinatory moment of "radiant vanishing consolations," and of younger women like Johanna Parry who secretly cling to "that preposterous hope of transformation, of bliss."[34] Munro remains fascinated by the dynamics of erotic fantasy, as she remarked in her Gzowski interview in 2001. Speaking of "Nettles" and "What Is Remembered" she managed to imply how the latter story is looking at romance from a new critical direction: "And the other story is about, of course, how our imaginations, how our fantasies can play such a terribly important role in our lives. Fantasies that never come true, but do come true in a way and then are misrepresented, and how we need these dreams to live by."[35]

What is remembered and forgotten only to be remembered years later, in this story that begins with a quotation taken from a newspaper and is then structured as a secret story about a woman's fantasy life hidden within the story of her real life? Who is Meriel, and how are her shifting subjective and social locations described within this text, which extends over a period of more than thirty years? The story opens in Vancouver with Meriel and her young husband Pierre at the funeral of his best friend Jonas, who died in a motor cycle accident up north, and it is at the lunch afterwards that Meriel, turning away from visions of the afterlife promised by the minister at the service, sees her husband speaking to the unknown bush doctor who had cared for Jonas after his accident. At that stage Meriel has no inkling that within a few hours time she and the doctor would come together in a passionate sexual relationship for one afternoon, which she would remember for the rest of her life. It is only when the doctor, who had driven her to visit an old family friend in a nursing home, makes the surprising offer to come in with her for the visit that she begins to understand the unspoken sexual chemistry between them, registered not consciously but entirely through the language of her body: "She had a sudden mysterious sense of power and delight, as if with every step she took, a bright message was travelling from her heels to the top of her skull" (p. 227).

Their visit to Aunt Muriel would seem like a digression though it turns out to be oddly complicitous with the romantic fantasy plot, for this almost blind old woman who sits smoking a cigarette while grotesquely wrapped in an asbestos cape, has an uncanny kind of second sight that unmasks their affair even before it has happened. Most disturbingly for Meriel, her much admired old friend changes before her eyes into somebody else, becoming "a suddenly strange old woman" who speaks with a new voice "not like any voice of hers that Meriel remembered." She tells them a story from her own youthful bohemian past in Vancouver, which uncannily foreshadows what will happen to them that very day. Perhaps Aunt Muriel is taking on the role of one of the Fates as she sits blindfolded by cataracts, remembering an erotic game that she once played in the dark, and wearing a blindfold: "Adventures.

Well...It looked like adventures, but it was all according to script, if you know what I mean. So not so much of an adventure, actually" (p. 230). This strangely parallel narrative coming from somewhere in the past and interrupted by the old woman's violent coughing fits challenges the younger woman's willed innocence in an old sexual game whose rules are well known and to which she has already consented. Meriel dismisses all this as "salacious fantasy," as she would have to do in order to go on playing the game at all. Given the time frames of this story, the reader will be aware that Meriel is now the same age as Aunt Muriel was at the time of that last visit, a suggestive parallel that reminds us of the extraordinary number of proliferating stories which are interwoven with Meriel's—not only Aunt Muriel's story, but also the doctor's, Pierre's, Jonas's (none of which Meriel or the reader will ever know) as well as her own fantasy narrative in its different versions, which is at the center of the plot.

It is not so much the affair itself as how it is remembered and what this reveals about Meriel's double life that interests Munro most: "In fact, I'm never absolutely sure of anything, and that's probably why I write stories, because every story is an investigation for me."[36] After their one passionate afternoon together nothing else happens, for there are no dismaying twists of consequence here—at least not in the real world. Meriel never sees the doctor again and she returns to the familiar social spaces of her marriage, which ends only with Pierre's death thirty years later. Yet that affair retains all its vitality as the erotic subtext of her life, endlessly revisited in daydreams as the secret space beyond respectable domesticity where Muriel's other self, that fantasy self which confirms her sexuality and her desirability as a woman, continues to exist with "every cell in her body plumped up with a sweet self-esteem" (p. 239). What she remembers most clearly are her own words to the doctor at the beginning of their affair, which are a woman's words of surrender: "*Take me somewhere else*, not *Let's go somewhere else*. That is important to her. The risk, the transfer of power...The start for her— in all her reliving of this moment—of the erotic slide" (pp. 233–34), where "Yielding had been the order of that day" (p. 239). The doctor had taken Meriel to his friend's Kitsilano apartment, a "small, decent building, three or four stories high," though she deliberately reconstructs the memory of that place to fit in with her own romantic scenario: "Why did she conjure up, why did she add that scene?" Of course she is always adding to and revising her memories: "She would keep picking up things she'd missed, assailed by sudden recollections."

Meriel's addiction to her fantasy script represents a form of feminine creativity where she edits her own plot and rejects other plots like the tragic romance plot, "not the kind that anybody wrote any more" (p. 239), or Turgenev's plot in *Fathers and Sons* that she discusses with Pierre when he is dying. She would like to revise the romantic climax of that novel because she feels offended by Turgenev's distortion of the woman's position: "I feel it's just Turgenev coming and yanking them apart and he's doing it for some purpose of his own" (p. 236).[37] Meriel is resisting not only Turgenev's nineteenth-century discourse of femininity but also Pierre's late twentieth-century masculinist construction of a woman's identity: "When it was over she'd love him all the more. Isn't that what women are like? I mean if they're in love?" he asks. And Meriel, "cornered," still manages to answer, "No" (pp. 236–37). Her fantasy has an independent imaginative life of its own, proved by the fact that the news of the doctor's death makes no difference to her daydreams, "if that's what you could call them" (p. 238). Moreover, her fantasizing throws up a seemingly endless fund of memories, one of which surfaces only after Pierre's death, when she suddenly recalls not the goodbye between herself and the doctor at the ferry terminal but his parting words that were both a lie and a "kind and deadly caution" designed to keep her from making a serious mistake and losing her emotional balance. Their secret affair needs to remain in a space deliberately shut off from reality, which was exactly where the doctor was placing it for them both. Meriel recognizes the doctor's gesture of self-preservation, just as she is aware of her own survival mechanisms and the fact that "prudence" had always been her guiding principle, though in her case enhanced by romantic fantasy. Now an old woman casting a retrospective glance over her life, she quite coolly contemplates the doctor's ghost: "She wondered if he'd stay that way, or if she had some new role waiting for him, some use still to put him to in her mind, during the time ahead" (p. 241). After all, as Atwood remarked in *The Robber Bride*, "The dead are in the hands of the living," and Meriel is positioned here as the historian who is outside the event manipulating her own script. She offers perhaps unwittingly a savage anatomy of the narcissistic self-serving quality of romantic fantasy, which imaginatively reverses the dynamics of power in a sexual relationship while paradoxically guaranteeing its vitality as a crucial component of the feminine imaginary.[38]

As the last story in the collection, "The Bear Came Over the Mountain" resonates against the others as it traces the fragmentation of a seventy-year-old woman's identity through Alzheimer's Disease and the end of her marriage when she is placed in a nursing home. Alzheimer's would seem to be the test case for studying the relation between identity and memory, as this psychotic illness fractures connections while in the process revealing the multiplicities of a self, obliterating some layers of recent memory and uncovering other forgotten layers hidden in the past. In a strange way, this story represents another version of multiple mapping: "How many maps...might be needed to deal exhaustively with a given space, to code and decode all its meanings and contents?"[39] or in this case, how many narratives might be needed to map one person's identity and her shifting subjective locations over a lifetime? The story is told not from Fiona the woman's point of view but focalized through her husband Grant's perspective, with some commentary from an omniscient narrator. Beginning with a history of Fiona and Grant's life as a couple, it ends with the aftermath of marriage in a nursing home; the story is structured as a retrospective of their long married life, including the day Grant commits Fiona to the institution and an account of his regular visits to her over several months. It follows Munro's characteristically metonymic narrative construction, proceeding by an accumulation of fragments linked tenuously by associative processes through which a married relationship and a woman's loss of her social identity are figured out. Is the narrative suggesting that Fiona no longer has an identity, or does it merely indicate that the balance of her personality has altered, so that what look like dislocations or blanks in memory might be interpreted as relocations in a different area of subjective space?

Once again the reader is challenged by Munro's unsettling mixture of the familiar and the unfamiliar in a narrative set within a detailed realistic framework, which at the same time exposes the limits of realism with its glimpses of alternative realities, dream lives, secret lives, and a proliferation of subsidiary themes around one main event, that of Fiona's Alzheimer's and her removal to a nursing home. Seen through Grant's eyes, it might be read as a husband's narrative of loss and memory that circles around his wife's absence; but Fiona is not dead. She is still alive and now living in an institution from which he is shut out most of the time so that her life has become a mystery to him, as he is reminded on every visit. Confronted with the evidence of her changing identity and her new emotional relationship with a fellow patient called Aubrey, Grant is forced to consider how that affects his own relationship with his wife, so that his story of mourning slips into a different genre altogether as it assumes the configurations of a plot about marital infidelity and a husband's jealousy. Yet Fiona seems perfectly happy and without guilt in her new identity as Aubrey's close companion. Viewed from her perspective (which is only ever implied), this could be read as the story of a wife's escape through dementia from the prescripted plot of her married life. The narrative keeps all those possibilities in play through its sideways slippages into fragments of other remembered stories, defying resolution in a manner best described by Ajay Heble when he speaks of Munro's "awareness that for any utterance, for any claim to be inhabiting a particular realm of meaning, there are always potential levels of meaning, and alternative ways of formulating ideas and ordinary experiences."[40]

Fiona's residence at Meadowlake Nursing Home (or "Sillylake" as she had once jokingly named it) forms the center of Grant's narrative as he speculates endlessly on what is happening to her behind those closed doors. It is his recognition that he is now an outsider to her life that is the generative principle behind the stories he tells himself as he comes to realize that he does not know who she is or who she ever was. It is as if Alzheimer's has merely exaggerated the elusiveness that had always been her most seductive quality: "She's always been a bit like this" (p. 277). Grant finds it impossible to decide whether she has really changed or not, or whether she is playing a game to test his love and fidelity, "a game that she hoped he would catch on to. They had always had their games—nonsense dialects, characters they invented" (p. 277). However, he becomes increasingly bewildered by Fiona's behavior, for while she retains her social mask and always greets him with her "lopsided, abashed, sly, and charming smile" (p. 288), he can never be certain whether Fiona recognizes him or not: "He could not decide. She could have been playing a joke" (p. 291). Yet, as he reflects, it would have been a cruel joke and out of character. Despite the nurse's warning that with Alzheimer sufferers what is remembered and forgotten shifts from day to day, he persists in believing that Fiona is not lost to him, for he is a man who has always been slow to notice changes in his women— either in his female students in the 1970s or in his wife's present psychological condition. His visits become a torment to him as Fiona continues to treat him with a "distracted social sort of kindness that was successful in holding him back from the most obvious, the most necessary question" (p. 293). Does she remember that he is her husband of nearly fifty years?

Above all, Grant is tormented by jealousy as he is forced every visit to contemplate his wife's devoted attachment to Aubrey, an old boyfriend from her distant past, as the two of them unselfconsciously enact their parody of adolescent love at the card table and in the conservatory (and where else?). Grant is forced into a new role as voyeur and stalker of his own wife, "like a mulish boy conducting a hopeless courtship" or like "one of those wretches who follow celebrated women through the streets" (p. 296). While the nurses and other patients treat it as a joke, "That Aubrey and that Fiona? They've really got it bad, haven't they?" (p. 292) and the medical opinion would be that Fiona was not fully in control of her emotions, the sight of them together provokes Grant's furious anger and "a truly malignant dislike" of Aubrey. His jealousy is exacerbated by unease as Grant finds himself looking back through the spaces of memory to his own numerous secret affairs during the 1960s and 1970s, which he had always taken pride in concealing from Fiona under a masquerade of faithfulness: "He had never stopped making love to Fiona in spite of disturbing demands elsewhere. He had not stayed away from her for a single night" (p. 285). Now this complacency is shattered as Fiona's affair with Aubrey appears to him like an open demonstration of his own secret liaisons, just as in the past her jokey voices had "mimicked uncannily the voices of women of his that she had never met or known about" (p. 277). Meadowlake may be "short on mirrors" though Grant is forced to look at the reflection of his own past behavior, feeling increasingly "as if he were suffering some mental dislocations of his own" (p. 298). The nursing home starts to assume hallucinatory dimensions as Grant wanders around, getting lost in its labyrinthine passageways and always wondering if the different women he sees could be Fiona dressed up in somebody else's clothes. Tormented and confused, it would seem that Grant does not escape punishment for his infidelities but that Fiona all unwittingly (or wittingly, who knows?) is turning the tables and playing a cruel joke on him after all. Munro's readers may wonder if that is perhaps one of Fiona's remaining wifely functions: "Is this the last function of old women . . . making sure the haunts we have contracted for are with us, not one gone without?"[41]

The story loops backwards and sideways in unexpected directions, though it is Grant's perplexing relations with Fiona and his inability either to accept or to represent her changed identity that I shall focus on here. In the last episode when he visits Fiona, he has brought her a "surprise" though it is he who is surprised and not her. (The surprise is Aubrey whom Grant has brought back to visit Fiona, but she has already forgotten about him and he remains absent, presumably outside the door.) Suddenly Grant catches the look on Fiona's face, that of a woman marked with the indelible signs of Alzheimer's: "She stared at him for a moment, as if waves of wind had come beating into her face. Into her face, into her head, pulling everything to rags" (p. 321). Yet, despite these symptoms of decay, Fiona still retains some of her old "bantering grace" as she stand up and throws her arms about her husband in seeming recognition. She then makes one of her old word jokes, which is heart-breaking, not for its faint echoes of her former self but for the way it codes in her inarticulate fears and anxieties: "You could have just driven away," she said. "Just driven away without a care in the world and forsook me. Forsooken me. Forsaken" (p. 322). As Freud said of dreams, so too of jokes, "If we succeed in turning the dream into an utterance of value... we shall evidently have a prospect of learning something new and receiving communications of a sort which would otherwise be inaccessible to us."[42] The story ends with Grant's reply, "Not a chance," which in its turn is an echo of his old duplicitous reassurances. It is as if this final scene is a replay of a relationship that has already vanished, where in the peculiar social spaces of Meadowlake, "people were content to become memories of themselves, final photographs" (p. 296).

Like Grant, the reader is left in a space of indeterminacy where Fiona's behavior is as mystifying as ever. What is going on in the mind of this woman who thinks today that she is in a hotel and about to check out? It seems like a real encounter between husband and wife, but is this genuine emotional warmth on Fiona's part or just in Grant's imagination? Does Fiona, who is wearing a bright yellow dress, which is not hers, resemble the yellow skunk lilies in the swamp that Grant observed driving home one day? She once told him that they were supposed to generate a heat of their own but that she doubted the truth of this state-ment: "She said that she had tried it, but she couldn't be sure if what she felt was heat or her imagination" (p. 316). Has Alzheimer's Disease at last cost Grant Fiona in a way that his marital infidelities never did, and is this loving embrace nothing but a mirage, or another of those "radiant vanishing consolations" that Munro sometimes offers?

It would seem that this last story offers a more complete version of the shifting locations through which identity might be represented though never defined in the multiple dimensions of Munro's narratives, just as it appears to figure the final episodes in that story of female destiny spelled out in the schoolgirls' word game at the beginning. With its own title based on a childish rhyme,[43] it confirms that promise of unpredictability coded into the opening game, in its artful arrangement of fragments that make up the narrative of a husband and wife's rela-tionship over many years. Like most of the other stories in this collec-tion it ends in the narrative present, this time marked by a joke and a moment of reconciliation, which may be nothing more than a simulacrum of reality. That indeterminate ending is so characteristic of

Munro's stories, which are constructed like floating bridges across the spaces between what is real and may be imagined: "I wanted these stories to be open. I wanted to challenge what people want to know. Or expect to know. Or anticipate knowing. And as profoundly, what I think I know."[44]

# CHAPTER 4

## IDENTITIES CUT IN
## FREESTONE: CAROL SHIELDS,
## *HE STONE DIARIES*, AND *LARRY'S PARTY*

> She's sick of her identity; in fact, she's afraid of it. She has all the identity she wants, all she can absorb. Daughter, sister, girlfriend . . .
> She's learned, too, how unstable identity can be, how it can quickly drain away when brought face to face with someone else's identity . . . It was exhausting, the battle to give yourself a shape. It was depressing, too, like an ugly oversized dress you had to go on wearing year after year after year.
> 
> (*The Republic of Love*)[1]

Where is here? Who are we? These are the questions that have formed the codes of the debate over national identity in English Canada for the past thirty years, a debate that shows no signs of diminishing in the contemporary context of multiculturalism, Quebec nationalism, and the political claims of the First Nations. Indeed, non-Canadians might interpret this anxiety over identity as one of the most distinctive marks of Canadianness. Within this contemporary context, Carol Shields's two novels of the mid-1990s, *The Stone Diaries* and *Larry's Party*, offer interesting alternative angles, for these texts mount a radical critique of the foundational fictions through which identities, both national and individual, are constructed.[2] Adopting the genres of fictive biography and autobiography and writing about both male and female subjects in narratives that move as easily across the Canada/United States border as they cross the Atlantic to Europe and back again, Shields challenges any essentialist concepts of identity, just as she challenges the classic fictional genres of identity representation. Wishing her fiction "to become a container for what it was talking about—which was the randomness of a human life, its arbitrary and fractured experiences that nevertheless strain toward a kind of wholeness,"[3] Shields adopts a performative concept of identity where her subjects are engaged in refiguring themselves in response to an endless series of coincidences, ruptures, and dislocations, though all within the seemingly safe confines of a realistic fictional frame and the outlines of a traditional romance plot. Shields writes about unassuming subjects, for her stated concern is with the "diurnal surfaces" of ordinariness, though registered with an eye sharpened "beyond ordinary vision, bringing forward what might be called the subjunctive mode of one's self or others, a world of dreams and possibilities and parallel realities."[4] Through this combination she translates large public concerns about identity into personal terms, as my initial quotation suggests with its connections between fabric and fabrication, where the female protagonist contrasts her fixed identity imposed by socially determining forms with her subjective sense of continually shifting identities, perceiving that identity is both unstable and relational ("How quickly it can drain away when brought face to face with someone else's identity.") Such perceptions give an individual focus to postmodern theoretical concepts of multiple shifting identities, which are always provisional, under construction, and open to revision. As I shall argue, it is Shields's unpretentiously postmodern approach, her unassuming feminism, and her revisioning of sacred myths of identity that are significant factors in accounting for the popularity of her fiction in Canada, the United States, Britain, and Europe. Her novels are symptomatic of a particular moment in Western cultural history, with its widespread skepticism about the metanarratives of history and nation, its questioning of the terms on which identities are formulated, together with an intense interest in gender construction and the revised dynamics of sexual relationships, while her use of a hybridized fictional form, which combines life-writing with social history and diurnal trivia, locates her protagonists within a familiar frame of social, professional, and family relations.

Shields is a Canadian writer and all her fiction has been published first in Canada, though she is herself a "border crosser," being an American immigrant to Canada. Born and brought up in Oak Park, Illinois (where her mother as a young woman boarded with Ernest Hemingway's parents), she moved to Canada in the late 1950s after her marriage to a Canadian postgraduate student in engineering whom she met on an exchange visit to Britain. She has lived in cities across Canada (Toronto, Ottawa, Vancouver, Winnipeg, and now Victoria) and in Britain and Europe for longish periods of time. Her novels have won prizes in three countries: in 1993 *The Stone Diaries* won the Governor General's Award in Canada and the Pulitzer Prize in the United States, as well as being shortlisted for the Booker Prize in Britain, while *Larry's Party* won the British Orange Prize for Fiction in 1998, her Jane Austen biography won the Charles Taylor Prize for nonfiction in Canada in 2002, and her most recent novel *Unless* was shortlisted for the Booker Prize in 2002. As she said in an interview in 1993, "I've never evolved a theory about the difference between Canadian and American writing... the border doesn't mean much to me."[5] That disarming comment typifies her slyly subversive attitude to the restrictiveness of a Canadian cultural nationalist agenda, an issue about which she had already ironized in her first novel *Small Ceremonies* back in 1976. In that novel, a popular male prairie writer's secret identity is revealed: "It's this: Furlong Eberhart, Canadian prairie novelist, the man who is said to embody the ethos of the nation, is an American!"[6] As British critic Faye Hammill remarks: "The figure of Eberhart exposes one of the myths behind interventionist attempts to create a national literature: the myth that the spirit of Canada will only emerge in the writing of Canadian-born citizens."[7] That dismantling of the territorial myth of national identity based on place of origin is amplified by the mobility of the characters in *The Stone Diaries* and *Larry's Party*; clearly, the border doesn't mean much to them either.[8] Speaking from her own position as a white middle-class woman, Shields does not engage with questions of racial or ethnic identity to any significant extent, though it would not be true to say that she leaves racial identity unexamined. Rather, she deconstructs whiteness as a category through her scrutiny of the process of identity formation based on family background and inheritance, class, education and profession, age, and above all assumptions around gender identity with its "complex network of cultural meanings that the sexed body assumes."[9] While in her recent collection of stories *Dressing Up for the Carnival* (2000), the disruption of myths of personal and cultural identity attains at times a surrealistic celebratory dimension in what we might call a postmodern version of the carnivalesque, *The Stone Diaries* and *Larry's Party* foreshadow these instabilities of the subjective "I" within the genre of postmodern biographical fiction.

When *The Stone Diaries* was published, Shields who has written two biographies of literary women (one of the nineteenth-century Canadian pioneer Susanna Moodie, author of *Roughing It in the Bush*, and one of Jane Austen) spoke about the reasons why she preferred the fictional mode of life writing: "Biography and history have a narrative structure, but they don't tell us much about the interior lives of people. This seems to me to be fiction's magic, that it attempts to be an account of all that cannot be documented but is, nevertheless, true."[10] This passage has a curiously modernist ring with its echoes of Virginia Woolf's criticism of the Victorian biographies against which she was writing her own memoir: "Here I come to one of the memoir writer's difficulties—one of the reasons why, though I read so many, so many are failures. They leave out the person to whom things happened. The reason is that it is so difficult to describe any human being."[11] Like Shields a generation later, Woolf adopted a deliberately digressive form, using loosely associated retrospective scenes to represent the disconnections within her own life story. There are also similarities between *The Stone Diaries* and Woolf's fictive biography *Orlando*, with their challenges to generic conventions in an attempt to represent the multiple layerings within a single identity, though Woolf the modernist writer had to cast her explorations of indeterminacies of identity in fantasy form, whereas Shields contains her representation of a woman's fluid identities within a realistic postmodern autobiographical fiction. Her next novel *Larry's Party* revises the genre of fictive biography in a different way by offering a spatial rather than a temporal figuring of a man's life story, in both cases taking into account the oscillations and oddities of the subjective life with all its digressions in narratives, which combine surface reportage with shifting angles of vision, leading readers through a multidimensional account of the undocumented experiences of her fictional protagonists' lives.

As she described it in an interview, Shields "usurps the genre of biography," appropriating it to question the very foundations on which the biographical project is structured.[12] Biography or autobiography, factual or fictional, is concerned with the construction of the identity of the biographical subject and his/her representation in the text, but as Shields speculates, the very concept of individual identity may be nothing more than a fictive construction. Her radical critique brings her novel writing practice very close to Judith Butler's theoretical discussions about postmodern constructions of identity:

> What can be meant by "identity" then, and what grounds the presumption that identities are self-identical, persisting through time as the same, unified, and internally coherent? . . . To what extent do *regulatory practices* of gender formation and division constitute identity, the internal coherence of the subject, indeed, the self-identical status of the person? To what extent is "identity" a normative ideal rather than a descriptive feature of experience?[13]

Butler's questions are also Shields's questions, though for the novelist they have significant narrative implications: how do you tell the story of someone's life so as to represent the instabilities within personal identity construction? *The Stone Diaries* is the autobiography of a woman called

Daisy "with a talent for self-obliteration"[14] and *Larry's Party* is the biography of a man who feels like "a man condemned, no matter what his accomplishments, to be ordinary."[15] Both novels appear to conform to the chronological arrangements of conventional biography, with chapters in *The Stone Diaries* arranged from Daisy's "Birth, 1905" to her "Death" in the mid-1990s, while *Larry's Party* covers the years of his life between 1977 and 1997 from age twenty-six to forty-six, when he suffers his mid-life crisis. They both look like family chronicles, for *The Stone Diaries* has all the biographical paraphernalia with a family tree and family photographs (though there is no photograph of Daisy herself), and *Larry's Party* has a frontispiece of him as a baby in a high chair. However, it soon becomes clear from the temporal disruptions within chapters with their flashbacks, associated clusters of remembered events and shifts in narrative voice, that Shields is exposing the limits of biographical convention as yet another regulatory practice in the construction of identity: "What is the story of a life? A chronicle of fact or a skillfully wrought impression? The bringing together of what she fears? Or the adding-up of what has been off-handedly revealed, those tiny allotted increments of knowledge?" (*The Stone Diaries* (hereafter *SD*), p. 340) This emphasis on the artifice of life writing recalls Paul De Man's suggestively deconstructive critique, "that the autobiographical project may itself produce and determine the life—that what the writer does is in fact governed by the technical demands of self portraiture."[16]

Those generic compulsions and distortions of biographical writing have their parallel in a subjective realization of the fabricated quality of a life as it is being lived. Daisy does not write her autobiography but thinks it instead: "It's just a thought construct of what her life is, the kind of construct that I think we all carry around with us."[17] This auto-biography is "written with imagination's invisible ink" (*SD*, p. 149) as an ongoing narrative rather like a diary, and not as a retrospective project. Shields keeps close to the shifts and changes within Daisy's subjective life: "She understood that if she was going to hold on to her life at all, she would have to rescue it by a primary act of imagination, supplementing, modifying, summoning up the necessary connections" (*SD*, p. 76). Larry on the other hand feels that he stands outside his own story: "This was his history, but none of it, it seemed, reflecting *him*. Was he a sexy man? Question unanswerable. Who is he, this shadowy, temporary self?" (*Larry's Party* (hereafter *LP*), p. 171). I have chosen these two brief passages of indirect interior monologue, one from the autobiography and one from the biography, to illustrate the way that Shields erodes the boundaries between two subgenres while negotiating across the gender divide, as both Daisy and Larry register the disparities between fictive constructions of identity and the vagaries of their subjective lives in that exhausting battle to "give yourself a shape." Shields too is engaged in the battle to give the lives of her fictional subjects a shape within her revised versions of the biographical genre, and I shall now take a closer look at the way she figures out identities in process in *The Stone Diaries* and *Larry's Party*: "It's occurred to her that there are millions, billions, of other men and women in the world who wake up early in their separate beds, greedy for the substance of their own lives, but obliged every day to reinvent themselves" (*SD*, p. 283).

## The Stone Diaries

The Dutch critic Hans Bak has focused the problematic issue of identity construction in *The Stone Diaries*: "As a piece of autographic fiction perhaps the most startling feature of *The Stone Diaries* is the highly tenuous and problematic status of Daisy Goodwill as a narrative self. *The Stone Diaries* confronts us with a peculiar paradox: it is a diary fiction with a vanishing writing subject, an autobiography with a floating center, a biography with a vacuum at the core."[18]

Though the narrative begins with Daisy's definitive statement of origin, "My mother's name was Mercy Stone Goodwill," this is an autobiography that slips in and out of first person narrative so that it quickly becomes a multivoiced text registering a dazzling range of different narrative perspectives, telling the life stories of many other people as well as Daisy's own. The cumulative effect of this method is to represent a woman who is "crowded out of her own life" (*SD*, p. 190) from the moment of her birth, which was indeed unexpected because her mother did not even know that she was pregnant: "Accident, not history, has called us together, and what an assembly we make. What confusion, what a clamor of inadequacy and portent" (*SD*, p. 39). So says Daisy, the "uninvited guest" who begins her life with the trauma of loss, for her mother dies in childbirth. Critics have drawn attention to Daisy's silences and her frequent absences from the text, arguing that the disrupted narrative with its flow of undifferentiated voices represents Daisy as a decentered subject whose identity is invented for her by others—both within the text and by the readers as well. How are we to reconcile this with the autobiographical project? I would argue that this is precisely Shields's intention to demonstrate that through the opinions of others in the social and cultural discourses surrounding us, our identity is constructed as intelligible and therefore representable.

After all, Shields is interested in the potential of fictive biography as an account of "all that cannot be documented" about the subjective life, but she also insists that subjective lives belong to embodied selves who live in and respond to specific historical and social environments. That environmental frame is provided here through a mass of realistic detail in which Daisy's life is embedded—newspaper reports, letters, recipes, household lists, as well as bits of local or national history—all supplemented by the gossip of Daisy's family and friends who comment on the various crises in her life. We are given a plethora of information: "That's the age we live in, the documentary age. As if we can never, never get enough facts" (*SD*, p. 330). These facts tell the reader a great deal about changing conditions in the lives of white North American middle-class women like Daisy during the twentieth century, but this social history like biography itself is "full of systemic error" for it leaves out so much. In conversation with an interviewer who pointed out that *The Stone Diaries* was divided into ten chapters, corresponding to the ten decades of the twentieth century, Shields denied that she set out to give a kind of summation of the century, explaining that her novel was "more of a journey through it."[19] That perspective highlights a different set of facts about Daisy's life, showing how it is filled with disruptions, journeys, and relocations. Born in Tyndall, Manitoba, the orphaned Daisy is taken as a baby by her self-appointed foster mother to live in Winnipeg, and then at the age of nine she is reclaimed by her father and travels with him across the border to Bloomington, Indiana, where she grows up and gets married for the first time. After a disastrous honeymoon in France where she is left a young widow, Daisy remarries and goes to live in Ottawa for over thirty years, and in her retirement moves south to Sarasota, Florida, making one trip to the Orkneys before she dies. Such mapping does not explain Daisy's life, though it does chart her changing social identities. At no point does Daisy question the categories that mark her female life as daughter, wife (twice), mother (of three), widow (twice), grandmother, or great aunt. She lives inside these social inscriptions as her name changes from Goodwill to Goodwill Hoad, to Flett, later to Grandma Flett. She conscientiously learns the appropriate behavior for these various domestic roles through reading books and magazines like *Good Housekeeping*, *McCalls*, and *The Canadian Home Companion*. Daisy takes an infinite amount of trouble learning to be normal: "You learned and you never forgot. You were like other people, you could do the same things other people did" (*SD*, p. 338).

Is Daisy totally trapped inside these social fictions of a woman's identity, like a houseplant that "thrives in a vacuum of geography and climate" (*SD*, p. 192)? If that were the case, there would be no autobiographical imperative: "You might like to believe that Daisy has no gaiety left in her, but this is not true, since she lives outside her story as well as inside" (*SD*, p. 123). Daisy's imaginative life exceeds and sometimes contradicts the facts of her existence, casting into doubt, I believe, the opinions of her family and friends and also of some literary critics that she is a woman erased from the center of her own existence. On the contrary, there is a centering principle in Daisy's life, which paradoxically looks like the absence of a center, and that is the death of her mother. That primary sense of loss, inseparable for Daisy from the trauma of birth is, as I shall argue, the foundational fiction of her identity.[20] The novel demonstrates the imaginative power of such a concept, though it also locates it emphatically within the dimension of private fantasy, for Daisy's is a version of the general desire to return to lost origins.

De Man's "figure of deprivation" becomes Daisy's figure for her own identity (or lack of it) and the explanation for her terrifying sense of inauthenticity, which runs as the secret subtext beneath her life story. Feminist theorists like Julia Kristeva and Helene Cixous have written extensively about the bond between mothers and daughters, but Shields writes about the lack of that sense of plenitude that Cixous celebrates as basic to a woman's physical and emotional sense of self: "It is necessary and sufficient that the best of herself be given to a woman by another woman for her to be able to love herself. . . In women there is always more or less of the mother who makes everything alright, who nourishes, who stands up against separation."[21] Instead, Daisy is obliged to construct her identity upon the traumatic separation from her mother, and throughout her life that loss figures in the formless form of "dark voids and unbridgable gaps" (*SD*, p. 76) or "the emptiness which she was handed at birth" (*SD*, p. 281). Her vocabulary of grief has striking similarities to Kristeva's language for thinking through the separation between mother and child in "Stabat Mater" though Kristeva registers it from the mother's point of view: "This abyss that opens up between the body and what had been its inside: there is the abyss between the mother and the child. What connection is there? . . . Trying to think through that abyss: staggering vertigo. No identity holds up."[22] Rethinking that trauma of separation from the daughter's point of view, Shields intimates that outside the story of Daisy's social identities she experiences that "staggering vertigo," for she lives in a condition of radical alienation and loneliness in the recognition that "she belongs to no one" (*SD*, p. 281).

Paradoxically it is out of this deprivation and yearning for what is lost that Daisy discovers her creative energies: "In the void she finds connection, and in the connection another void—a pattern, of infinite *regress* which is heartbreaking to think of—and yet it pushes her forward, it keeps her alive" (*SD*, p. 281). The mother may be a metaphor, as Cixous suggested, though that loss supplies the imaginative dimensions of Daisy's narrative quest, which is focused on her perpetually deferred desire to feel the warmth and the touch of her lost mother's body: "It's this wing-beat of breath I reach out for. Even now I claim it absolutely. I insist upon its literal volume and vapors, for however hard I try I can be sure of nothing else in the world but this—the fact of her final breath . . . burning, freezing against my sealed eyelids and saying: open, open" (*SD*, p. 40).

If by a primary act of imagination, the eleven-year-old Daisy managed to take hold of her life's story, so we may be tempted to wonder whether there is any final act of imagination by which Daisy's claim on her lost mother might be redeemed. Does her life's story confirm De Man's figuration of autobiographical discourse as "a discourse of self-restoration?"[23] The answer would appear to be yes, for on her death bed Daisy reinvents herself for the last time within the private spaces of her interior monologue as a stone effigy, an imposing funerary monument like the ones she had seen years before in Kirkwall Cathedral—or, the reader may think, like her father's stone tower built in memory of her mother. But Daisy does not think of her father and his tower; instead at this crucial moment of border crossing from life to death she thinks of her mother and manages to make the longed-for identification that will restore her to herself. Finally Daisy reimagines her identity not as an empty space of longing but as a bodily figuration set in stone: "The image is, at the very least, contained: she loves it, in fact, and feels herself merge with, and become, finally, the still body of her dead mother" (*SD*, p. 359).

I have called this loss of the mother Daisy's "foundational fiction of identity," but in what sense is it a fiction? I believe that Daisy makes fact into fiction by magnifying this primary loss into a metaphor of disablement through which to account for her sense of inauthenticity, and so she avoids having to acknowledge that this might also be the result of her social conditioning. Those regulatory practices of femininity within which she saw her identity inscribed are represented most clearly in the social arrangements for her "good marriage" back in 1927. Why, she wonders at the time, is she going to marry Harold Hoad? It is not a question of love, but she knows that it is the socially expected time for her to marry, and "She wants to want something but doesn't know what she is allowed" (*SD*, p. 117). On her second marriage nine years later, Daisy does not tell anyone until after it has taken place, but even then she still doesn't know what she is allowed and follows prescribed social rules for wifehood and motherhood. As a result, after years of marriage she finds herself lying in bed beside her husband with "the debris of her married life raining down around her" (*SD*, p. 191), and once again retreats into her search for the "slender and insubstantial connection" with her lost mother. To take this originary sense of loss as the all-encompassing explanation for Daisy's malaise is to take her at face value, adopting her own foundational fiction that is reductive of the complex negotiations through which a woman's identity is continually refigured.

Daisy may have felt erased from her existence, but *The Stone Diaries* is a multivoiced, not to say a multiplot, novel and we are bound to ask whether Daisy's indeterminate sense of identity is peculiar to her or whether it has correspondences with the other life stories woven in with her own. Is Daisy's problematical identity a gender issue, and does it reflect that "misalignment between men and women," which she believes is the source of the real troubles in this world? Do "men behave in one manner, and women in another" (*SD*, p. 121)? Shields pulls apart this binary myth of essential difference, though she also emphasizes the significance of socialized gender construction:

> I have a romantic belief that men experience life very much as we [women] do emotionally. There is the question of language, but that just requires paying attention to how language operates and what is really behind it. But men are as damaged as women are by power, by power-lessness, by loss, by loneliness, by their need for the other.[24]

The narrative structure allows for the fragmented representation of many men's and women's lives with whom Daisy has come into contact over her eighty years. All of them have the same randomness as her own: her guardian Mrs. Clarentine Flett, who suddenly left her husband after twenty-five years to bring up the orphaned Daisy is accidentally killed when she is knocked down by a boy on a bicycle in Winnipeg, and that same boy later becomes a millionaire who builds the Clarentine Flett Horticultural Conservatory in her honor; the "old Jew," one of the witnesses at Daisy's birth, advances from being a nameless foreign peddler to reassuming his name and becoming "founder and owner of a nationwide chain of retail outlets" (*SD*, p. 258). There are also the checkered histories of Daisy's girlfriends and of her own children. For all these people, stories "erupt in their lives" (*SD*, p. 21), but the stories of Daisy's two fathers, Cuyler Goodwill and her father-in-law Magnus Flett, offer the fullest accounts of shifting constructions of identity where characters reposition themselves, assuming different identities in different places at different times in their lives. Both would seem to demonstrate that "the 'coherence' and 'continuity' of the 'person' are not logical or analytical features of personhood, but, rather, socially instituted and maintained norms of intelligibility."[25]

The trajectories of these two men's lives form a contrastive pattern, with Magnus Flett making his homeward journey back to Scotland for no apparent reason after fifty years in Canada, while Canadian-born Cuyler Goodwill becomes an American and is buried in Indiana. Both these stories are told in a narrative mode which is as dislocated as the lives recounted, with a mixture of omniscient narrator's voice (which may or may not be Daisy's) and a large measure of indirect interior monologue ("all that cannot be documented but is, nevertheless, true"). A summary of Cuyler's life is given by his daughter, who sees him as a nomadic subject who traveled "from one incarnation to the next. In his twenties he was a captive of Eros, in his thirties he belonged to God, and still later, to Art. Now, in his fifties, he champions Commerce" (*SD*, pp. 91–92). Though this account emphasizes the mobility of Cuyler's life, it leaves out the emotional intensity of his feelings as a young man whose rapturous mysticism found its expression in his building of the Goodwill Tower, "a dream structure made up of sorrow mingled with bewilderment" (*SD*, p. 58). However, that omission does highlight the peculiar waywardness of the subjective life, for Cuyler reinvents himself in America as a man without a past: " 'People change,' he has been heard to say, or 'Such and such was only a chapter in my life' " (*SD*, p. 92). Embracing the progressive 1920s American ethos, Cuyler now sees himself—and is seen by others—as an American, a "citizen of a proud, free nation," a border crosser who "has not spent one minute grieving for his lost country" (*SD*, p. 93). He never returns to Canada, even when his daughter goes to live in Ottawa after her second marriage to Barker Flett.

The reader knows nothing of Cuyler's inner life during his prosperous years as a businessman, which makes an interesting comment on his relationship with Daisy (if she is the narrator here) who lived in her father's house almost without interruption until the time of her second marriage in 1936. That life seems to have been effectively obscured by his public speeches, where earlier mystical apprehensions of cosmic forces are translated into a homespun rhetoric of "time teaming up with that funny old fellow, chance, to give birth to a whole lot of miracles"

(*SD*, p. 80). In his most memorable speech, Cuyler expounds on his favorite metaphor of Salem limestone and its peculiar properties: "I say to you young women as you go out into the world, think of this miraculous freestone material as the substance of your lives. You are the stone carver . . . You can make of your lives one thing or the other" (*SD*, p. 116). An inspiring commencement speech though his graduating daughter finds it an embarrassment, but given the facts of Cuyler's life, the reader is inclined to see in it the dimensions of his self-delusion. It is both true and untrue—true in the sense of the shifting frames of his identity, but untrue when we consider the randomness of those shifts. Who or what is the stone carver? Certainly not Cuyler, though possibly his imagery of time and chance provides a fitter explanation for the coordinates by which his life, like all the other lives here, has been shaped. Only at his death, when at the age of seventy-eight he suddenly finds himself lying flat on his back in the garden one April morning, does the interior monologue allow the reader and possibly Cuyler himself to glimpse his inner life, when "his angle of vision was radically altered" (*SD*, p. 276). Striving to perceive a continuity in his identity, he realizes the power of the repressed life that goes on below the level of consciousness: "(There are chambers, he knows, in the most ordinary lives that are never entered, let alone advertised, and yet they lie pressed against the consciousness like leaf specimens in an old book)" (*SD*, p. 279). He dies, remembering at last the name of his young wife, Daisy's mother, for whom he had built the tower more than fifty years ago: "Ah, Mercy." And her name comes to him like a blessing.

The ruptures in Cuyler's life are paralleled in the life of Magnus Flett, whose wife also suddenly left him (not because she died but because she walked out) though his response to loss takes a strikingly different form. Whereas Cuyler's grief is transmuted through his creative effort in building the memorial tower, Magnus becomes obsessed with Clarentine's memory as he embarks on a quest to "find" his lost wife by reading all the romantic novels she had left behind. In the process Magnus finds himself seduced by the language of *Jane Eyre*: "There were things in the story that filled the back of his throat with smarting, sweet pains, and in those moments he felt his wife only a dozen heartbeats away" (*SD*, p. 100). His imaginative life is transformed, and he reads Brontë's novel so many times that he learns it by heart. As Shields explained, "I think he took the book into his body and soul, and made it his. It was a whole other dimension, another world to live in besides the one he was stuck in."[26] Unlike Cuyler, Magnus turns away from the world, sloughing off his identity as father and abandoned husband and going home to the

Orkneys, where he decides to become a hermit and live forever. Oddly enough, he becomes a national celebrity instead, partly because he is the oldest man in Britain and partly because of his astonishing ability to recite the whole of *Jane Eyre*. Like the Goodwill Tower, Magnus's recitation becomes the expression of a deferred desire as intense as Daisy's for her lost mother, though perhaps men do inhabit their stories differently, or at least their language of longing assumes different forms of expression. Daisy never finds out what these differences might be, for when she meets the one hundred and fifteen year old Magnus Flett, he is no longer the romantic wanderer she had imagined him but a "barely breathing cadaver" (*SD*, p. 305), wheezing out part of the first sentence of *Jane Eyre* and mechanically repeating Daisy's name when she says it. What does Magnus represent for Daisy? A legend? A foundational fiction? In any case, "a conscious revisioning will be required of her: accommodation, adjustment" (*SD*, p. 307).

Perhaps up in the Orkneys, like her great niece and her boyfriend scraping away at rocks on their paleobotanical project, Daisy has been seeking "to find a microscopic tracing of buried life," in an impossible search for origins. Like them she fails, as for a moment the borders blur between biography and biology, just as they do between the novel's dominant images of flowers and stones in the realms of paleobotany: "Biology . . . will always frustrate the attempt of specialists to systematize and regulate; the variables are too many" (p. 293). That statement could be taken as emblematic of Shields's project in this fictive autobiography, and it is to this autobiographical dimension that I wish briefly to return. To what extent does this postmodern narrative bear the marks of Daisy's consciousness? Or to put it another way, could this text be said to have a "feminine" identity? To that contentious question I would answer yes, if we "pay attention to the way that language operates."[27] In the same year *The Stone Diaries* was published, Shields wrote about the alternative structures that characterize women's storytelling: "I noticed that women tended to deal in the episodic, to suppress what was smoothly linear to set up digressions, little side stories which were not really digressions at all but integral parts of the story."[28] Her first experiments with that alternative narrative method in her short-story collection *Various Miracles* (1985) suggested the communal quality of women's gossip, though it seems to me that *The Stone Diaries* with its shifting narrative voices elaborates and refines this principle while maintaining the fiction of Daisy's autobiography: "It was true that every anecdote we exchanged had a different structure and feel to it, but afterwards I wondered if they didn't add up to a larger, more complex image, an image that commented in its prismatic way on the nature of women and their ability to care for something beyond themselves, and in their caring create a strategy for survival."[29]

## Larry's Party

Turning to *Larry's Party*, we are obliged to look again at this topic of gender difference in writing, for the question now is not how to write a woman's life but how to write a man's life when you are a woman writer. Crossing gender lines in her fictive biography of a male subject Larry Weller, the florist from Winnipeg who becomes an internationally famous maze designer, Shields explores the foundational fictions on which Larry's identity is constructed, a project that culminates in the question asked in the final chapter: "What's it like being a man . . . in the last days of the twentieth century?" (*LP*, p. 315). In this discussion I shall highlight the issue of gender identity, asking how masculinity is signified, for this, I believe, is at the center of Shields's biographical project rather than sexual, racial, or even national identity. Those are not problematical issues for Larry as a white heterosexual male whose profession allows him to assume a "North American" identity as he moves easily across the Canada/United States border, relocating from Winnipeg to Chicago and then moving back to Toronto during the twenty years of his working life from 1977 to 1997. As a novelist Shields has always been interested in writing across gender boundaries, "not just writing about the other sex, but speaking through its consciousness, using its voice."[30] Half of *Happenstance* is written from a man's perspective, and Larry's is the main focalizing consciousness in *Larry's Party*. (There is no intrusion of the female biographer here, just an anonymous recording voice that is elided into Larry's indirect interior monologue.) Such "gender-hopping" as Shields calls it, is symptomatic of her speculative inquiry into gender difference. It is not a question of impersonation, but Shields does interrogate the concept of masculinity as foundational to a man's sense of identity, showing how it is constructed as a social fiction. In tracing the parameters through which Larry is formed as a masculine subject Shields is exploring the territory mapped so suggestively by Virginia Woolf's *Orlando* and more recently by feminist and gay theorists like Judith Butler and Peter Dickinson: "The abiding gendered self will . . . be shown to be structured by repeated acts that seek to approximate the ideal of a substantial ground of identity, but which in their occasional discontinuity reveal the temporal and contingent groundlessness of this ground."[31]

Shields domesticates such gender theory through her fictive biography. Like *The Stone Diaries* this novel is structured chronologically, starting with "Fifteen Minutes in the Life of Larry Weller, 1977" and working through fourteen chapter titles like "Larry's Work, 1981," "Larry's Penis, 1986," "Larry's Threads, 1993–4," up to "Larry's Party, 1997." Glancing at the contents page, we might assume that this is the biography of a centered male self, very much in control of his own life and his possessions—but how is the reader to interpret the maze designs, which together with the dates preface every chapter, in a manner similar to the quilt patterns in Atwood's *Alias Grace*? There is a chronological grid, but the mapping of Larry's interior life is a spatial one, constructing a man who is a wanderer in his own life—indeed, someone who experiences life as a maze and who earns his livelihood as a mazemaker. And what is any reader to make of chapter 1, which begins with a mistake? "By mistake Larry Weller took someone else's Harris tweed jacket instead of his own" (*LP*, p. 3)? It soon becomes evident that this is no story of stereotypical masculinity, for Larry's is an accidental life; he is a man to whom things happen and his identity is shaped by coincidence, random circumstance, and social pressures over which he seems to have minimal control. In the course of this biography, Larry like Daisy before him assumes many identities: he is a son, a husband (twice), a father (once), and a lover (three times, or is it four, if we count the time he was seduced at college?), and his professional name changes from "Amazing Space Inc." in Chicago in the 1980s to "Larry Weller, Mazemaker" in Toronto in the 1990s. Far from taking control of his life, Larry's most characteristic state is a mixture of bewilderment and anticipation, always waiting for "the next thing that was going to happen to him" (*LP*, p. 13).

We might begin this inquiry into masculinity by citing Simone de Beauvoir's famous statement about femininity in *The Second Sex*: "One is not born a woman, but becomes one." To this we could add Butler's subversive gloss on gender construction: "As an ongoing discursive practice, it is open to intervention and resignification,"[32] much as the name Larry is regarded as a construction site by one of Larry Weller's Chicago friends, a homosexual who is also called Larry: "I made up my mind I'd hang on to the name Larry. I'd force it, by God, to take a new shape. I'd give it some gender stretch, some fiber, a few brain cells even. It's a dopey name, let's face it, but it's ours and we can learn to love it" (*LP*, p. 257). Is gender no more than a name, an attribute of one's social identity, and if so, how does Larry learn to become a man? The answer is through processes of socialization within the normative heterosexual framework of his family and community:

> Larry listens. This is how he's learning about the world, exactly as every-
> one else does—from sideways comments over a lemon meringue pie,
> sudden bursts of comprehension or weird parallels that come curling
> out of the radio, out of a movie, off the pages of a newspaper, out of
> a joke—and his baffled self stands back and says: so this is how it works.
> (*LP*, p. 58)

Much of the social matrix is verbal (or what might be referred to as
the "symbolic" register of language) and it is within this framework of
the symbolic that Larry learns to assume his masculine identity: "The
symbolic is understood as the normative dimension of the constitution
of the sexed subject within language. It consists in a series of demands,
taboos, sanctions, injunctions, prohibitions, impossible idealizations."[33]
If gender is a social inscription rather than a foundation of personhood,
it may be likened to a social performance where Larry learns the scripted
meanings that his sexed body assumes, together with the appropriate
gestures and costumes for his masculine roles. But what happens if he
has feelings and desires that do not fit these gender roles? That is Larry's
problem, for he is always "a subject in excess" so that his identity performance often looks like a masquerade. That term is frequently used in
feminist theory, and here Shields deftly turns it around to reveal that
masculinity is as much a fabrication as femininity. Does masquerade set
out to conceal (as in hiding behind a mask), or does it set out to pretend
(as in dressing up to be someone else)? These are the questions that
Shields addresses from the very first chapter of this fictive biography, as
she encourages readers to think about the terms through which social
identities are constructed.

The opening episode of the Harris tweed jacket taken by mistake
introduces Larry's life story with a masquerade of masculinity as, wearing someone else's borrowed clothes, he strides along the streets of
Winnipeg feeling like a new man. This top quality coat is the signifier
of the master codes of wealth, power, and privilege, so that anyone
seeing a man in that jacket would say "Here comes the Big Guy, watch
out for the Big Guy" (*LP*, p. 4). However, inside that jacket is Larry, the
humble twenty-six-year-old floral designer worrying about the fact that
the jacket is not his, so that there is a fundamental disunity between
social image and subjectivity established right from the beginning. This
is part of a deliberate narrative strategy, which emphasizes identity as a
staged performance. Just as Larry has taken the coat by accident, so there
are lots of other things in his life that are accidental as well, like his

college course in floral design or his girlfriend Dorrie who becomes his wife and the mother of his son, who is conceived by accident: "It was sort of a mistake the way they got together" (*LP*, p. 10). While wearing the expensive jacket Larry finds temporary release into a more positive vision of himself, and significantly it is in this heightened state of masculinity that Larry decides to fall in love with Dorrie: "You can fall in love all by yourself. You don't have to be standing next to the person; you can do it alone, walking down a street" (*LP*, p. 12). However the young Larry cannot sustain his masquerade for more than a few blocks, so that before meeting Dorrie he takes the jacket off and stuffs it into one of the city's big rubbish bins; he is not ready yet to "move into this jacket and live there" (*LP*, p. 12). Larry will have to undergo many transformations before he will feel at home in clothes like this, a process ironically foreshadowed by the wind whipping around him on the Winnipeg street, alternately puffing up his shirtsleeves turning him into Superman, and then pressing them flat, all "puny and shrunk-up." When Larry recalls this episode twenty years later, he misremembers it through a glamorous haze of nostalgia: "He'd felt the force of the wind and impulsively he'd whipped off his tweed jacket, offering himself up to the moment he'd just discovered, letting it sweep him forward on its beguiling currents" (*LP*, p. 331). That unreliable aspect of life writing is one of the reasons for Shields's fascination with it: "I'm interested in how we describe our own lives, how we think them into existence. The construct of your life that you carry around in your head changes every day."[34]

Pursuing her semiotic reading of clothes as social signifiers of gender and status, Shields returns to the topic in the chapter called "Larry's Threads," when nearly eighteen years later Larry has become a prosperous white male professional, a Chicago-based maze designer ("A/Mazing Space Inc.," as his business card reads, p. 145), who tours Europe and America looking at ancient and contemporary mazes. He is also a man at the end of his second marriage, to an American feminist art historian called Beth Prior who is a specialist in images of the Virgin Mary and who has accepted a job as Head of Women's Studies at the University of Sussex in England: "Is this then, a man incapable of holding a woman's love?" (*LP*, p. 231). At the age of forty-three Larry has learned to wear the costumes of successful masculinity, though the dimension of masquerade is still evident as his clothes are used to map not only his changing social identities but also his subjective life. When the prosperous middle-aged Larry, recent winner of the state of Illinois Award for Creative Excellence, boards a plane for Boston, he wears his "stone-washed jeans, perfect for a man feeling stone-washed and stone weary" (*LP*, p. 234). Those jeans and that weariness are counterpointed by his memories of the clothes he had worn in the last days of his marriage to Beth—a dark grey doublebreasted suit, which he had felt were his "grave clothes" and a pair of maroon silk pajamas bought in Paris, which made him feel "like someone in a porno film" (*LP*, p. 237). In his misery Larry remembers nostalgically some of his earlier clothes, especially his beloved Harris tweed jacket, though he seems to have forgotten how he lost it. What he remembers is that it made him look like a normal person. Larry has now become a man who wears "important threads" like a tuxedo and expensive Italian loafers. He is the kind of man who wears the uniform of male professionals, with his beige raincoat and dark suit, though it is his shoes that confirm his generic status: "They announce the presence of a man coming forth in all his adult sobriety and good sense and prudence and leather-enriched masculinity" (*LP*, p. 241). It is as if Larry continually seeks reassurance of his status through his clothes and through his body hair, even boosting his confidence at the time of his separation from Beth by growing a moustache. As he reflects, "Beth . . . would no doubt be ready to offer a range of theories, psychological and mythical, about male hair and its importance to a man's self image, but Larry isn't interested in any of these theories, not these days" (*LP*, p. 243).

However there is within this chapter on clothes and masculinity one short aberration, when Larry thinks about transvestism. He remembers his dying father, that pattern of traditional heterosexuality and homophobia, sitting in hospital wearing his wife's quilted pink dressing gown, indifferent at the last to "funny-bunny looks" from other patients, and Larry remembers his own heterosexual anger at the indignity that his father suffers. However, his second and much more ambiguous memory is of himself, alone after his wife's departure for England, dressing up in one of her floral nightgowns and looking at himself in the mirror. What does this cross-dressing signify? "Nothing much," Larry would say, though it is a moment when one of those "wayward chips of himself" (*LP*, p. 237) floats to the surface, calling in question the unity of his gendered subjectivity. Of course for Larry it is recuperated as parodic performance accompanied by a "lewd wink," though it sits there as a visual supplement that unsettles the dominant heterosexual script, tentatively opening up spaces for possible alternative meanings.

For Larry as for Freud anatomy is destiny, though even Freud conceded that "the majority of men are also far behind the masculine ideal," and that all human beings "combine in themselves both masculine and feminine characteristics, so that pure masculinity and femininity remain theoretical constructions of uncertain content."[35] The chapter on male sexuality is called appropriately enough, "Larry's Penis." Set in the early days of Larry's second marriage, the focus is on heterosexual desire and the material specificities of male and female bodies. Instead of a celebration of that privileged male signifier the Phallus, there is a detailed anatomical description of Larry's penis ("average in size. At least he thinks it is," p. 124), together with a list of the multiple names by which the penis is known in English. Certainly "phallus" occurs in that list, though its supreme status is undercut by terms like "cock," "pendulum," and "prick," which precede and follow it. Its status is further undermined by his new wife's feminist critique of the male sexual organ, which she compares unfavorably with the beauty of women's breasts and lips, not to mention women's moral superiority as the empowering consequence of their lack of penises. Not surprisingly in this context, Larry retreats in memory to his earlier sexual experiences, notably his seduction by a fellow college student when he suddenly, gratefully found his maleness confirmed: "He could do what his fellow human beings did, what they were meant to do. He was like other people" (*LP*, p. 131). Certainly for Larry his penis is neither a sacred nor a privileged signifier but a familiar body part like his pancreas or his brain, though it does sometimes point the way to rapture. There is a wonderful image of Larry briefly attaining the "secret heart of the maze" in an orgasmic moment of lovemaking with Beth: "Forget the past, forget the future, the real music is spilling out of now, out of here. . . . The savor of this minute—which will not come again" (*LP*, p. 139). Under Beth's relentless intellectual analyses of sexual and gender difference, Larry shrinks into silence. Instead of joyous sexual affirmation, the chapter ends with his forlorn conviction of his male otherness and his premonition that he will always "in one way or another" be a failure in Beth's estimation.

It is in the final chapter "Larry's Party," arranged by his new partner Charlotte Angus in honor of his two ex-wives who are both visiting Toronto, that the gender debate takes center stage, though it is diffused (defused?) as dinner party conversation:

"What is it like being a man these days?"
"Yes, what's it like? In the last days of the twentieth century?"
"Tell us." (*LP*, p. 315)

Interestingly, though all the women ask that question, which is repeated three times during the conversation, only one man (not Larry) attempts an answer: "Being a man in 1997 means walking on eggshells" (*LP*, p. 319). However, that statement is possibly the wrong point to enter this debate, for even if one were to neglect the complicated emotional subtext of the occasion, the dinner party discussion develops as a kind of historical overview of the changing cultural meanings associated with gender identities, demonstrating how much social practice regulates the way people see themselves: "But at least we all knew who we were and what was allowed" (*LP*, p. 321). The man who tries to answer the question begins by reminding his listeners of their historical context, registering the loss of traditional roles for men as providers and guardians, while even their biological role is in danger of being made redundant by new reproductive technologies. Beth, that ardent feminist, bears witness to that for she appears at the dinner party "exuberantly" pregnant through artificial insemination. Though none of these men believes he is a "typical man," what emerges through their shared masculine perspectives is a combination of diffidence and resentment at the way men have been demoted to the role of "buffoons." (We may recall Larry's gay friend Larry Fine making a similar point earlier: "You know something? There's a sense in which, deep down, all men in the world are named Larry," p. 261.) The image is one of male bewilderment, "Of being off-balance half the time" (*LP*, p. 321), or indeed of "walking on eggshells."

When the women enter the debate, they present the other half of the picture. Their parallel anecdotes reflect changing concepts of femininity across two generations, for none of these women have followed their mothers' advice about what a wife should be, and both Larry's ex-wives make it plain that they would like to move beyond gender stereotypes, for themselves and for their children: "Anyway, this baby of mine is going to be a person first and a man second" (*LP*, p. 325). Though the women's conversation has a fluency and a lightness lacking in the men's contribution to the debate, it would appear that masculinity and femininity are both in process of revision: "All I meant to say is that men and women at the end of our century should treat this period of uncertainty as an experiment. We can try things out. Men can cook up a batch of soup if they want and not have to give up their penises" (*LP*, p. 324). This debate underscores what the narrative has already revealed, that gender categories are only foundational *fictions* of identity, a position summarized by Judith Butler (which I shall quote, even at the risk of sounding like Beth): "This 'being a man' and this 'being a woman' are internally unstable affairs. They are always beset by ambivalence precisely because there is a cost in every identification . . . the forcible approximation of a norm one never chooses, a norm that chooses us, but which we occupy, reverse, resignify to the extent that the norm fails to determine us completely."[36]

Against such postmodern constructions of identity, the question of "what is it like to be part of the company of men at the end of our millennium?" remains unanswered, fusing with unanswerable metaphysical questions about the meaning of life: "What do they [men] want once their names are inscribed in the book of life? Wait a minute—there isn't any book of life" (*LP*, p. 331). Yet this is a book about one man's life, and within the social space of the final dinner party Larry does find the answers to some important questions in his life as he looks across the candlelit table and exchanges glances and a smile with his first wife Dorrie, the mother of his son Ryan. It is one of those quiet moments of revelation when the diurnal surface splits to "reveal another plane of being, which is similar in its geographical particulars and peopled by those who resemble ourselves,"[37] a slight slippage sideways like a momentary distortion of vision, or as Shields describes it here like a "mirage." Alice Munro used the same image to describe a husband's moment of insight in his marriage in "The Bear Came Over the Mountain," though with opposite consequences to the ones envisaged at Larry's dinner table. (Or is it Beth's dinner table?) The visual effects confound reality and desire, as Larry sees the years of separation between himself and Dorrie collapsing into an imaginary shared life: "They are, in this alternate version of reality, partners in a long marriage, survivors of old quarrels long since mended" (*LP*, p. 328). It may be a "perceptual accident" brought about partly by the candlelight and partly by social interaction (and most significantly by Larry's refusal to act as foster father to Beth's unborn child), but the mirage serves as a blurred vision of a reconciliation that has already taken place and as the image for a future that conforms to the secret desires of both husband and wife: "A vision, a blur of what rightfully is theirs."

Interestingly, this reconciliation is confirmed through Larry and Dorrie's after dinner conversation on the topic of mazes, as they recall their visit to Hampton Court maze on their honeymoon when Larry first got lost, and he makes the momentous declaration that he no longer wants to be lost but found. Typically, Larry's statement is hedged about with indeterminacy: "This is not quite true, but what's true he doesn't yet trust" (*LP*, p. 336), for Larry's subjective life is as full of evasions as the mazes he designs are full of winding paths, and where the notion of a centered self is as elusive as the secret goal at the heart of a maze. There is much to be said about mazes in this novel, both as features of landscape architecture and as artificially constructed spaces where the design invites multiple symbolic readings. Shields plays across the boundaries between realism and the symbolic in her construction of Larry's life, through a narrative form which itself mimics the backward and forward loopings of a maze.[38] As mazemaker and mazing subject, Larry lives his professional and subjective life on the borders between reality and imagination, and his life derives its meaning from his passion for mazes. However, it is not the growth of his "maze craze," which develops "like a ripe crystal growing in his brain and taking up more and more space" (*LP*, p. 92) that I wish to trace here, but rather to consider the significance of mazes as the force shaping Larry's identity as a creative artist, where "his freakish profession is the only thing that keeps him from disappearing" (*LP*, p. 180). It is inside the maze, that fabricated order of art deriving from the living organic world of hedges and earth but deliberately sequestered from life that Larry manages to transcend the socially scripted boundaries of his identity: "It was essential that those threading their way through shrub-lined paths be boxed in by barriers to their vision and enclosed, too, by silence. In a maze you had to feel doubly lost, with exterior sensation cut so cleanly away that nothing remained except for the sound of one's own breath and the teasing sense of wilful abandonment" (*LP*, p. 153). Only when wandering inside a maze does Larry find that simulacrum of an order missing from his real life, while the creative work of designing a maze spells for him his only true liberation of spirit, "thinking how happiness lurks between the hand and the eye, and between the objective design and the abstractions that bloom in his head" (*LP*, p. 180).

Larry's joy is a reminder if not an echo of Shields's comments on her fiction writing activities: "Nothing is more wonderful than being in the middle of a novel, carrying this big thing around in your head all the time. I love to be in the middle of a novel...It makes your other burdens easier."[39] Larry's passion and his profession are fused together in what Shields has called "the rhapsody of work" (*LP*, p. 68), and it seems to me that in this highly self-conscious narrative construct there are evident analogies to be drawn between Larry the mazemaker and Shields the novelist as creative artists, for within the a/mazing space of the text the novelist gains a similar freedom, entering an imaginative dimension beyond the limits of personal identity, or what Shields in her essay "The Ticking Clock" calls "the tight little outline of our official resumes."[40] As she writes in that essay, "What is needed is permission to leave our own skins, worrying less about verisimilitude and trusting the human core we all share" (p. 90). Larry, like Daisy Goodwill before him, has managed to find a way of living "outside his story as well as inside it" (*SD*, p. 123) through his mazemaking, just as Shields has managed through her fiction making to move outside the enclosures of time, geography, and gender, with a glimpse into "the inaccessible stories of others" (p. 87). Like Larry, she works within established traditions using everyday materials, though always seeking through the powers of art to move beyond realistic representation into spaces of the imagination, or what she refers to as "the subjunctive mode" of being.[41] Here narrative representations of such border crossings introduce a principle of psychological mobility that challenges any foundational myths about identity. This opening up of a/mazing spaces within the subjective lives of her protagonists shows a way of casting off that "ugly oversized dress" of fixed identity "that you had to go on wearing year after year after year":

> We want, need, the stories of others. We need, too, to place our own stories beside theirs, to compare, weigh, judge, forgive, and to find, by becoming something other than ourselves, an angle of vision that renews our vision of the world.[42]

# Chapter 5

## "How do we know we are who we think we are?": Ann-Marie MacDonald, *Fall on Your Knees*

He opens his knapsack and takes out a sealed cardboard tube. "When Miss Piper died, she left me a note with your name and address, and instructions for me to give you this personally."

He hands the tube to Lily. She breaks the seal at one end and withdraws a paper scroll. She spreads it out on the table.

Anthony asks, "What is it?"

"It's the family tree," Lily says. "Look. We're all in it."

Rose flicks off the TV, scuffs over on her dilapidated slippers, fishes for her glasses.

. . .

"I don't understand."

"There you are, there."

Lily points to the issue of Frances Euphrasia and Leo (Ginger). Sprouting from the union of their branches is his name in green ink, "Anthony (Aloysius)."

*(Fall on Your Knees*, p. 565)[1]

Ann-Marie MacDonald's Maritime Gothic novel ends far away from the small Nova Scotia town of New Waterford, Cape Breton Island, in an apartment in Harlem, New York, where the secret histories of a New Waterford dynasty stretching over four generations are finally laid out to view as names written on the family tree. A young Afro-Canadian ethnomusicologist and a middle-aged white woman who have never met before discover that they are cousins (their mothers were sisters) and the novel ends with the woman, Lily Piper, inviting the young man, Anthony Piper, to "sit down and have a cuppa tea while I tell you about your mother" (p. 566). This invitation throws the reader back to the opening of the novel, for it is Lily's voice that begins the narrative as it loops back into the past: "They're all dead now" (p. 1). The family tree would appear to be the emblem for this novel, the goal of the quest at its center, for storytelling as MacDonald reminds us constitutes a search for wholeness and reconciliation, as the protagonists strive

> to put something back together again, something that should never have been dismantled in the first place. Something that's missing, a part of the truth, part of themselves... I guess what the book says is that you can try to resist reconciliation—at your peril. But it's going to happen, something's going to be born. Something's going to come together.[2]

The family tree represents this wholeness laid out like a map, where relationships between the names on it are not spatial but temporal and genealogical, and where identities are constructed through the bloodlines of family history. The image of the "tree" is peculiarly appropriate in a novel that is obsessed with tracing roots, unearthing buried secrets repressed in private lives, or covered over in communal histories, a point that is emphasized here through the imagery of branches and twigs and sprouts recorded in green ink, which transform the chart of connected names into a living organism. That "tree" is the gift bequeathed by one Piper sister to the last two surviving family members, Lily and Anthony, who bear the Piper name.

Interestingly, the true history only emerges after the survivors have left Nova Scotia, for they meet unexpectedly in cosmopolitan New York, to be confronted with the baggage of a shared secret history that they carry in their genes. In the light of these revelations (and the last chapter is called "Sudden Light"), we have to look into the implications for individual identity and at the extent to which futures are inextricably connected to the past. As one interviewer asked MacDonald when the novel was published, "Is everyone at the mercy of family history, or is it possible for us to 'invent' ourselves to some degree?" Perhaps the question should be turned around: how much of family history itself is invented? And might a true family history necessitate reinventions of identity when what was previously unacknowledged leads to unforeseen multiplications in the discourse of identity? That family tree may represent a return to origins but it also means a refiguring of identity, at least for Anthony, the orphan from the Nova Scotia Home for Coloured Children in Halifax, who suddenly finds his place in a large extended family. What is foregrounded here is the hidden multicultural and multiracial identity of one Canadian family, offered as a revisionary version of settler history that unravels English-Canadian colonial myths of whiteness and cultural unity through a dynastic narrative. This is the story of two Cape Breton families brought together by a racially mixed marriage—the Scottish Pipers and the Lebanese Mahmouds—from 1900 to the mid-1960s when the family tree is finally made available to Lily and Anthony. However, those bare facts of genealogy are in themselves not enough; they need to be supplemented by Lily's storytelling voice, where events are lived through again so that Anthony may emotionally connect with the members living and dead of his newly discovered family, and especially with his mother. It is no wonder that when Lily shows him his own name and the names of both his parents, the knowledge is so disturbing to the young man that he feels "seasick." Paradoxically, the written genealogical map that ought to confirm identity leads here to a radical reassessment and sudden proliferation of identities for the last of the Pipers.

The narrative begins in Lily's voice, introducing all the different members of the original Piper family: "Mumma," "Daddy," "Lily," "Ambrose," "Mercedes," "Frances," and "Kathleen," and an uneasy feeling develops in the reader that there are mysteries and secrets here that will need to be explained. On the surface this looks like a traditional narrative about a house and its benevolent paternal head (with chapter titles like "The Children's Hour," "Little Women," or "The Shoemaker and his Elves"). However we soon discover that this is an illusion, for underneath there is evidence of terrible family scandals, domestic violence, and child abuse, as well as many dissenting women's voices, and altogether a great deal of wrong that has gone unpunished and unforgiven. MacDonald's multivoiced storytelling project sifts through layers of deceit and half-truths, as she explained:

> For me—and this is part of my love of stories—nothing is ever completely what it seems. You have to keep peeling back and peeling back. Perhaps the person who has been considered an incorrigible liar has been giving you a message all along, and the persons who are above reproach in that respect have been lying to you ... They're trying to confuse you with mere facts.[3]

As Maritime fiction, the novel evokes a strong sense of Cape Breton Island as geographical place, opening with Lily's "Silent Picture" of New Waterford in the moonlight:

> Here's a picture of the town where they lived. New Waterford. It's a night bright with the moon. Imagine you are looking down from the height of a church steeple, onto the vivid gradations of light and shadow that make the picture. A small mining town near cutaway cliffs that curve over narrow rock beaches below, where the silver sea rolls and rolls, flattering the moon. Not many trees, thin grass. The silhouette of a colliery, iron

tower against a slim pewter sky with cables and supports sloping at forty-five-degree angles to the ground. Railway tracks that stretch only a short distance from the base of a gorgeous high slant of glinting coal, towards an archway in the earth where the tracks slope in and down and disappear. And spreading away from the collieries and coal heaps are the peaked roofs of the miners' houses built row on row by the coal company. Company houses. Company town. (p. 1)

This is a realistic description of a small coal-mining town where, as one of the characters remarks, if you scratch the surface of the island what you find is blackness underneath: the blackness of coal. Initially it could be mistaken for one of D.H. Lawrence's small mining communities in Nottinghamshire or Derbyshire, though this panoramic view contrives to introduce dark holes and a graveyard together with hints of the supernatural: "That sighing sound is just the sea," before focusing in on the "white, wood frame house with the covered veranda" where the Piper family lived. The reader cannot quite escape the sense that the place is haunted, though that fantastic dimension is held in check by the framework of realism. In the interview when MacDonald described her discovery of the location for her story, there is a similar shift from photographic realism toward the mysterious:

At the beginning, I saw sepia tones, that kind of yellowed photograph look, and it's a kitchen table. Okay, it must be an old photograph. Pull back a little bit (living in the twentieth century, it's hard not to think in filmic terms), so we pulled the camera back a little bit—oh, it's a house, it's a clapboard, it's white. Pull back a little bit more, it seems to be on this sort of scrabbled, tough landscape. Pull back more, it's an island, and you think, Oh my God, I know that island, I know where that is, and now I know when it is. This house is where I'm going to start, and it's going to start with these people...and I know there's a secret in the garden.[4]

Family history and regional social history are intertwined throughout, for the novel traces the fortunes and decline of the Nova Scotia coal mining industry in the early twentieth century with its strikes, lockouts, and occasional outbreaks of violence, together with widespread poverty and epidemics of infantile paralysis and influenza. After World War I, economic conditions on the island worsened and instead of the Roaring Twenties, Cape Breton staged "a dress rehearsal for the Great Depression" of the 1930s (p. 192). The narrative voice switches frequently between Lily's voice and omniscience, for as MacDonald found, history requires a wider perspective than Lily's: "I soon realized that I wasn't going to be able to exercise the narrative scope that I wanted if I stayed with that."[5]

It is the voice of the social historian that records the illegal bootlegging traffic between the island, Newfoundland, and the States during Prohibition, just as it comments ruefully on out-migration from the region and its consequent depopulation during the 1920s: "There is no such place as 'down home' unless you are 'away.' By November 1929 the process is underway whereby, eventually, more people will have a 'down home' than a 'home'" (p. 241). In this historical context it is emblematic that the novel should end not in New Waterford but in New York, where the last descendants of the Piper family finally meet. These are stories of identity that are set within the frame of Cape Bretoners' multicultural inheritance. The island has always been a place of immigrants and exiles since it was colonized by the French in the seventeenth century; in the eighteenth the Scots and the English came to settle, as well as ex-slaves from the plantations of America and the West Indies. At the end of the nineteenth, Lebanese fleeing the Turks arrived, as well as blacks from Barbados to work in the coal mines, and later Jewish refugees from Europe before World War I. It is this racial and cultural mixture with its attendant hostilities and hybridized identities that constitutes the Piper–Mahmoud inheritance. What the family tree reveals as it names relationships across cultural, racial, national, and sexual divides—Scottish, Lebanese, black, and lesbian—is the blurring of borders by its inclusion of excluded or marginalized groups. A similar reconciliation is achieved at the end of the narrative by James Piper, the white patriarch and by his daughter Mercedes, the most conventional of the Piper sisters. We need to remember that it was Mercedes who compiled the final version of the family tree that she sent to Lily by the messenger to whom she left the old Piper home in Cape Breton. As MacDonald has remarked, the aim of her storytelling is "to make the world larger, not smaller, to welcome what is, not what we'd prefer."[6] The multicultural theme with its related ideological dimensions has attracted most attention from reviewers and critics, who see MacDonald's novel as a significant text in the development of "new paradigms for exploring identity in Canada."[7] (It is perhaps worth adding as a marginal note that MacDonald herself, born on a Royal Canadian Air Force base in Germany, is the child of a Scots Canadian father and a Lebanese Canadian mother who both came from Cape Breton Island, and that she regards the island as her "spiritual home" although she now lives in Toronto.)

Certainly the thematics are important, though it seems to me that the extreme difficulty the protagonists have in getting their story of multiracial inheritance told merits our attention. And what is the significance of the fact that the storytellers are all female? I would argue that the narrative appeal is that of Gothic fiction, for this novel is full of stories of remembering, misremembering, and forgetting, but always marked by the refusal of the past to stay buried. It works as a kind of negotiation with the dead (to evoke Atwood's phrase about the origins of storytelling) which leads to their fictive resurrection, as the very first sentence of the novel reminds us: "They're all dead now." What is unearthed is a tangle of contradictory stories and revised versions of stories told from different narrative points of view. There were after all two earlier versions of the Piper family tree, one made by an adolescent Mercedes and the other by Lily at the age of six, but both of them flawed by missing information or deliberate omissions. Mercedes intended hers to be a surprise gift to her father in the hope of restoring to him the story of his own lost white family, and as she piously explains to Lily, "It tells us where we came from. But it doesn't tell us where we're going. Only God knows that" (p. 208). Lily is recorded on Mercedes's first tree as the sister of herself and Frances, for Mercedes has repressed the memory of her elder sister Kathleen's pregnancy and the possibility that Lily is Kathleen's illegitimate daughter. Indeed, the secret of Lily's parentage is not revealed till much later, while that pregnancy is obscured by Kathleen's death in childbirth. Mercedes connives in the socially accepted fiction (or what one chapter calls "The Official Version") that Kathleen died of influenza and that Lily is the child of James and Materia. While that is a benign falsehood, it prefigures a much more damaging lie told by Mercedes years later. Fearing the social stigma of an illegitimate colored child when Frances becomes pregnant, Mercedes arranges to have the baby sent to an orphanage, telling Frances that her infant son died and so depriving her sister of her maternal role and Anthony of his mother's love. Ironically it is Lily, the illegitimate offspring of an incestuous relationship, who makes Mercedes's rigidly drawn chart into a nonsense with her own childish revisions. She turns the Family Tree into an apple tree, which is actually more accurate in a cartoonlike way, though her comic inventions of red apples with gold and silver wings obscure any Biblical connotations of the Tree of Knowledge together with the ancient names of her father's family, which Mercedes has laboriously rediscovered in dusty chapel registers and provincial archives. Frances describes it as "a dry diagram covered mostly with names of dead Scottish people" (p. 199), whereas Lily's multicolored tree is a living tree, which has its tangled roots in the earth, twined around a treasure chest containing the remains of her dead twin brother who was christened Ambrose by the sisters, as she figures family memories and legends together with Frances's fairy stories about the family.

When Mercedes is so upset at Lily's desecration, Frances and Lily decide to hide her artwork by burying it in the garden late at night under a rock, which is already the repository of a secret that Frances has repressed. When the final version of the family tree appears in New York, it is not only Mercedes's gift to Lily and Anthony of the truths she has learned but also her confession of the lies she has told and her plea for forgiveness. By placing this at the end of the novel, which is also the end of the original Piper family saga, MacDonald highlights the difficulties in acknowledging relationships that transgress conventional sexual and racial boundaries. However, that ending also holds out the promise that "something will get born" from old roots through Anthony's new story as it looks toward a different future founded on the knowledge of his family past.

This is a novel that flaunts its multiculturalism, not only thematically through family history but through the prose texture as well, in its use of multiple languages and the heterogeneity of its intertextual allusions, vigorously resisting myths of cultural purity. Mothers speak to their children in Gaelic or in Lebanese Arabic, though the maternal "semiotic" language is forbidden by the fathers in favor of the "symbolic" order of English. (The maternal language of primary bonding is retained however in the secret subtext of children's yearning for lost mothers, which constitutes one of the most important emotional imperatives in this novel.) James Piper may forbid his wife to speak or sing to their baby daughter Kathleen (named after his mother) in Arabic on the grounds that it will "confuse" her, yet he teaches Kathleen to sing in Italian at the age of three and by the time she is six or seven he encourages her to sing a whole verse of Verdi's *Rigoletto* in the garden at midnight to dispel a nightmare. Incidentally that song about a daughter's intense love for her father is the same one with which Kathleen makes her debut as a concert performer at the Lyceum Theatre in Sydney, Nova Scotia, on the evening when World War I is declared. Kathleen sings in Italian and in French during her training as an opera singer in New York, though it is in Harlem that she discovers jazz and negro blues as well: "I love Verdi and Mozart, but I love the Rhythm Hounds and I love Sweet Jessie Hogan, she is the reigning diva of this city... I love it all. But I love Rose's music best" (p. 487).

Songs and music pervade this novel. There are allusions not only to Italian opera and Harlem jazz but also snatches of Materia's Arabic songs, which she sings to her younger daughters when James is not at home, as well as a West Indian lullaby and music hall numbers. Most hauntingly, fragments of the Irish song "I'll Take You Home Again, Kathleen" recur throughout the text as well as references to the Nativity carol "O Holy Night" ("Cantique de Noel"). Taken together, the musical allusions constitute a subtext that resists the fabricated narratives of "The Official Version," commenting critically or sometimes directly contradicting it. While opera singing is Kathleen's vocation and holds out for her the glamorous promise of fame, freedom, and independence, it also opens the way to her romantic lesbian relationship with the black pianist Rose Lacroix, a transgressive love for which they are both horribly punished. For Kathleen's mother, Materia, piano playing was also her form of rebellion against her husband's tyranny. He was a piano tuner, but she created musical chaos with her wild impromptu medleys and later developed this into an art form when she began to play professionally for the silent movies and traveling vaudeville troupes at the local cinema: "Materia was happy as long as she could play" (p. 53). However her rebellion was cut short by James's jealousy; he made her quit her job, so reducing her to silence. However, their teenaged daughter Frances uses her inherited musical talents as a more effective form of defiance against her father with the song and dance routines that she performs at a speakeasy run by one of her Lebanese uncles in the neighboring town of Sydney—and many years later, Frances's illegitimate son becomes an ethnomusicologist. Music spells out a feminine discourse of resistance against male tyranny, but it can also have more sinister connotations, like the description of Frances being beaten by her father, which is represented as a choreography scored to music: "In the shed the performance has begun. The upbeat grabs her neck till she's on point, the down beat thrusts her back against the wall, two eighth-notes of head on wood...Cue finale in the gut. Frances folds over till she's on the floor. Modern dancer" (pp. 262–63). Perhaps the most devastating musical allusion of all is to the Christmas carol, "O Holy Night" from which the novel's title is derived; the first lines are, "Fall on your knees, Can't you hear the angels singing." This celebration of the Nativity, ironically recalled in the chapter "O Holy Night" where Kathleen dies in childbirth (p. 135), gestures toward the gap between fictions of femininity and the reality of suffering female bodies, just as it points enigmatically toward the mystery at the center of the plot.

Among the dazzling range of intertextual allusions here, where fairy stories and nursery rhymes are mixed with Roman Catholic legends of the lives of the saints and the melodramatic plots of silent films, all matted together like the tangled roots of the family tree itself, the father's boxes of Great Books (a hundred and three volumes, not including the *Encyclopedia Britannica*) assert the image of patriarchal ambition and authority. That his books are largely unread rather undermines this image, though there is one book in the pile that would seem to fore-shadow the tragic destiny hovering over this family's history. That book, Dante's *The Divine Comedy*, is the one James uses to teach Kathleen to read: "At the age of three and a half she'd shared his lap with a terrify-ingly illustrated book more than half her size and sounded out 'In the midway of this our mortal life, I found me in a gloomy wood, astray'" (p. 40). Kathleen's reading begins ominously with the opening lines of *The Inferno*, and though *The Divine Comedy* is not referred to again until near the end, the plot enacts stories of sin and suffering within the Piper family as intense as Dante's transcendent visions.[8] Like Dante, the novel allows its main protagonist to progress through repentance to reconciliation though unlike Dante he is allowed to do it in the world of the living, and when a much chastened James returns to the book in his retirement, he decides "to cheat and skip over *Purgatorio*, eager for the beatific vision and the reunion with Beatrice" (p. 428). In fact, life has not allowed him to cheat on purgatory at all, but he dies with Dante's *Paradiso* in his hands (p. 449). James is discovered sitting in his armchair by his gentle daughter Lily, who picks up the fallen book "and places it carefully in his lap. She bends and kisses his forehead, but she doesn't ask him the question [she had intended to ask] because he is dead" (p. 449). Just as Lily has already "forgiven him for what she does not yet know" (which is the secret of her own incestuous origins), so Frances affirms at the end of her life that "Daddy died in peace because he made his confession. And I forgave him" (p. 557). Although the staunchly Roman Catholic Mercedes accuses Frances of heresy, denying that she has the power to dispense the Sacrament of Penance, the daughters whom James has most wronged have no doubts that their father has been forgiven. *The Divine Comedy* seems to be a hidden structural principle behind this human comedy, which at the same time manages to transform the reader's view of James from incestuous tyrannical father to fatally flawed tragic figure.

However, the most sustained intertextual relationship is with the nineteenth-century English Gothic novels of Charlotte and Emily Brontë, *Jane Eyre* and *Wuthering Heights*. That relationship is a self-conscious gesture of "filliation," as feminist critics like Barbara Godard and Suzanne Becker have asserted.[9] This seeking out of literary foremothers on the female writer's part is paralleled by the fictive protagonists themselves who select models for their life stories from the heroines of fiction, film, or history. Kathleen's somewhat contradictory idols are opera stars like Malibran or Emma Albani (who was also a Canadian like herself) or the American blues singer Jessie Hogan. Although Frances loves reading the Brontës' novels, her true *alter ego* is Louise Brooks, the smoldering star of 1920s silent movies like "Diary of a Lost Girl" or "Pandora's Box," for she is "the best and the worst girl in the world. She is also the most modern. Frances longs to be sold into a 'life of sin,' forced on to the stage and into 'houses of ill fame' where life is tragic but so much fun" (p. 246). All these stories of adventuresses and exceptional women focus on female rebellion against male authority, and it is no accident that in the novel's epigraph from *Wuthering Heights* the heroine answers back:

> "Why canst thou not always be a good lass, Cathy?" ·
> "Why cannot you always be a good man, father?"

A copy of *Wuthering Heights* features as an important prop in the novel (hollowed out by Frances as a hiding place for the money that she earns at the speakeasy), but it is the copy of *Jane Eyre*, defaced by Frances's sketches of Rochester's dismembered hand, which circulates among the sisters and bridges the generational gap between a mid-nineteenth-century novelist and a late twentieth-century one. As MacDonald commented in relation to her indebtedness to this novel:

> I just identified with the much-abused heroine who keeps at it. She may be frail but, my God, she's walking those moors, she's eating pig slop, and it all works out in the end... That's why the book lasts. Because the woman is enraged, and she's going to live her own life. And it's all within the strictures of the time and place.[10]

In this novel about rebellious daughters the Jane Eyre presence is always there: "Jane is in the attic! Jane is in the building!" MacDonald's joke made in her interview with Eve Tihanyi marks Jane as the prototype for Frances, the "bad sister" who is a trickster, a liar, a thief, a sexually abused child, and a teenage "slut" (as her father calls her). Frances's duplicitous twinning with Jane Eyre signals dimensions of difference in this novel, which does have a haunted house and an attic that contains scandalous secrets but there is no madwoman, only women trapped in silence. Likewise, there is no Mr. Rochester figure here and there is no heterosexual romance ending in happy marriage, for MacDonald's narrative trajectory is preoccupied with different issues from Brontë's. Here issues of racial and sexual identities related to hybridity, lesbianism, incest, and illegitimacy matter most, though this updating also looks back to the domestic framework of *Jane Eyre*, where women's traditional roles of mother and homemaker are assumed by the Piper sisters in slightly deviant versions. The childless Mercedes assumes a possessive mothering role toward Frances, which is later transferred to Anthony; Frances herself when a child takes on her dead mother's role as "mother" to Lily and much later, deprived of her own motherhood and living in the family home with Mercedes, she parodies the role of home-maker with her excessive quantities of baking; Lily and Rose after living together for thirty years in New York might be mistaken for "a senile old couple." (Indeed, that would be a mistake, as I shall discuss later.) It is that mixture of unconventionality and tradition, which had so delighted MacDonald in *Jane Eyre*, that is celebrated here, not only in the narrative but in the character of Frances herself, for she like Jane is the female hero and the one member of her family who dares to go digging literally as well as metaphorically for the secret knowledge of what has been buried or deliberately forgotten: "Once again, it is the female subject's gaze at the family community that brings out its gothic patterns."[11]

To describe the paradigmatic female Gothic plot as a "narrative of disclosure and reparation" where "the weight of the past...may be escaped only when its secrets are brought to light through the process of discovering connections between past and present"[12] serves to highlight the overall pattern of MacDonald's novel and the hidden dynamics of Frances's quest. To define the female Gothic tradition and contemporary neo-Gothic by its emphasis on female subjective experience, character-ized by "excess" and by women's desire for "escape"[13] points directly toward MacDonald's rebellious daughters and their transgressive desires. Gothic motifs might be summed up as figuring the "unspeakable" and "live burial,"[14] which in this novel may be taken quite literally with Kathleen's months of silence up in the attic at home all through her preg-nancy, as well as figuratively with its imaging of suppressed traumatic memory as something that is "deeply familiar but which has become alienated through repression."[15] Gothic discourse inhabits the perma-nently unstable territory of the "uncanny" (Freud's *unheimlich*) where what is familiar threatens to collapse into unfamiliar spaces or black holes, generating a high level of anxiety and suspense. Unsurprisingly, as several recent critics have suggested in their revisionary readings of the uncanny, the scariest Gothic place is the home, which becomes an "unhomely" space haunted by monstrous memories and abusive father figures.[16] For MacDonald, Gothic horror is family horror and the domestic space of the Pipers' white house, which replaces the Gothic castle or abbey, becomes the dominant architectural metaphor. Here the attic and the cellar, and even the kitchen and the sitting room, become multipurpose spaces of refuge and protection but also of entrapment and anguish. That same duplicitous topography extends to the garden, which doubles as a Gothic burial site, and beyond that to the creek, which serves as the place of infant baptism, drowning, and disease: "There have never been any fish to be caught in the creek. The only thing anyone's ever got to catch in that creek is polio" (p. 151), and Lily does. The creek marks the boundary between inside and outside worlds and its trickling sound is "like a girl telling a secret in a language so much like our own" (p. 3), but which remains untranslatable till near the end of the novel.

The most shocking Gothic motifs have traditionally related to distortions of the family romance plot with their violent tyrannical fathers, dead or absent mothers, daughters who are imprisoned or married off against their will, and daughters who try to escape. MacDonald's plot presents a revisionary version of this Gothic romance, for James Piper who is the ambitious head of the new Canadian branch of the Pipers and Mahmouds is both a devoted father and an incestuous one, cherishing his daughters but also sexually abusing them. James is cursed by his sexual desire for young girls, having seduced and married Materia Mahmoud when she was thirteen, and later abusing Frances and raping his favorite Kathleen when he visits her in New York and discovers her relationship with Rose. She dies in childbirth of the twins she conceived. The twin who survives is Lily, whose identity is built on lies: "Lily doesn't know whom she looks like. She knows she had a sister who died, and Mumma died of a broken heart right after, and Daddy loves us very much" (p. 188). If the white father is a Janus-faced figure then so also is the dark Lebanese mother, the child bride who is disowned by her wealthy father for marrying the "enklese bastard."[17] Materia seems trapped in her silent maternal role, though in truth she is not silent at all but secretly speaks her Arabic mother language to Frances and Mercedes. She tells them wonderful stories of her "Old Country," the Lebanon, and teaches them Arab songs and dances like the *dabke*, so bequeathing to them their "other" inheritance. A fanatical Roman Catholic, she murders her daughter Kathleen in a mercy killing on the terrible night of childbirth in the attic, and two days later, overcome with guilt, she commits suicide by putting her head in the gas oven, leaving her daughters to the mercy of Daddy whom they idolize. As family romance, the novel keys into infantile fears and desires that are played out through the sisters' childish games and as jokes, which mix Celtic superstitions with Roman Catholic beliefs in saints and miracles. Perhaps the most grotesque of these syncretic images is that of the devil baby in the baptismal gown, which so terrifies Mercedes and which turns out to be their black cat Trixie, dressed up by Frances. It is this strain of dark comedy and childish fantasy that constitutes one of the most rebellious features of this text, for it always exceeds classification within any conventional genre category.

To return to the dynamics of disclosure and reparation within Gothic storytelling, there are three interconnected mysteries here that I would like to explore: the story of Lily's origins, the story of Anthony's origins, and the story of Kathleen's reinvented identity in New York. All of them run counter to official narratives of family inheritance, for they are stories of identity constructed "out of bounds, exceeding prescriptive means of belonging." As one critic has recently argued, *Fall On Your Knees* questions the very knowability of identity by exploring the transgressive effects of desire, where "racial and sexual proprieties are crossed and questions of belonging become questions of longings...From the implications of incest on family relations to the desire for the other and to the impurity of race, MacDonald fuses questions of national belonging, racial fictions and sexual fantasies."[18]

The mystery of Lily's parentage is the secret scandal at the center of the novel, and it is also the imperative that provides the hidden connection between Lily and Anthony through the creative imaginings of the novel's most adventurous storyteller. "Frances is the biggest liar in the book, but her lies are really attempts to get at the truth...She is actually giving Lily more of the truth than she can get anywhere else."[19] Kathleen dies when Lily is born, and Lily is brought up as the daughter of James and Materia: "Everyone agrees to this fiction...And as the years go by the facts are eroded and scattered by time, until there are more people who don't know than people who do" (p. 166). The only person who refuses to believe the convenient social lie is Frances, for she is dimly aware that the "facts" do not fit with the "truth" and that in some unspoken way it is she who is responsible for Lily's welfare. This enigma is signaled to the reader at the beginning in the strange black and white silent movie scene when Frances is first introduced: "What's she doing in the middle of the creek, in the middle of the night? And what's she hugging to her chest with her chicken-skinny arms? A dark wet bundle. Did it stir just now? What are you doing, Frances?" (p. 3). What was she doing in the creek? And how does it relate to Lily? It takes Frances most of the novel to remember, and her efforts to disinter her deeply repressed childhood memories become the motivating force behind the fantastic tales she tells Lily, just as it provides a shadowy map for a quest whose meaning is hidden in Frances's unconscious:

> She has no intention of leaving the island until she has made enough money for Lily. And accomplished something else too. What, Frances? Something.

She will know it when she sees it. She is a commando in training for
a mission so secret that even she does not know what it is. (p. 307)

The narrative reveals that six-year-old Frances was there on the terrible
night of Lily's birth and Kathleen's death through Materia's impromptu
Caesarean performed with the kitchen scissors. The episode is recorded
vividly in the present tense, as Frances creeps into the attic room where
she sees her dead sister's mutilated body with its opened womb looking
like an "abandoned bootleg mine" (p. 136). She also sees two wriggling
babies wedged between the dead woman's legs "for safe-keeping, until
the priest can be dug up" (p. 146). And it is Frances who, out of love
for the babies, takes them carefully down to the creek to baptize them.
However, things go wrong and she drops the boy baby, who drowns.
Frances has to stand naked holding the baby girl while her father wraps
the nameless boy in her nightgown and buries him in the garden, placing
a heavy stone over the shallow grave. These are the traumatic memories
that are relegated to Frances's "cave mind" in a process of repression,
which is described in detail: "The cave mind has entered into a creative
collaboration with the voluntary mind, and soon the two of them will
cocoon memory in a spinning wealth of dreams and yarns and finger
paintings... Fact and truth, fact and truth..." (p. 151).

Yet every time Frances looks at her beautiful crippled sister Lily, she is
on the verge of remembering what she has never understood nor come to
terms with, and every time she tells Lily another story about her origins,
she is weaving a kind of daydream out of what Gaston Bachelard has
described as "the complexity of mixed revery and memory."[20] In these
stories Frances is always the heroine who saves Lily from a variety of
bizarre deaths—from being thrown out with the garbage, being smoth-
ered by an orange cat, or being drowned in the creek by Mumma
"because your father is a black man from the Coke Ovens" (p. 249). As
the narrative voice comments, "Every time Frances tells the true story, the
story gets a little truer" (p. 249). From a psychoanalytic point of view,
those stories are very close to the analyst's constructions whereby
repressed memories are brought to light, and Frances's storytelling looks
very like some of Freud's case histories. Interestingly, there are several allusions to Freud in the text, notably when her father tries to discover the
reason for Kathleen's "perverse" desire for Rose: "He has dipped into
Dr Freud in an effort to discover where to lay the blame for Kathleen's perver-
sity. Freud calls women 'the dark continent.' James couldn't agree more.
He doesn't hate blacks, he just doesn't want them near his bloodline"
(p. 359). Was he reading *Three Essays on the Theory of Sexuality* (1905)?

We do not know for sure, but after he has his stroke, Lily reads to him aloud from "Fairy-tales and Freud" (p. 421), which makes a suggestive link between Freud's theories and fantasy narratives. That is the connection I wish to explore here, through the implications of Frances's quest for the truth through storytelling.

Frances gives Lily her life story in different versions, and her own daydreaming finds its oneiric resonance in Lily's unconscious memories as she too starts to dream back to her origins, first in nightmares of drowning: "You were in it, Frances" (p. 255) and then gradually expanding under the influence of Frances's storytelling into dreams of her dead twin brother. Frances is a great dealer in dreams, and it is she who gives Lily the dream of Ambrose as her big brother and her guardian angel. (The dead baby is named by Frances after Saint Ambrose whose name appears beside the prayer on the Roman Catholic funeral mass cards.) Frances's stories take the uncanny and transform it from something frightening that occurs "when infantile complexes which have been repressed are once more revived by some impression, or when primitive beliefs which have been surmounted seem once more to be confirmed."[21] Ambrose is Frances's gift to Lily, restoring to her a missing part of her identity and providing one of the two most important talismans of her imaginative life: "Frances does not need to tell Lily any more Ambrose stories after this because he has become Lily's story. Frances has finally succeeded in giving him to her. Lily is okay. For now. Frances can get on with other things. Her life" (p. 278).

Perhaps the most resonantly Gothic of all the sites on Frances's quest for buried secrets is the old French mine, where she first takes the ten-year-old Lily one afternoon on a mysterious expedition. Instead of escorting her to Brownies as her father had asked her to do, Frances in Girl Guide uniform and still bearing traces of her father's latest beating leads Lily up the hill and into the "abandoned bootleg mine," ostensibly to visit Ambrose. The imagery here of the cave and the mine with its subliminal associations of "cave mind" and Kathleen's emptied womb transforms the sparse regional landscape into a theatre of psychic drama (and after all, what could be more "mine" than the repressed memories of the unconscious?).[22] As Frances drags a very frightened Lily along the dark tunnels carved into the rock under the earth and down to "a pool of still water inches from their feet, dear God, how deep is it?"(p. 267), the two girls are entering the topography of Frances's forgotten dreams. The omniscient narrative voice tells the reader that "There's no treasure associated with the old French mine, it just happened to be the first hole excavated for the purpose of extracting 'buried sunshine'" (p. 265), and the mine seems to be a kind of "black hole" or psychic space without limits in which unnameable desires and fears operate and where fantasies are played out. Lily thinks she sees a dead miner (or is it a soldier from the trenches of World War I?), while Frances declares that the dark pool is where Ambrose "lives." Through Frances's act of imaginative transformation the mine becomes a chthonic space where birth and death are intertwined and where intimate connections unite this womb–tomb with the spaces of home via an underground river that "turns into our creek." Overcome with fear, Lily first wets her pants and then she faints, for she is only the innocent witness to Frances's obscure quest, which conforms to dimly apprehended imperatives of her own. However it is in that dark space that Lily performs one of her minor miracles, for when Frances in an access of misery and guilt declares to her sister that she is the devil, Lily immediately forgives her: "This is the moment Lily stops being afraid of anything Frances could ever say or do again. Stops being afraid of anything at all. She reaches out and takes Frances's hand" (p. 270). Frances breaks down and cries.

Frances's narrative imagination works incessantly to retrieve the secrets of Lily's origins: who were her mother and father, and what really happened to Ambrose? This disentangling of her web of repressed memories engenders the suspense of Frances's quest as she wanders into the transgressive spaces of her Lebanese uncle's speakeasy and then as an interloper into her grandfather's house. She returns home only to discover the secret hidden at the top of the attic stairs:

> On her narrow journeys up the attic stairs by night Frances has seen a picture she did not know she owned: Kathleen with a black-red stomach, sweaty hair, two tiny babies alive between her knees. There is no one else in the picture except the person who is looking at it—*that must be me*. There is a voice way at the back of Frances's mind, hollering into a wind. (p. 321)

Out of these fragments of traumatic memory comes Frances's sudden realization that Kathleen is Lily's real mother, though it is out of her own imagination and suppressed longings that she creates the identity of Lily's secret father. On her quest for forbidden knowledge, Frances sometimes makes mistakes, and it is when hiding in her grandfather's kitchen cupboard watching his black housekeeper Teresa talking to her brother Leo (Ginger) Taylor that she tells herself another story just to see if it is true. For once, France believes her own story: "*There was a secret father, it was Ginger*" (p. 322), the young man who had driven Kathleen to school and who still drives a truck for her father. Frances fails to heed the warning given by the narrative voice at the end of the old French mine episode: "But memory plays tricks. Memory is another word for story, and nothing is more unreliable" (p. 270).

It is out of this false memory that Frances's eerie pursuit of Leo Taylor begins, as she embarks on the second stage of her psychic quest to restore the losses of the past, and once again the way leads back into the dream topography of the cave mind. As if compelled to give back to Lily her drowned brother in a living physical form, Frances takes Leo to the old French mine in order to seduce him, and nowhere else in the novel are the obscure conflicting energies of her subjective life so clearly imaged—her longings for her lost dark mother and her deep guilts as well as her repressed hatred for her abusive father and her defiance of his white master narrative. Staged as a parody of drowning and rebirth in the black space of the mine, this scene of Anthony's conception figures the return of the repressed in a transgressive act of healing that crosses the boundaries of sexual and racial codes, mediating between past and present, the living and the dead. While I am not going to explore the wider resonances of this act, which spreads out across the generations of the Piper and the Taylor families like the ripples of a stone thrown into the deep dark pool of the mine, there is one particularly interesting feature in this cryptic crossword of a novel that I would like to mention. When the "rescue party" consisting of Mercedes and Lily arrives, it is Lily who traces the way (miraculously, as Mercedes thinks) up the steep slope to the mine, following the fragmented letters that she remembers Frances had blazed on the tree trunks the day Frances first brought her to this place. While those letters apparently spell out the name "AMBROSE," the reader is only given the last four letters ("ROSE"), which forms a doubly coded message. Those letters show Lily the path she needs to follow now, just as later Frances will also give Lily the clues to reach another Rose, her dead mother's lover in New York. Like so many of Frances's messages, memory and desire are both veiled and revealed "under the rose" (which etymologically means "in secret").

By the time Frances finds out who Lily's real father was through James's confession to her, she is already pregnant and her father has lost his terrible patriarchal authority over her. There is briefly the possibility of reconciliation, where the Pipers' Gothic family history might be domesticated in ways that are only slightly at odds with normalcy:

> At last, Mercedes thinks, we are a family. Daddy is senile. Frances is crazy, Lily is lame, and I'm unmarried. But we are a family. Soon to be one more. And for the first time it crosses Mercedes' mind to keep Frances's child. (p. 431)

However, the colored child whose name was to have been Aloysius is stolen away from Frances by Mercedes who lies to her sister about the baby's death, and their father dies while reading Dante's *Paradiso* (p. 449). It is in this context of multiple loss that Frances makes her final sacrifice for Lily. Not only does she tell Lily her lost mother's name and give her back Kathleen's diary but she also gives Lily the means to escape from Cape Breton forever and to travel to New York to find Rose, the black jazz musician who was her mother's lover twenty years earlier. As Mrs. Luvovitz, one of the Piper's neighbors remarks, "Nothing in life is not mixed" (p. 560), and Lily's departure is a traumatic leavetaking from Frances who has been her "real mother." It is Frances whose "face first looked you [Lily] into existence," and as if to confirm that maternal relationship the last thing Frances gives Lily before sending her away is her own milk: "Frances opens her nightgown and guides Lily's mouth to drink" (p. 451). So Lily leaves, protected by her family talismans, for she is wearing her dead mother's green silk dress and the new red boots that her father had finished for her just before his death (in which Frances's gift of three thousand Canadian dollars are hidden). She is carrying her mother's diary, which she reads on the way to New York.

The section of the novel that tells of Lily's journey is called "Hejira," the Arabic word for "escape" or "flight," though Lily's journey is embedded in or indeed overshadowed by the story of her mother's flight. Kathleen's ghostly voice speaking out from her diary dominates this part of the narrative, finally divulging the beginning and middle of the story whose ending in the attic we already know. It is only through the diary that the reader comes to understand Kathleen's narrative of desire as she awakens to womanhood in the urban spaces of cosmopolitan New York, where she is sent by her father to train as an opera singer. Freed from her family for the first time and filled with ambition, she welcomes the whole world opening up at her feet: "1:12 am [February 29, 1918. New York City]—I am burning. I have to live, I have to sing, I want to transform myself into a thousand different characters and carry their life with me onto the stage where it's so bright and so dark at the same time"(p. 455). Enormously talented, Kathleen undergoes the torment of daily singing lessons with a male teacher whom she refers to as "the Kaiser," though increasingly her vision enlarges with her excitement at the "whole amazing world" of New York, where "you can walk for an hour and never hear a word of English, you can eat in five different countries in five blocks, you can hear music everywhere" (p. 463). In counterpoint to the music of classical opera, the strains of Harlem jazz, blues rhythms, and the piano playing of Rose Lacroix her black accompanist, begin to transform

Kathleen's awareness as she allows herself to feel those currents of emotion and erotic desire, which formerly she had only mimicked in her singing: "Saturday [May 4]—He asked me today if I knew the difference between sentiment and emotion" (p. 468).

Kathleen learns that difference through her tempestuous relationship with Rose, which develops as a potentially lethal power game bedeviled by racial prejudice and a kind of appalled fascination on both sides, until they both realize that they have misinterpreted visible differences and that they are both of mixed race. Kathleen's shock at discovering Rose's mother is white and Rose's when she discovers that Kathleen's mother is Lebanese brilliantly exemplifies the fallibility of conventional identity markers and the breaking down of artificial barriers, just as it opens the way for the two young women's carnivalesque night out at the Mecca night club where Kathleen wears her new green silk dress and Rose dresses up in her dead father's suit for the first time. Looking like a beautiful young man, Rose is most truly herself when she is in disguise. The lyrical description of their lovemaking is also the mutual confirmation of their most secret identities: "I forget where we were. That we were anywhere. We just looked at each other . . . So that's who you are" (p. 523). The diary entries for September and November are filled with promise for Kathleen as a newly liberated twentieth-century woman:

> [November 1, 1918]—Oh Diary. My loyal friend. There is love, there is music, there is no limit, there is work, there is the precious sense that this is the hour of grace when all things gather and distil to create the rest of my life. I don't believe in God, I believe in everything. And I am amazed at how blessed I am. Thank you.
> Love, Liebe, Amore, Kathleen Cecilia Piper. (p. 536)

Nowhere is it written for Lily to read what happened on the night of November 11, 1918 when the war ended and James took Kathleen home again, so ruining not only her career but her life, for that traumatic encounter reduces Kathleen's voice to a terminal silence.

The extent to which Lily's journey to New York is a retracing and a repeat-with-variations of her mother's journey only becomes apparent when she arrives at Rose's apartment in Harlem, still wearing the green silk dress now much the worse for wear. She is first of all cursed by two black cleaning women in the chapel in Rose's building who mistake her for the ghost of her mother: "That red-haired devil who ruined our Miss Rose has come back to life as a shrunk-down raggedy cripple" (p. 540), and then when she appears before Rose Lily is both herself and her double, as Rose's response suggests: "Rose puts forth her hands, slowly fingering the air as though searching for something in a dark wardrobe. Lily enters the embrace" (p. 541). Significantly, on this first meeting Rose suffers from a kind of distorted vision, seeing only her beloved Kathleen as she clings to Lily in an agony of grief. Indeed, the doubled identities work both ways, for when "Miss Lacroix" opens the door, Lily sees a tall black man looking down at her whom she politely addresses as "Rose." In New York Lily finds her new identity as Rose's partner and when Anthony arrives thirty years later, he sees the two women as an old married couple. We may recall that Lily's identity has shifted before, at least in Mercedes' eyes, when she changed from Lily the saint to Lily the demonically possessed. It would seem that Lily's identity is "always constituted within and not outside representation" by others,[23] though her origins are written on her face in her uncanny resemblance to Kathleen. Lily also carries the mark of her crippled leg, which she treasures as the sign of her individuality, in resistance to Mercedes's hopes of a miracle cure at Lourdes. Lily is finally both herself and Kathleen transformed, just as her home with Rose fulfills her mother's narrative of desire and escape and just as she also completes Frances's narrative of quest and restoration.

*Fall on Your Knees* is history told from a feminine perspective, and like Atwood's historical novels, which sprang from a fascination with "the mysterious, the buried, the forgotten, the discarded, the taboo,"[24] this too is history as Gothic tale telling. The Piper sisters have spent their lives resisting and revising the myths of their white father, which were the myths of Empire and patriarchal domination, in order to incorporate the stories of their dark silenced mother who figured only as the repressed other in their father's story. In the end they arrive at the recognition of their multiracial inheritance. Instead of the old incestuous fiction of the father and his little princesses, the family tree in its final New York version is more inclusive, for it tells the stories of rebellious daughters who have followed their own desires and defied patriarchal authority across the generations, beginning with Giselle Mahmoud their maternal grandmother, and continuing with their mother Materia's defiance before Kathleen and Frances were born. The love stories of both the Piper sisters mock the traditional heterosexual marriage plot while raising unsettling questions about the traumatic difficulties of women asserting their independence through personal relationships that transgress conventional social codes of sexuality and race.

This feminine history revises the white "master narrative," though it cannot rewrite the lives of all the rebellious daughters. There are a remarkable number of women's stories here, which begin with girls fired by ambition, talent, and the desire for escape, only to end in disappointment, entrapment, and early death. So, how can a novel restore the wasted lives of women whose identities have been subordinated in structures of biological and social determinism? The answer here is surely a Gothic one: a resurrection of the dead through stories that celebrate these women's energies of resistance and their rare moments of freedom and self-fulfillment, like Materia's elopement and later her piano playing for the silent movies in New Waterford, or Kathleen's liberation from the Law of her Father: "Kathleen is truly and utterly and completely Kathleen in New York" (p. 122). Kathleen's story of the failed woman artist is counterpointed by the story of Rose's success as a famous jazz pianist though ironically that success comes only through cross-dressing as she takes up the role of male performer, as Frances's record cover bears witness: "*Doc Rose Trio, Live in Paris: Wise Child.* A handsome black man, the angles of his face reprised by a fedora wound round with a gleaming emerald band" (p. 556). These stories provide a supplement to the bare evidence of women's names recorded on the family tree, just as the acts of these rebellious daughters have consequences that are like supplements to the patriarchal narrative of family inheritance, adding to but also altering it by putting back what was missing, "something that should never have been dismantled in the first place."[25]

The ending represents not only a complication but also a displacement in the narrative, spatially and temporally, for the meeting between Lily and Anthony happens in New York in the mid-1960s when all the members of the Piper family on Cape Breton Island are dead. Yet it is in New York that the Piper family history is reconstituted in a revised version of family, where both Rose's and Anthony's names are featured, as well as Leo Taylor's and Lily's dead twin brother Ambrose. The ending of this tragic narrative begins to look like comedy, as losses are restored and Lily gains a "father" in black (mixed race) lesbian American Rose and a "brother" in Scottish Lebanese Afro-Canadian Anthony. Indeed, Mercedes' final version of the Piper family tree bears a strong resemblance to Lily's tangled cartoon version buried so long ago in the garden "with its riot of golds and greens and ruby-reds" (p. 213).

Glancing beyond domestic history to a wider Canadian context, we might consider the implications of the Piper family tree in the light of Katarzyna Rukszto's essay to which I referred earlier, as to how the nation might become the site of a productive rather than a neurotic identity crisis. The 1960s was significant as a time of the liberalization of Canada's immigration laws and the decade before Trudeau's bilingual and multicultural policies began to change the nation's self-image and its narratives of heritage, though this novel lays bare the demographic realities to which Trudeau's policies might be seen as a late response. Maybe crossing the border allows a more objective view of the patterns in Canadian history, which has always been made of hidden immigrant histories and mixed race inheritance as this family saga shows. An image for contemporary Canada is likewise projected forward from social history of the 1960s when the German Jewish immigrant Mrs. Luvovitz, wife of the New Waterford pork butcher whose two elder sons were killed fighting for Canada in World War II, speaks about coming "home" and the complex processes surrounding concepts of identity and belonging. She also foregrounds generational differences between herself and her Canadian-born grandchildren, who quite happily live within multiple identities, negotiating between official discourses of nationality and discourses of the street and the local community. Interestingly MacDonald gives this a francophone inflection in what could only be interpreted as another gesture of reconciliation, for Ralph Luvovitz is one of the Cape Bretoners who has moved away from the region and is now living in Montreal, married to a Roman Catholic:

> Mrs Luvovitz looks at the sea and thinks, when did this become my home? When I buried Benny here? When the second war came? She cannot discern the moment. She just knows that every time she returns to Cape Breton, she feels in her bones, this is my home. That is why she has declined to move permanently to Montreal. She spends half the year there. She loves her daughter-in-law, would you believe? And her five grandchildren who are only each perfect. They speak French at home, English at school and Yiddish with every second shopkeeper. Real Canadians. (p. 559)

By uncovering hidden histories, *Fall on Your Knees* opens the way for more inclusive definitions of what being a "Real Canadian" means.

# CHAPTER 6

## MONSTERS AND MONSTROSITY: KERRI SAKAMOTO, *THE ELECTRICAL FIELD*

"Is that what you think of me? That I'm the monster?"
"Why not?" he reeled. "You'd do anything to stop me from having a life besides you and Papa. I can't even have a friend to myself. Even Yano!
(*The Electrical Field*)[1]

This heated argument between a brother and sister after the detective's visit following the murder of a neighbor and her lover goes to the heart of issues about identity and monstrosity that are explored in Kerri Sakamoto's *The Electrical Field*. In this discussion about contemporary Canadian literary traditions and the revision of national and cultural identities through fiction by racial minority writers, what might be the function of images of monstrosity in a novel written by a young Japanese Canadian woman in the late 1990s? Are they confined to the accusations hurled in a family quarrel? On the contrary, as I shall argue, the monster image has a wider resonance here, for this is a story that returns to a deliberately forgotten episode in Canada's recent past that casts its uncanny shadows over the present. This novel takes as its subject the psychological legacy of the internment of Japanese Canadians in World War II after Pearl Harbor, which was undergone by Sakamoto's parents and relatives and was first written about in fiction by Joy Kogawa in her novel *Obasan* (1981). Unlike Kogawa who was interned as a child, Sakamoto born fourteen years after the war looks back to an experience of which she saw only the aftermath. As she remarked in an interview, the internment "is part of our collective history,"[2] which I take to mean Canadian history, insisting that the Japanese Canadians' wartime experience needs to be accommodated within narratives of the nation.[3] This is where the concept of the monstrous comes in, and in this chapter I shall approach Sakamoto's novel as a historical critique of the identity crisis precipitated by the wartime construction of Japanese

Canadians as "others" in a narrative addressed to contemporary readers, which moves toward a reconciliation of differences, translating Japanese culture to outsiders while confronting the reluctance of a traumatized generation "to step outside one's own culture" [4] and arguing the need to move beyond that collective malaise in an effort "to rethink connections between history, representation and social change."[5]

The monstrous is always associated with cultural constructions of otherness as Rosi Braidotti's definition suggests, bringing us closer to the specificities of Sakamoto's novel: "The monster is the bodily incarnation of difference from the basic human norm: it is a deviant, an a-nomaly, it is abnormal."[6] Braidotti is talking in a feminist context about constructions of sexual difference and the historical devaluation of female bodies: "The monstrous as the negative pole, the pole of pejoration, is structurally analogous to the feminine as that which is other-than the established norm, whatever that norm may be,"[7] though she also remarks that such constructions of deviance and freakishness may conceal racist as well as sexist prejudice. Sakamoto insists on that broadening of definitions of monstrosity to include racial difference in the historical construction of Orientals as others within Canadian cultural discourse, which climaxed in the demonization of Japanese Canadians as "enemy aliens" in the early 1940s. Sakamoto's novel, which is both a social and a psychological history, focuses on that monstrous construction of Japanese Canadian identity at a time of national crisis and on its postwar consequences in the lives of individual victims. Not only does it deconstruct monster myths pertaining to a particular racial minority but it also offers a way forward out of the traumas of history so that *The Electrical Field*, like those other Asian Canadian novels by women—*Obasan* and Sky Lee's *Disappearing Moon Cafe* (1990)—offers "a 'theoretically informed and informing' contribution to the ongoing process of rethinking questions of history, narrative, and resistance."[8]

Set in the mid-1970s, the plot revolves around a murder mystery when one of those internment camp survivors, Masashi Yano, shoots his Japanese-born wife Chisako and her white lover, then his two children and himself. The mystery is not *who* did it, but *why?* The story is told by their neighbor, a middle-aged Japanese Canadian spinster Asako Saito who is also a camp survivor, and as Sakamoto commented at the time of the novel's publication, "I'd like to think readers were intrigued by Miss Saito's psychology, as it relates to internment."[9] We need to remember that this is a historical novel reflecting on the experiences of a previous generation at a specific cultural moment of deep demoralization for Japanese Canadians, a time now thirty years in the past in that wilderness period thirty years after the end of World War II and before the Redress movement had attained any momentum. Japanese Canadians were still trapped in a collective silence around the experience of internment, when rare activist voices like Yano's were assiduously ignored: nobody came to his redress meetings although he distributed hundreds of leaflets, having consulted the telephone directory for Japanese names. Traumatized by history and with no clear vision of a future, the scattered members of the Japanese Canadian community were caught in a defensive isolationism of which Asako is a prime example: "I think that what happened to her was that she became fearful of moving out into the larger world once she was let out of the camp, as the whole community was."[10] This is a novel about damaged lives, but in a curious way it is also about progress and the capacity of individuals and societies to change. Sakamoto is writing a revisionist history that engages in a critical reassessment of that negative othering suffered by the novel's protagonists as it strives toward a more comprehensive understanding of their predicament, addressing Japanese Canadians about their own history as well as readers who are outside that culture. It is within that specific historical frame of reference that the psychology of Sakamoto's characters makes sense and where the dehumanizing concept of monstrosity breaks down, as the novel represents a wide range of individual responses to internment history: "I wanted to portray these Japanese Canadian characters in a spectrum of experience that encompasses internment but also extends beyond it, and complicates their own particular psychology. I believe that preoccupation lies at the heart of the book."[11] In the late 1990s, precisely ten years after the Redress Settlement of 1988, Sakamoto writes her novel reflecting back on the lives (and deaths) of three families—the Saitos, the Nakamuras, and the Yanos—who live in a small white Ontario town, chronicling their interaction and its consequences in that period of social marginalization and mutual distrust, which is one of the tragic subplots within Canada's recent history.

Out of this context of hidden resentment and rage at social injustice, which finds its stifled expression only in silence and shame—two features of the collective Japanese Canadian postwar experience that are frequently commented on by Kogawa and Sakamoto—it is hardly surprising that domestic violence should erupt in its most extreme form. What is Yano's multiple family murder and suicide but a return of the repressed, the secret familiar thing that "ought to have remained secret and hidden but [which] has come to light" as Freud's definition of the Uncanny reminds us?[12] It is to the territory of the uncanny that monsters belong, and which Detective Rossi seems to gesture toward in his conversation with Asako about Yano the murderer: "I keep thinking he had to be some kind of. . ." (*The Electrical Field* (hereafter *EF*), p. 282). Asako supplies the word "monster" and then promptly denies it, for she has already taken that word upon herself: "What had I done? A monster, that was what I was, what I'd always been" (p. 239). Though the image implies an unspoken connection between herself and Yano, Asako's self-accusation hints at an area of private trauma that is only temporally related to his, in the sense of being part of the internment experience. Her narrative fills in the story behind the newspaper photos of the murder victims, but it also tells the story behind the portrait of her beloved elder brother Eiji who died of pneumonia in the camp. Asako's role in these two apparently disconnected stories constitutes the thread that her account follows through all its dislocations to the end. The novel prompts readers to wonder to what extent Asako's particular kind of feminine subjectivity is, like Yano's crime, the result of the ferocious othering of Japanese Canadians and their monsterization within official and popular discourse.

The vocabulary of vilification directed against Japanese Canadians was unambiguously racist, as any of the historical accounts of the period make plain, and Ken Adachi's focus on the abusive term "Yellow Peril" in *The Enemy that Never Was* is emblematic of the crucial role that visible difference plays in the construction of racist stereotypes.[13] *Obasan* documents a similar discourse of demonization through a Japanese Canadian's perspective:

> There's this horrible feeling whenever I turn on the radio, or see a headline with the word "Japs" screaming at us. So long as they designate the enemy by that term and not us, it doesn't matter. But over here, they say "Once a Jap always a Jap," and that means us. We're the enemy. ... Here at home there's mass hatred of us simply because we're of Japanese origin.[14]

Kamboureli's critical reading of *Obasan* usefully takes the discussion of racism one stage further with her reminder of how anti-Oriental hysteria was already embedded in the social system of British Columbia in a historical process of racialization dating back to the late nineteenth century when Asian workers (mainly Chinese) formed the majority of the cheap labor force in building the Canadian Pacific Railway. As she says, "What makes racism insidious is the fact that bodies are already racialized" (p. 185). As we shall see, it is this racialized self-perception with all the connotations of a negative othering that has shaped Asako's sense of herself as an embodied subject, and which may account for her disgust with her own physical body.

To return to images of monstrosity in Sakamoto's narrative is to return to the same order of white racist discourse that Kogawa had represented in *Obasan*, the most significant example of which is probably the description of the Japanese Kamikaze pilots, those young men who flew their suicide missions against American warships during the war in the Pacific during the 1940s. Asako's younger brother Stum who was only two years old when the war ended, has unthinkingly adopted the popular Canadian usage where "Kamikaze" has become a loosely derogative term synonymous with "crazy man." He frequently refers to the angry outspoken Yano as that "Kamikaze Jap," though for Asako who is fifteen years older the origins of the image are still vivid: "He clung to the word without knowing what it truly meant. It could only be a picture in his head, as it was in mine: a newspaper cartoon of hideous flying insect-men plummeting in flames. Photographs of Japanese soldiers in magazines, squashed faces, hundreds and hundreds of them, all the same. Not one recognizable. Not one Yano" (p. 256).

As a kind of balance in a text that negotiates very carefully between conflicting perceptions of otherness, on the very next page Asako recalls Yano's comments on the Kamikaze: "Kamikaze were very clean, Saitosan . . . The kamikaze cleansed themselves and prayed before they flew off to die for the emperor" (p. 257). Yano is referring to a Japanese cultural tradition of military honor that follows that of the samurai with its emphasis on spirituality as well as technical skill. As the American anthropologist Ruth Benedict explains in *The Chrysanthemum and the Sword*, "Their pilots who flew their midget planes in a suicidal crash into our warships were an endless text for the superiority of the spiritual over the material. They named them the Kamikaze Corps, for the *kamikaze* was the divine wind which had saved Japan from Genghis Khan's invasion in the thirteenth century by scattering and overturning his transports."[15] That juxtaposition of diametrically opposed cultural interpretations serves to highlight the fact that Asako's vocabulary of the monstrous is derived from the discourse and practices that have oppressed her and which as a Japanese Canadian she has internalized. From being constructed as an alien, she has become alienated from herself. Indeed, the most extreme form of self-alienation is figured in the text almost like a warning in the case of Yano's brother, another internee, who has been confined to a mental hospital for twenty years because of his strange fits, which began in the camp: "He can't stand the sight of an Oriental . . . It's shameful. Chinese, Japanese, man, woman, doesn't make a difference. Goes nuts" (p. 101).

Though Asako's condition is not psychotic, she clings neurotically to her racial and cultural identity within the domestic confines of her home and family, and her fractured autobiographical narrative reveals a fissured female subject who lives very uncomfortably inside her personal and collective history. As a result, her story becomes monstrous in the sense of always threatening to turn into something "other-than" itself,[16] caught in a constantly shifting negotiation between memories of the recent and distant past and a present in which so much is repressed. Asako's carefully fabricated narrative of her own life is finally shattered by the violent intrusion of the murders, but it is her pervasive sense of unease and the cracks that appear on the narrative surface that provide an index to her traumatized self-construction. If we read her narrative through the question with which I opened this chapter, what we discover is a split self who fears that she really is a monster but who also knows that she is not. Asako's self-perception is tied to the key issues of her gendered and racial identity seen through the distorting lens of her internment experience, which has represented her difference as monstrous to herself. She is and is not Japanese, being a "nisei" (second-generation Japanese Canadian) who has never been to Japan, her sexuality only finds a vicarious expression through voyeurism, while her maternal feelings are displaced onto fiercely possessive love for her younger brother and for Sachi, her neighbor's teenage daughter. To compensate for her borderline existence Asako takes refuge behind the feminine stereotypes available within Japanese traditional cultural patterns, where she is the dutiful daughter tending her bedridden old father, just as she is the responsible elder sister to her brother Stum, and in her fantasies the beloved younger sister of her dead elder brother Eiji.

It is within this traditional Japanese framework of family responsibility that Asako feels protected as she goes about her household tasks, isolated from the outside world in the old family home, which is cut off from the rest of the town by a stretch of waste ground full of giant electricity pylons, the Electrical Field of the title. She sees herself as the center of a peaceful domestic order: "I marvelled at that, the consolation of my quiet life, the getting on: my calm" (p. 16), and moreover she persuades herself that her life is vindicated by her compliance with traditional patterns of submission to family values.[17] Yet there are many hints that this is an outworn ethic and that the Saitos' way of life is disintegrating like their house, which is "turning to dust, like so many things" (p. 50). Asako is caught in a condition of emotional paralysis inside a house of decay pervaded by bad smells and the odor of the dying. Even when she escapes outside into her garden, she notices that the flowers are "a little ruined, a little imperfect" and that "everything is withered and rotting. Eating itself up" (p. 106). She has only limited contact with her white neighbors whom she regards with fear and suspicion and even with the two Japanese families in the row of bungalows across the field, though she constantly observes them from a distance through her front window. Indeed the novel opens with Asako in her characteristic position as a watcher who takes no responsibility for what she sees: "I happened to be dusting the front window-ledge when I saw her running across the grassy strip of the electrical field." But the second sentence slightly shifts away from that passive detachment: "I stepped out onto the porch and called to her," for the flying figure is Sachi Nakamura, the neighbors' thirteen-year-old daughter whom Asako has befriended after she caught her stealing her flowers. It is Sachi, who as Sakamoto affirmed in an interview, "unsettles everything," and yet there are other signs of unsettlement within the narrative, where like the first two sentences, an element of instability is introduced.

Asako accepts her family responsibilities with resignation, but she also resents them: "Yet I felt helpless. I gave in to this feeling in my weak moments; knowing that I must not surrender to it, this sense I'd carried for as long as I could remember, that I must look after everyone, as I had all my life" (pp. 98–99). With her older brother dead in the internment camp and her mother dying not long after their release, Asako has had to assume the sole responsibility for her father and younger brother, nor has there been any space for independent expression of her own desires or ambitions:

> There were never many chances for me. I knew that from long ago, from when we first got here. "On-ta-ri-o," Papa kept saying with his pitiful accent ... With Eiji gone and Stum just a baby, I was the first-born, born here; they pushed me out to the big city, to the world, thrusting my homely face to it when they were afraid ... I didn't know the right words to say, in English or in Japanese. I cringed at how I stumbled along. (p. 51)

Again Asako refers to her liminal position and her agonies of self-consciousness about her language and her "homely" physical appearance, which underpin her construction as a subject, both in her self-representation and in her relationships with others. The language issue is especially fraught, as it signals many of the contradictory emotions from which Asako suffers. Although she has always made great efforts to improve her English and still does the newspaper crossword every day, she preserves a sense of cultural identity in her narrative by scattering Japanese words and phrases throughout. While reminding readers of the narrator's otherness (or perhaps of the reader's otherness to Japanese culture) these linguistic signs of difference need not exclude non-Japanese readers. Most words are translated within the same or the following sentence, as on the first page with "we nihonjin, we Japanese," in itself an affirmation of a communal identity that does in fact exclude the "hakujin." Asako's ambivalence over the language question suggests a chosen othering on her part, related not only to her internment experience but also to her Japanese conservatism and what has been called "the strong exclusionary strain in the Japanese psyche."[18] Certainly the home language for the Saitos is Japanese, where within the social hierarchy the different forms of address make clear the position of every family member. Asako is called "ne-san" (elder sister) by her younger brother Stum, an acknowledgment of his respect and his dependence on her. He calls her by her English name "Anne" only to warn her of the intrusion of an outsider, as when Detective Rossi comes to interview her about the murder, and it is not until after Asako's breakdown when Stum finally has to take some responsibility for his sister that he stops calling her "ne-san" and addresses her by her name, "Asa." Interestingly, this change of address together with the shifting balance in the brother–sister relationship is encouraged by Stum's Filipino girlfriend Angel, who begins by calling Asako by her name at their first meeting when Stum is still addressing her as "ne-san." In turn, Asako's form of address to her brother shifts over time as a mirror of her perceptions of their changing relationship. At the beginning she is still calling the thirty-three-year-old unmarried Stum "my baby brother, my ototo-chan" (p. 7), signaling an emotional possessiveness that Stum increasingly comes to resent and which is at the heart of his denunciation of his sister with which I began this chapter. His accusation of her monstrous selfishness causes a rupture of the domestic surface that transforms Asako's familiar world into something uncanny, "as if Stum and I were at the helm of a spaceship approaching a strange planet" (p. 136).

How is the reader to understand the complex network of conscious and unconscious energies interacting inside the mind of a woman who always hides behind a metaphorical mask or quite literally behind her front window curtains? However, Asako does peer out through the glass, just as in her narrative she appears through partial refigurations in three other protagonists: Sachi, Chisako the Japanese-born wife of Yano her neighbor, and crucially Yano himself. In each of these relationships Asako would seem to occupy a conventional social role, as caring surrogate mother to Sachi, as female friend and confidant to Chisako, and as good neighbor to Yano. However, the relationships soon transgress those limits, opening the way to unhomely territory, which is both secret and familiar. These figures in their different ways all represent Asako's uncanny doubles.

Asako fancies that Sachi is the embodiment of her younger self: "Sachi was a perceptive child, gifted, really. She reminded me of myself in a way, a finely tuned receptacle for others' impulses and confidences" (p. 4). Yet Sachi more often than not disturbs such identification for as Asako watches the girl, her image shifts and she becomes "a scraggly urchin" remembered from the last day at the internment camp (p. 2 and p. 9), and on another occasion "my Sachi" is a cigarette smoking Canadian teenager who is not the least bit interested in "silly folding cranes or my heaven-earth-and-man flower arrangements" (p. 11). She is also the lover of Tam, Yano and Chisako's son, and it is her insistence on involving Asako in her restless searches for clues about his disappearance that takes the older woman out of the security of home and down to the wilderness beside the creek. This territory is soon to be officially marked out of bounds by ribbons of yellow police tape for it is the scene of the crime, but right from the start Asako describes it as "this private place, a forbidden place where too many things had happened. Who else had known about this spot?" (p. 42). The answer Asako does not give is that she had known, for it was here when hidden amongst the trees that she had spied many times on Tam and Sachi's sexual games—and for which, as she much later confesses, she had supplied Sachi with the Japanese words like "chi-chi" and "chikubi," the pet names for female body parts. It is also the place where she had spied on Chisako's illicit meetings with her lover, the "hakujin" Mr. Spears in his car, and it is here that Asako circles around the area of her own repressed sexuality, looking for something she has lost: "So instead I set down my handbag and slowly began searching the ground for something, anything, I didn't know what, futile as it seemed" (p. 44). Asako manages to avoid finding anything, although Sachi leads her back there again and again. It is also at Sachi's urging that she tells the stories about her beloved brother Eiji and his ghost hovers over that wilderness space, for Sachi, that dissident troubled teenager, wants to know the truth and refuses to stay inside the sheltering fictions that Asako and her parents insist on offering her.

Later in the novel Asako goes down to the creek several times on her own searching for Sachi, and on her final visit she even saves the girl from drowning though almost drowning herself. As the water closes over her head, Asako's most assiduously repressed memory of her brother's death almost breaks through, but the words will not come:

*Sachi*, I called feebly, but the sound died in my mouth. I know what's true, I know what's a lie, I meant to tell her. I know what I did and I will say it. For you I will. Sachi. I didn't save him. I longed to say this; to have these be the last words in her ears. Instead, I closed my eyes and sank. (p. 279)

Asako is rescued by Detective Rossi who praises her for her bravery and she is even thanked by Sachi's mother who had earlier resented their friendship, though it is an imperfect reconciliation after all. As Asako turns to offer Keiko Nakamura the roses she has been picking for her, she finds that the woman has already gone, overcome by embarrassment at her seeming neglect of her daughter. Asako is once again alone, left holding her flowers and contemplating "the prettiness of a thing that will soon die" (p. 289).

Evidently Sachi can unsettle Asako and lead her toward a recognition of her hidden secret life, but that slippery image of her younger self cannot engage with the adult woman's neurotic awareness of herself as an embodied sexual subject. It is Chisako who figures as the Other Woman here, reminding Asako of all that she desires and lacks: "I was not Chisako. No matter how many times I had wished it" (p. 16). Asako is haunted by Chisako's ghost afterward as fragmented memories of their encounters insistently recur, though she has a strong resistance to making connections between their friendship and Chisako's murder. Looking at these memory fragments it is not difficult to see how Chisako mirrors and indeed embodies all Asako's fantasies of femininity and race, which she has repressed. Chisako has the same racialized female body as Asako, which she has managed to transform into an image of exotic and desirable femininity. Worse still, Asako has watched the transformation process from the time of Chisako's arrival four years earlier as a shy and frumpy young Japanese mother into "the real thing," "a true Japanese lady from a Samurai family" (p. 22). Her account of that early "ugly duckling" unselfconsciously describes the source of her own jealousy and self-contempt:

> Chisako had made herself a beauty. Had grown into one, miraculously. She hadn't been one in the beginning. When she first came, she was plain, almost as plain as me. To see her, I didn't feel so badly about myself. Slowly it happened . . . My plain self had grown ugly even as Chisako had blossomed. (pp. 24–25)

As if to underline it a few pages later: "She was beautiful in anyone's eyes. A wife, a mother . . . I could not endure myself in her presence for one second longer" (pp. 28–29).

Chisako is not only beautiful but also excitingly sexual, as her affair with her white boss Mr. Spears reminds Asako. Ironically and very dangerously as it turns out, Chisako makes Asako her confidant, showing her the first present Mr. Spears gives her, a small glass dome containing a perfect pink rose: "A small bloom, really, a lovely hybrid tea, I guessed, but at certain angles it became monstrous" (p. 49). That telltale word encapsulates all Asako's hidden resistance and she first repulses Chisako's confidences, condemning the relationship as a moral transgression, a righteous position that she maintains to the end.[19] However her feelings are rather more ambivalent, for she spies on Chisako and Mr. Spears in the woods when they are making love and she even acts as accomplice in deceiving Yano. Watching Chisako magically transformed as an object of desire and a sexually satisfied woman is for Asako to suffer her own obliteration in a torment of jealousy that becomes unbearable:

> I could see she was savouring some private moment, reliving it even as I sat there, and I was even more ludicrous, if that was possible... I felt nauseated watching her with her eyes closed too long. I felt like some peeping Tom... I wanted to punish this greedy woman, she who thought she could have everything she ever desired. (p. 207)

This is the vindictiveness of a woman who sees herself as lacking in all that she has ever desired: "All my life, what I'd felt had been the promise of nothing. The risk of nothing, which had frozen me to ice" (p. 209). However, perhaps Chisako's greatest crime in Asako's eyes is her outspokenness when she dares to speak frankly and sympathetically about the sexual act:

> "You have never been with a man, have you?"
> Now I was stunned; I was—there were no words for the distress, the shame I felt at being asked such a thing. But she would not let me go, and her face hovered so close; I could not conceal myself... "Please, Chisako. Please," I pleaded, barely audible to myself. "Do not embarrass me." (pp. 214–15)

Chisako's sexuality has to be construed by Asako as dangerous in order to justify her betrayal of Chisako on the grounds of duty: "She got what she deserved" (p. 216).

Asako transgresses the rules of social decorum as grossly as Chisako has transgressed sexually, for unasked she takes the responsibility of telling Yano about his wife's affair that same evening when they are walking together in the electrical field. Though consciously she justifies it, the imagery tells a different story: "I shouted each loathsome word louder and louder, as loud as I could, to make Yano understand. The secret torn from my throat, cast to the wind. How grateful I was for the cover of night" (p. 233). (Which is "loathsome?" Chisako's act, or Asako's telling?) It is Yano who reminds Asako next morning of her social transgression in telling him what she should have left for Chisako to say: "Why did you tell me? Why?" and "I wish you hadn't told me. I didn't need to know. But it's done" (pp. 235–36). The last words Asako hears him say are "Mottai-nai . . . What a waste" (p. 236). Later that day, he shoots Chisako and Mr. Spears when he finds them together in the woods and then shoots his two children and himself.

To lay out the dynamics of Asako's relationship with Chisako in this way is to simplify a narrative fractured by repression and guilt, and whose meaning Asako only comes to realize when she is pressed repeatedly by Detective Rossi to recall her last meetings with the pair before the murders. Her confused telling, where her mind is like a buzzing hive of bees, constitutes the struggle out of a kind of traumatic amnesia but Asako is then confronted with the terrible realization of her own betrayal of them both: "A monster, that was what I was, what I'd always been" (p. 239). Actually she exaggerates her responsibility, as her brother and Sachi both strive to make her see, but that image of monstrosity telescopes all the shame associated with her racial and sexual difference as well as her moral transgression of the boundaries of friendship and loyalty. Perhaps the most ironic gesture of reconciliation is that of the white detective, who in a simple act of kindness gives Asako the glass dome with the pink rose inside, which was found at the scene of the crime: "He slipped the glass dome into my hand. Quietly said: 'It was a brave thing you did, Miss Saito. You saved that girl'" (p. 287).

If Chisako and Sachi are incomplete doubles for Asako because of their individual differences from her, the person who is most like her is Yano, though it is only after the murder suicide that Asako can acknowledge their affinity. Yano's face with his angry eyes and his broad smile hovers over the narrative from the beginning, when in the quiet of her garden Asako's carefully assumed calm is interrupted by thoughts of the "wild, crazy man" whom her brother casually refers to as "that Kamikaze." Though gradually details of their friendship emerge, Asako's first memory sketches the man and those qualities that make him so disturbing: his sexuality and his outspoken anger at the social injustice inflicted on Japanese Canadians by internment. If his obsessional campaigns as a lone activist trying to rally support for governmental redress irritate Asako, it is his unwashed male body that worries her far more: "it was alive and pungent, insistent, a man's odour probing you all over" (p. 5). Asako has an almost pathological sensitivity to bodies— their shapes and odors as well as their signs of race and sex—which constitutes her unspoken discourse of sensuality as a kind of displaced sexuality. Yano's overpowering physical presence as he stands too close or suddenly appears beside or behind her on her daily walks in the electrical field makes a strong impression, which Asako cannot afford to acknowledge as anything other than a threat: "Remembering too how he unsettled me each time, repelled as I was by him" (p. 72). As Chisako had personified desirable femininity, so Yano's masculinity represents the forbidden area of sexual desire that Asako can experience only as a voyeur. Indeed it is Chisako who translates her feelings into frankly sexual terms, much to Asako's embarrassment: "You want to think badly of him. You want to believe he is a monster so you can hate him, ne?" (p. 284). Chisako also points out that he is not a monster but a man: "Nothing to be afraid of" (p. 285) and that Yano would never be unfaithful to her.

What Chisako as a Japanese bride coming to Canada after the war does not understand is that there are emotional affinities between Yano and Asako that date back to their wartime experiences, and it is this shared psychological legacy that forms the bond between them. Though Asako initially resists Yano's overtures of friendship, precisely because she sees in him the mirror image of her own racial characteristics, which she cringes to contemplate, Yano follows her around like her shadow: "Over and over he'd ask me about the camps. He'd say the government owed us money and an apology. Badger me with where this, when that, and how long" (p. 5). He insists on their communal identity as members of an oppressed racial minority group, for Yano sees clearly the connections between large historical events and personal relationships in a localized present context, which Asako and most of the scattered Japanese Canadians steadfastly refuse to see. His is essentially a political commitment, though his passion draws Asako toward him as an ally in abjection, in a gesture that excludes Chisako at the same time as affirming her superiority as the true inheritor of Japanese culture: "Not like the rest of us homegrown nisei; not like him and me, neither here-nor-there stock" (pp. 92–93). Once more Yano's comparison impresses Asako with the sense of her own inferiority, even within her own racial group:

"She [referring to Chisako] doesn't know what it feels like to be ashamed, you see" . . . "Not like you and me," he finally said, his eyes drilling into mine. "She doesn't know what it's like to get herded up. She doesn't know what it feels like to be ashamed to be nihonjin." (p. 94)

Yano's sense of offence is fuelled by his conviction of Japanese superiority to Westerners, which makes him vehemently resentful about social injustices and those who inflicted them on the Japanese, so that again and again he refers to that communal sense of shame and the wasted potential of a whole generation who have suffered persecution on racist grounds:

> He started walking again, striding as he spoke. "Same with your papa, sweeping up on that chicken farm. Your brother, all those years. We'd be doing something else. Something important, ne? You too, Saito-san. All of us. We were too good. We were doing too well, so they had to set us back, didn't they?" (p. 122)

It would seem that we are being shown that Yano too is guilty of a negative othering and that through displaying the attitudes of Yano and Asako, Sakamoto is taking the debate about Japanese Canadian identity forward in original ways that could only be undertaken from the relatively detached position of a writer belonging to a later generation, as she strikes a precarious balance between the otherness resulting from white prejudice against the Japanese Canadians and the Japanese Canadians' deliberate othering of themselves. Yano's insistence that internment survivors "have to stick together" is eminently understandable after the destruction of their community, though that insistence on group support also carries a negative charge in its strongly exclusionary strain.[20] Asako is critical of this communal commitment, "As if being nihonjin in the same neighborhood could melt every disagreeable difference between us" (p. 108), and yet she acknowledges "We were bound together, that was true" (p. 95). Yano insists on more than a mutual social support group when he gestures toward a bonding that is psychological and spiritual and beyond the power of language to describe: "He sighed, then pointed from me to him in a continuous loop, implying some sort of connection that was beyond words" (p. 94)[21] and which Chisako would not understand.

That "continuous loop" signals all that is unspoken and unspeakable in this narrative as it charts the emotions that shaped Japanese Canadian identities for a whole postwar generation, trapped in what Sakamoto calls "the residue of the internment experience."[22] From this angle it is possible to see the relation between Yano and Asako as a psychodrama where the electrical field assumes a symbolic meaning. That strip of barren ground has a dual existence in the text, for not only is it a real place in a rather dreary landscape where Asako and Yano meet and talk on their daily walks, but it is also a space where violent psychic energies are unleashed. In physics an "electrical field" is a field of force between two highly charged bodies, one positive and one negative, where patterns of movement might be diagrammed as a series of concentric circles. This is the image that haunts Asako when she remembers her last meeting with Yano the morning after her double betrayal:

> We'd been circling, circling, once, twice, three times around the field, looping the towers. I'd grown tired. We'd halted at the north tower. Suddenly Yano grabbed hold of the steel rails and shook, shook with all his might, so that a rattling echoed into the thickly clouded sky . . . But he kept on, as if trying to uproot the whole tower. (pp. 234–35)

In his distress Yano tries to tear up the pylons, so that as if by a kind of metonymy his wild emotions are associated with the lethal currents overhead. It is a revelation of the tragic subtext of Yano's life, the failed idealist, the angry politician who had tried unsuccessfully to rouse the Japanese Canadian community to seek reparations, the husband who has been deceived and who finally turns killer and suicide in an attempt to redeem the shame brought on his family name by his wife's infidelity. A comment by Ruth Benedict on the phenomenon of "Giri" in traditional Japanese culture may help to elucidate Yano's position:

> Giri to one's name is the duty to keep one's reputation unspotted . . . Giri to one's name also demands acts which remove a slur or an insult; the slur darkens one's good name and should be got rid of. It may be necessary to take vengeance upon one's detractor or it may be necessary to commit suicide . . . But one does not shrug off lightly anything that is compromising.[23]

And so, there in the electrical field Asako recognizes the significance of Yano's headshake, "in that manly way that shows regret for an action that must be taken, whatever the consequences" (p. 236). From one perspective Yano's crime could be seen as honorable, though it is also as an ironic fulfillment of the fate that he had angrily vowed to avoid: "They were hoping we'd all commit hara-kiri in the camps, don't you think, Saito-san?" (p. 258).

Yano's appalling defeated humanity is only perceived after the crime when Asako finally acknowledges their affinity: "All along I'd understood. How one thing turns everything bad, taints all of it, and there is no going back. There is no return. For hadn't I longed for that too, a hundred, a thousand times?" (p. 244). Yano is Asako's uncanny double in its masculinized version, refiguring her own sense of alienation and her repressed desire for revenge in the magnified form of murderous violence. Are they the monsters in this text as their twinned images would suggest, or are they victims caught in a field of force that has predetermined their fate?

> We rounded a corner and the electrical towers, Chisako's cages, my
> giants, swung into view, and I saw myself there, foolish and clinging,
> beneath those monstrous beams. Clinging to another, no less dwarfed—
> to Yano, on that morning as grey and early as this: two ants struggling in
> that empty field. (p. 286)

So, from monsters to ants, but where do Yano and Asako assume their
proper identities as human beings? The answer has to be that Yano
assumes it through Asako's narrative, which is in a sense a memorial to
him, just as her telling restores her own. Perhaps the clearest signal is when
Asako resists the image of Yano's monstrosity in her last conversation with
Detective Rossi as she remembers their conversations in the electrical
field:

> I thought of the nod I'd given him on our morning walks; the smile to
> loosen the clenched fist, to tell him that I knew there was an impressive
> man inside who'd had his chances taken away. How I held back, the time
> when it counted most.
> "No, no," I said quietly. (p. 282)

The novel acknowledges that human beings may be crushed by the
weight of vast historical forces, but it does not stop there; instead it insists
that life moves on beyond tragedy. Yano and his family are all dead, and
Asako has to learn to move outside her willed amnesia back into the
living world of human relationships. Things have already changed as
even she realizes, when her brother and his girlfriend take her to visit the
chicken hatchery where they both work. There, speaking with Stum's
Japanese boss, Mr. Fujioka, who had married a girl whom Asako knew in
the internment camp, she finds her memories of the camp challenged by
his different view. His wife's relatives still live there: "What do you call
that place? A shangri-la?" He laughed. "Folks there don't seem to age
much" (p. 298). Stung by his comments, Asako replies: "The sky, the
clouds. It was always dark," though when Mr. Fujioka contradicts her she
has to admit that he is right: "Yes, that was true. I'd forgotten; if it wasn't
dark it was bright, ice bright. . . I didn't remember things the way Kaz's
wife did" (p. 297). From that unreliable memory and a haze of wordless
unease Asako is once again rescued by Yano, or rather by her memory of
Yano's social outrage on her behalf, which acts like a catalyst in her mind.
Finally the last "closed door, closed even to myself" (p. 298) opens,
revealing the secret that she could never admit to herself—her own
responsibility for Eiji's death in the camp: "I did not tell Yano it was me,
selfish, hungering child that I was. It was me wanting the world my way,
never to change, ever. It was my fault, all my fault—not the war, not the
government, not some hakujin stranger named Mackenzie" (p. 301).

In that uncanny moment outside the hatchery Asako is released from her most secret guilt, and now finds that she is free to accept her living brother's love for her and also the loving relationship between him and his girlfriend Angel without jealousy. She is learning to forgive herself, and though this is a human centered secular narrative, there are echoes here of the text from a sermon that Asako had heard long ago in the internment camp, which she had never understood: "*Look within Buddha's deep waters, to be healed, to forgive*" (p. 63). It comes as no surprise to the reader to find Yano's eyes hovering over her memory. The novel ends very quietly in the real world of work and love as Asako sits in the car listening to Stum and Angel's description of sexing chickens. She has to acknowledge that though things change, everything may still be in order: "Girls here, boys there. It was simple, really" (p. 305).

Contrary to Asako's optimistic assertion, there is not much that is simple in this very politically conscious novel, just as there are no simple solutions to charting the problematic relationship between personal and collective history in the formation of identity for someone belonging to an oppressed racial minority. Sakamoto makes her points obliquely through her choice of Asako as narrator, for it takes almost the entire novel before she can move beyond her bewildered and frightened silence to acknowledge the multiple layers of her repressed memories. Certainly she and Yano, both permanently scarred by their internment experiences, have little sense of being Canadians; both are deeply suspicious of the white community and the government and cling to their racial identity: "We are so full of shame, aren't we, Asako? We hide away, afraid that they'll lock us up again. That's it, isn't it?" (p. 231). Yano is very proud of his Japanese wife whom he married during his time in Japan when he was deported there after the war, yet there is a tragic irony in the fact that Chisako married him because he was not Japanese: " 'That's why I married him. He is Canadian, not nihonjin . . . He's a nisei,' she said, as if she had to explain that to me" (p. 119). Once again Chisako has managed to touch on a raw spot as she highlights the precarious balance of otherness experienced by Yano and Asako, who despite their affirmation of Japanese identity are neither purely Japanese nor purely Canadian, but both. Looking back to that lost generation, Sakamoto sees such haunted identities as forms of entrapment leading to catastrophe. Against the impulse of its main narrator, the novel by taking a retrospective historical view manages to imply that such perspectives would have to change, and that Japanese Canadians themselves would need to take a closer look at their cherished myths. This revisionary impulse to look into "the closed box of our inheritance" is a position not unlike

Atwood's, though this time seen from a different cultural and racial perspective. It emphasizes the necessity for opening a way through to the future beyond positions of negative othering, not only for the younger generation like Stum and Sachi but also for Asako as survivor: she must remember her own past as well as that of her community in order to outface all her monsters.

How, given a figure like Asako, is it possible to tell a narrative oriented toward the future rather than the past? The answer for Sakamoto writing in the late 1990s is to retell the old story of a murder committed twenty-five years earlier, registering the repression and anger of the victims and their self-destructive violence, and then to put it behind. Sakamoto believes that "writing is a hopeful act. And it's a very active thing. If you don't believe that change can come about, you won't write."[24] The story is told as an exorcism of ghosts and Asako's narrative manages to gesture, however tentatively, beyond loss and trauma into wider social spaces, which the "sansei" of Sakamoto's third generation of Japanese Canadians now occupy in their native land of Canada. Yet *The Electrical Field* is also a memorial, which remains as a site of otherness within the discourse of Canadian nationhood, suggesting that there are no simple solutions and certainly no homogeneous answers in the construction of multicultural Canadian identities.

# CHAPTER 7

## CHANGING THE BOUNDARIES OF IDENTITY: SHANI MOOTOO, *CEREUS BLOOMS AT NIGHT*

Who we are as Canadians is contingent upon how we move from one context to another, how we cross the thresholds of memories, how we embrace or, for that matter, keep away from the differences we encounter, how we negotiate our histories, in the context of other histories.[1]

Who is the "we" being addressed here? Smaro Kamboureli, one of Canada's best-known literary theorists of multiculturalism, in the introduction to her 1996 anthology *Making a Difference*, encodes a recognition of heterogeneity and dynamic process within the national collectivity, which opens up new critical directions for conceptualizing Canadian identity and Canadian literature within the contemporary context. My inquiry into this refiguring centers like that anthology on the role being played by immigrant writing in English in shifting the boundaries of Canadianness. By choosing to discuss the writing of Shani Mootoo, a lesbian visual artist and video maker, as well as a short-story writer, a novelist, and a poet, who describes herself in transcultural terms as "Indo-Caribbean-Canadian," I have deliberately chosen someone whose own lived experience of border crossings between countries, cultures, and fields of artistic activity informs her constructions of identity in her texts. Born in Ireland, brought up in Trinidad, now living in Vancouver, and publishing all her work in Canada, Mootoo has adopted a Canadian nationality, though her fiction and her poetry range across all the cultures that intersect in her own hybridized identity. As one of the characters in her short stories describes herself, she is

> Not properly Trinidadian (she could not sing one calypso, or shake down her hips with abandon when one was sung—the diligence of being a goodBrahmingirl), not Indian except in skin colour (... in her family a sari had always been a costume), certainly not White and hardly Canadian either.[2]

Mootoo is one of the many women of Caribbean origin now writing in Canada, though as Indo-Caribbean, her affiliations of race and inheritance are different from Marlene Nourbese Philip, Nailo Hopkinson, or Dionne Brand, whose backgrounds are Afro-Caribbean. However, all these different voices draw attention to "the disjunctions of representation that signify a people, a nation, national culture."[3] Mootoo's texts are especially interesting because working across three genres, she pays attention to the disjunctions within the subjective experience of liminality, in a range of representations where the politics of gender and sexuality are deeply implicated with race and the heritage of colonialism. My inquiry will center on *Cereus Blooms at Night*, Mootoo's first and only novel to date, though I shall frame it by beginning with a brief analysis of one short story from her collection *Out on Main Street* (1993) and ending with her recent poetry collection *The Predicament of Or* (2001), in order to illustrate the generic range in her figuring of the presence of the "other" in Canadian writing.

"The Upside-downness of the World as it Unfolds," which is the last story in *Out on Main Street*, typifies Mootoo's wittily intimate engagement with the question of what it feels like for a nonwhite woman to live in contemporary multicultural Canada. The title, incidentally, reads like an idiomatic version of Bhabha's "instability of cultural signification," the term he uses when theorizing heterogeneous representations of the nation, but here Mootoo is referring to the representation of one particular subject's experience. There is a certain self-reflexiveness here for she is writing about a woman writer, an Indo-Caribbean immigrant now living in Vancouver who contemplates her own liminality in an endless process of negotiating her multiple identities as a transcultural subject. We are also reminded that we are reading a story in process, for this is writing as performance where the "tdrrrrring!" of the typewriter punctuates the ongoing narrative. The focus of this story is language, the English language, which this writer is using in the performance of her craft, though it is also a language freighted with trauma for her. The story begins with an obstacle in the shape of a "back-home" memory that hinges on a mysterious word. (What is this word, and why should it evoke the memory of a sharp whack across the knuckles with a ruler?)

Mootoo manages to be both comic and serious in her consideration of a Trinidadian colonial education—comic in her use of narrative form with its shifting multiple perspectives and its ironic reversals, and serious in the way she highlights the English language as the emblem of Empire, the master discourse of authority with its power to engender that feeling of "otherness" and inferiority, which is perhaps the paradigmatic colonial experience. The story begins with the narrator's memory of her terrible private tutor, Mrs. Dora Ramsey, a retired English headmistress who personifies Britishness in the Trinidad of the 1960s when the narrator was growing up, and it proceeds through associated memories of a Caribbean childhood where ripe juicy mangoes, flowering jacaranda and bougainvillea were inextricably mixed with Hindu religious music and the mysteries of English grammar, administered by Mrs. Ramsey with the aid of her wooden ruler, which was imperially named Rudyard. The narrator and her sister are subjected to rituals of social humiliation as soon as they enter the white colonial space of Mrs. Ramsey's house, where "Nothing was mongrel . . . and everything was trophy-and-certificate-winning" (p. 108). Mootoo dramatizes the deformations of this educational system, which so many postcolonial theorists have analyzed—the self-alienation of the colonial subject as these girls are encouraged to devalue their Indian heritage and the Hindi language as "old and backward" compared with superior English values, though they are also taught to reject America and Americanisms as well. The terrible word at the center of the narrator's traumatic memory is the American slang expression "*okay*," vilified by Mrs. Ramsay as a butchering of "our Oxford English Dictionary." However her lesson misfires, for it is through that word with its loaded cultural signifiers that the narrator learns to deconstruct the concept of whiteness into "English" and "American": "It went unchallenged for me that in the hierarchy of Whites, British was Queen and American was peasant" (p. 111). With delicate irony the narrator enacts her resistance to the values displayed so parodically by Mrs. Ramsey, displacing her colonial otherness on to the "American underdog." ("India was not 'Other' enough for me," she remarks, recalling her Brahmin grandmother's silent guerrilla warfare at home, with her insistent reminders of the family's Indianness in her saris, her poojas, and her singing of bhajans.) The narrator emerges from what is described elsewhere in this collection as "national cultural chaos" (p. 59) as a postcolonial transcultural subject, first choosing to study in North America rather than in England and now living in Vancouver where "the word 'okay' is no longer italicized, even though there is a faint ringing in my knuckles still" (p. 112).

As the story shifts in time and place from the Caribbean to Canada so the ironies around otherness multiply, for in Vancouver fashions in race have changed and her "White friends . . . no longer want to whiten me but rather they want to be brown and sugary like me" (p. 112). Otherness is clearly a cultural construction, depending on who and where you are: "Now that I live in North America 'Otherness' is elsewhere" than it was in Trinidad (p. 112). The narrator plays across the boundaries of race, nationality, and sexuality, confessing that her enthusiasm for "love-sick Sudanese musicians" (who are always male) springs from her broken love affair with Zahara, a young Muslim woman from Zaire ("close enough to Sudan"), and that it was in the World Beat music shop that she first met Meghan and later Virginia, a white Canadian middle-class lesbian couple who are passionately interested in "other" cultures.

The narrator's account of her friendship with these women enacts a multiple critique of identity categories based on culture and race as she contemplates white fantasies of exoticism and her own transcultural ambivalence, as well as a critique of colonialism where history comes unraveled even as it repeats itself in different versions. Meghan and Virginia fantasize about being South Asian, and they have the financial means to put these fantasies into practice. With their visits to India (where the narrator has never been able to afford to travel), their "Indian" gestures and their perfectly pleated saris, together with Meghan's skill in speaking Hindi, their imitation Indian identities look more authentic than the narrator's own: "They were better Indians than I" (p. 118), in a cultural context where identities are "always constituted within, not outside, representation."[4] The narrator has constantly to remind herself of the dimensions of masquerade practiced by these two very well off "good-looking White dykes" who have the privilege of slipping in and out of cultural identities in ways not available to the narrator herself, whose skin color is always the signifier of an otherness that she cannot escape, whether she wears blue jeans or a sari.

It is on the visit to the Hare Krishna temple in Vancouver where Meghan and Virginia invite the narrator to "come and learn a little about your culture" that the mood shifts from playful irony to satire, as the significance of these cross-cultural games comes sharply into focus. As the narrator confesses, she had thought that Hari Krishnas were white (having been introduced to the movement by the Beatles), and she records her own mixed responses as they change from embarrassment to anger, from feeling "shown-up as a cultural ignoramus" to intense resentment at the charade of exoticism that she witnesses in the temple, with its cultural cross-dressing and its Indian religious rituals presided over by the white guru and his white devotees. In another revelation not unlike the one centered on the word "okay" she suddenly glimpses the dimensions of loss within her own colonial inheritance, remembering her grandmother's "panic and distress at the unravelling of her culture right before her eyes" (p. 120). Seeing from this new perspective, she begins to interpret the Hare Krishna ceremony as another mode of imperialist appropriation where the old agendas are repeated with mini-mal transformation, for in the temple it is still the brown men and women who are at the back and on the periphery and it is only the brown women who are called into the kitchen to prepare the free vege-tarian meal for the worshippers. This is the narrator's moment of crisis, where memories of her colonial past in the Caribbean confront the post-colonial present in the new space of Canada, as she feels the familiar tingling in her knuckles. However, this time it is not from physical pain and humiliation but "from too tight a fist wanting to impact with history. An urgent rage buzzed around my head" (p. 123). But what is to be done? How to unseat traditional patterns of racial hegemony? The narrator's choice would seem to be rebellion, indifference, or irony, and here she chooses irony in her demonstration of disparities and reversals. Contemplating her two friends sitting at her side, "genuine in their desire to find that point where all division ceases and we unite as one" (p. 121), she takes the measure of the disjunctions between the liberal agendas of a dominant white culture so secure that it does not feel threatened by history or the present, and the entirely different agenda of a nonwhite postcolonial subject like herself. Both of them see the same phenomenon but interpret it in radically different ways: whereas for the narrator the brown women walking single file to the kitchen signify the repeat patterns of colonialism, for Meghan they speak to an infringe-ment of her feminist ideology: "Pretty sexist, eh! That's a problem for us too" (p. 121).

The final twist to the story comes with a letter from the narrator's mother in Trinidad announcing the death of Mrs. Ramsey, whose wish was of course to be buried in England. However times have changed, bringing in a series of ironic reversals, for Mrs. Ramsey's stepson no longer lives in England but has married an Indian woman from East Africa and emigrated to Philadelphia. So, Mrs. Ramsey with her outdated values is buried in a country that she hated and despised, and the mother's letter written in her careful English ends with a sentence where the traumatic word sits in triumph: "We sincerely hope this arrangement was okay..." Within the mode of comic irony Mootoo engages with the themes of colonial history and its postcolonial inheri-tors, with hybrid genealogies and transcultural immigrant subjectivities, using the English language, which is itself always in the process of change, to articulate positions of liminality, playing across the borders of race, nation, and gender in such a way that the boundaries themselves are put into question, opening up new ways for the representation of identity.

*Cereus Blooms at Night*, while engaging with the same themes as the short stories, constructs a far more ambitious narrative agenda that begins by implicitly questioning definitions of a "Canadian" novel, for *Cereus* is set on the fictive Caribbean island of Lantanacamara, and Canada, which is mentioned only at the end, is located outside the text. By centering her novel elsewhere, Mootoo displaces territoriality as the marker of Canadian identity, introducing instead the multiple cultural affiliations that are figured within Canadianness, or what Bhabha calls "the structure of cultural liminality—within the nation"[5] as prelude to her explorations of individual identities, which elude issues of nationality altogether. Yet despite its specific narrative location, *Cereus* manages to position itself "in-between" the Caribbean and Canada by its narratives of desire for escape and its transformations of identity: "You grow up here and you don't realize almost everybody in this place wish they could be somebody else? That is the story of life here in Lantancamara."[6] In this story of a Caribbean postcolonial culture damaged by its colonial inheritance, Canada represents the place beyond an immobilized present, which Bhabha has described in his study of the postcolonial diaspora:

> "Beyond" signifies spatial distance, marks progress, promises the future; but our intimations of exceeding the barrier or boundary—the very act of going *beyond*—are unknowable, unrepresentable, without a return to the "present" which, in the process of repetition, becomes disjunct and displaced.[7]

This comment might be read as a sketch for Mootoo's novel, which from one point of view looks like a return to origins with its story about domestic violence and different kinds of social alienation, but which from another perspective may be read as a "return to the present" where ghosts of the past have to be exorcized in order to move "beyond" into a different future.

This is a postcolonial text that confronts the binary structures inherent in colonialism and in sexual politics through a narrative that first explores the traumatic effects of such polarization on individual lives across several generations, and then in an effort of displacement sets out an alternative narrative of transgressive desire, which opens up spaces for new identity constructions. Though it is inscribed within the Indo-Caribbean historical experience of British colonialism, Mootoo's shifting perspective manages to engage with traditional emphases on race and then to move beyond these, focusing instead on issues of gender and sexuality and their social repercussions in Lantanacamara. Bodies alive and dead are very important here, but skin color and racial identity, which were the defining markers of difference under colonialism, no longer have the same significance in a racially hybridized postcolonial Caribbean context. Mootoo does not disavow race; she just does not include it as a primary classification of identity in present day Lantanacamara, whereas issues around sexuality and gender are much more socially relevant. The old colonial mechanism of violent othering has not vanished, but has only been transformed into the social ostracism of certain individuals who are seen to transgress the heterosexual norms of their community.

To focus my discussion of "otherness" in Lantanacamara, I shall begin by highlighting the phrase used by one of these marginalized outsiders, "a shared queerness" (p. 48). Who says it, what does it mean, and what is its significance? The words are spoken by Tyler, a gay Afro-Caribbean male nurse at the Alms House in the small town of Paradise, Lantanacamara, to describe his affinity with an elderly Indo-Caribbean patient Miss Mala Ramchandin. She has been committed to the home as a crazy old lady and possibly a murderess as well, though criminal charges against her have already been dismissed: "No victim, no evidence, no witnesses—no crime," as the judge summarized the case (p. 8). Both Tyler and Miss Ramchandin are regarded as scandalous figures in Paradise, he because of his homosexuality and she for two reasons—the suspicion that she has murdered her father and the open secret that she lived in an incestuous relationship with him for many years before he disappeared. It is through the stories of these two protagonists who are struggling to formulate their identities on the boundaries of social definition that concepts of liminality are explored, though in the process terrible secret histories are unearthed, so revealing those "unhomely moments" that "relate the traumatic ambivalences of a personal, psychic history to the wider disjunctions of political existence."[8] In other words, this novel translates the historical traumas of colonial inheritance into domestic terms of dysfunctional families and damaged individual lives. Within the immediate context, Tyler's phrase situates himself and Miss Ramchandin as two marginalized figures whose "queerness" refers to sexual practices that transgress cultural codes of heterosexuality and masculinity, placing them outside social limits of acceptability. Whereas public opinion in Lantanacamara does not bother to distinguish between different kinds of what is loosely called "perversion," it is Tyler who seeks to understand the bases of normative heterosexuality and to clarify the crucial differences between kinds of transgressive sexuality:

> Over the years I pondered the gender and sex roles that seemed available to people, and the rules that went with them...I was preoccupied with

trying to understand what was natural and what perverse, and who said so and why. Chandin Ramchandin played a part in confusing me about these roles, for it was a long time before I could differentiate between his perversion and what others called mine. (pp. 47–48)

Tyler's investigation provides an important dynamic in the restoring and re-storying of Miss Ramchandin, reconstructing her history of sexual abuse from the victim's perspective against the falsity of social opinion, while at the same time Tyler's self-confidence is restored through Miss Ramchandin's unconditional acceptance of him: "She knows what I am, was all I could think. She knows my nature," and he calls her his benefactress. Storytelling has mutually restorative functions here as it weaves different kinds of sexual transgressiveness into the wider context of Tyler's grandmother's tale told twenty years earlier about one of the casualties of colonial history:

I wonder what Nana would think if she knew the positions I was in that enabled me to gain the full story. For there were two: one, a shared queerness with Miss Ramchandin, which gave rise to the other, my proximity to the very Ramchandin Nana herself had known of. (p. 48)[9]

This novel might be read as an attempt to unhide the hidden psychic damage of Caribbean colonial history before venturing into new living spaces for the future, perhaps as an alternative to the desperate choice proposed earlier in the text: "I wonder at how many of us, feeling unsafe and unprotected, either end up running far away from everything we know and love, or staying and simply going mad" (p. 90). Tyler's is the main narrative voice, for he becomes the recorder of Miss Ramchandin's story, which he sends out like an open letter to her long lost younger sister Asha in Canada, though his own position is an oddly liminal one. Being on the periphery of Miss Ramchandin's story, he uses that marginal space to establish himself as the center of his own life story, while events in their yearlong relationship lead to the intermeshing of their two lives. Tyler's position is liminal in another way too, for though his voice is central in the narrative present, his story is continually interrupted by large fragments of his carefully reconstructed narrative of Miss Ramchandin's life. That narrative opens out into a family saga that goes back three generations through the story of her childhood and that of her lover Ambrose Mohanty, to the early lives of her parents, and then further back to the history of her paternal grandfather who came from India to Lantanacamara as an indentured laborer on the sugar plantations in the 1840s.[10] Whose voice tells these histories? Tyler's grandmother begins the Ramchandin narrative, but she leaves it poised on an enigma: "Hmmm, I wonder what become of him?... It's like he disappeared off the face of the earth" (p. 25). Her voice blurs into an omniscient narrator's voice, while the scandals of recent history immediately preceding Tyler's acquaintance with Miss Ramchandin are recorded dramatically through her own indirect interior monologue and the voices of the other major protagonists, which Tyler could not possibly have known. Toward the end, Tyler's voice is overlaid by the voice of the absent Asha as he reads out her old letters to her sister. Though he reassumes the storyteller's authority to offer his narrative in the hope that Asha will answer, there are so many voices haunting the present that Tyler seems to be caught in a space between traumatic narratives of the past and more optimistic as yet unrealized narratives for the future.

Questions of liminality—of being positioned in an "in-between" space between cultures or countries, or between identity categories of race, sexuality, and nation—have frequently been addressed to the immigrant condition as Mootoo does in her stories, but in her novel she transposes these questions to examine liminal identities in her home place. Lantanacamara's population includes a seemingly disproportionate number of people who suffer from identity confusions, double namings, split identities, or traumatic symptoms such as excessive passivity, sleepiness, muteness, or alcoholism. Many of these conditions are transformed in the course of a narrative, which itself hovers between realism and allegory in the shifting spaces of magic realism, balancing the tragedies of colonial history against the optimistic resolutions of romantic comedy. Mootoo seeks to represent the complex dynamics operating within a postcolonial society as the context for her study of different subjectivities, so that her protagonists occupy a series of changing positions in between different identities or roles. Such instability extends beyond issues of gender, sexuality, and race to include a questioning of boundaries between criminality and innocence, madness and sanity, and of the borderlines between reality, fantasy, and daydream. Indeed, the key image of the text is that of the rare nightblooming cereus plant; it circulates like a gift from a different dimension of experience, mingling its fragrance with the stench of bodily and moral corruption in the Ramchandin garden, opening up spaces for vision and hope. The cereus plant is intimately associated with Mala Ramchandin who has lived for most of her life beside it in the garden of the house filled with dark secrets, and it is her liminal identity that is the central focus of the text.

Who is this mysterious woman whose existence on the periphery of Lantanacamara has been almost forgotten except by one man, her old lover Ambrose Mohanty? Is she a criminal or a crazed victim, or is she something else entirely, as Tyler believes on the first night he sees her? "My intuition was that the woman on the bed was going to prove herself to be neither crazy nor failing in health, and that she would fare better given more freedom" (p. 20). As Mala's story unfolds, we discover a strong feminist politics in this tale of a woman who is both victim and survivor in an appalling history of loss and sexual violence and who finally takes revenge on her incestuous father by locking him up to die in a room underneath the house. She continues to live for many years in that haunted domestic space. When her release finally comes it reads like a flawed version of the Sleeping Beauty fairy tale, for her Prince Charming is not the man she thinks he is and she has to suffer the invasion of her privacy and the violation of her secret by the police before being forcibly carried from her home under arrest for murder. Her place is burned down by the same person who set out to rescue her, as the familiar Caribbean trope of the ruined house in a fallen paradise is given a savagely ironic twist. No wonder that when Mala arrives strapped to a stretcher at the Paradise Alms House she refuses to speak; it is her only possible response to the bullying and victimization she has endured at the hands of men in the immediate past and throughout her life history. Clearly she is suffering from what Tyler diagnoses as "symptoms of trauma" (p. 13), but equally she is acting out her role as silenced female victim just as she is expressing her distrust of language and of those who have used it so duplicitously against her. It is Tyler's self-appointed task to restore this damaged woman to trust and hope, and the story ends with their mutual rehabilitation. It will be evident from my brief account that Mootoo's agenda is neither exclusively feminist nor entirely "queer." It includes gender troubles of the male sex too, as she analyzes the kinds of oppression suffered by men who fail to conform to their Caribbean society's norms of masculinity, while heterosexuality is given a range of representations from failed marriages through the traumatic violence of incest to the traditional scenarios of true romance in Mala's garden.

Yet for Mootoo's protagonists whose life histories are inscribed within Caribbean colonial history problems of gender identity and sexual transgression are inevitably bound up with the discourses of colonialism, as Tyler hinted in his comment about his grandmother's unfinished story of Chandin Ramchandin. The origins of Mala's terrible story lie far back in her father's story in his double betrayal by the English Christian missionary, the allegorically named Reverend Ernest Thoroughly and his daughter Lavinia. Ramchandin is one of colonialism's casualties (while Mala's lover Ambrose is another), a tragic figure who turns into a monster through grief and rage and self-loathing. As the clever son of Hindu Indian laborers, the eleven-year-old boy was taken from his parents and "adopted" into the Reverend's family, to be educated as a Christian convert destined to become a theological teacher to the Indian population of Lantanacamara as part of the "civilizing" project of Empire. Chandin's education teaches him white manners and aspirations, but it also teaches him to despise his own race and the color of his skin. Seduced by the master narrative of colonialism, he becomes the stock figure of colonial otherness where "the white man's artifice [is] inscribed on the black man's body. It is in relation to this impossible object that the liminal problem of colonial identity and its vicissitudes emerges."[11] When Chandin falls in love with Lavinia Thoroughly, the disastrous ambiguities of his position become apparent: as adopted "son" he is both a member of the family and outside it, playing the role of Lavinia's brother as she and the Reverend insist, and yet not her brother as Chandin knows, though he is denied a voice to plead his own case. The confused kinship relations here foreshadow the nightmare of incest in the next generation, for Chandin is already "an in-between unnamed thing" within colonial discourse long before he becomes a father and the sexual abuser of his daughter. Frustrated and confused, when he hears the news of Lavinia's engagement to her English cousin, Chandin marries her friend Sarah, an Indian Christian convert like himself. Even his imitation of desirable family life—with a wife and two daughters and a crystal chandelier like the one in the Thoroughlys' house—is destroyed by the love affair between Sarah and Lavinia, and his ultimate rejection comes when the two women run away together, Sarah being forced to abandon Mala and Asha to their father's care. In his profound humiliation, Chandin completely rejects his former identity and becomes a recluse and an alcoholic, physically and sexually abusing his helpless young daughters. He begins his incestuous abuse in a kind of nightmare fantasy when he mistakes Mala for his lost wife, but then continues in the full rage of consciousness not out of love but out of hatred and a mad lust for possession and domination. It is symptomatic of Mootoo's multiple critique of colonialism that she would trace not only its terrible legacy of violence across several generations, but that she would also demonstrate the limits of power within the master narrative itself through the lesbian love affair between Lavinia and Sarah, where a discourse of female desire transgresses colonialism's prescribed racial and sexual boundaries. The two women disappear and the Thoroughly family fade out of the story, though they leave a trail of disaster in the damaged psyches of those most favored by them in Lantanacamara.

To return to the Ramchandin family saga, it is Mala who becomes her father's victim in a classic case of identity confusion, caught between the typically feminine roles of submissive daughter, abused wife, and "mother" to her little sister while she herself is still only a child. When Asha runs away in her early teens, Mala is left alone with her father in a house that could only be described as "unhomely," as Ramchandin recreates in his distorted domestic relations a Caribbean history of enslavement and where the psychological legacy of colonialism is refigured as sexual violence in the family: "The recesses of the domestic space become sites for history's most intricate invasions. In that displacement, the borders between home and world become confused; and, uncannily, the private and the public become part of each other, forcing upon us a vision that is as divided as it is disorienting."[12]

Mala is powerless and friendless in a community that remains indifferent to her plight. If anything, the townspeople have a kind of residual sympathy for Ramchandin, whom they see as having been driven to insanity: "Such a man would take to the bottle and to his own child, they reasoned, only if he suffered some madness. And, they further reasoned, what man would not suffer a rage akin to insanity if his own wife, with a devilish mind of her own, left her husband and children" (p. 195). Indeed, the novel is strongly critical of the town's neglect, for though the incestuous relationship is an open secret, nobody challenges Ramchandin's abuse of his paternal authority and instead they ostracize his daughter for the father's transgression. Even the letters from her sister are never delivered, as we learn years later, "because the righteous postman, deeming the Ramchandin house to be a place of sin and moral corruption, refused to go up there" (p. 243). Surely this is the reason why the pall of smoke from the Ramchandins' burning house and garden hangs symbolically over Paradise in a "thick, black cloud" until Judge Bissey publicly exonerates Mala from the charge of murder. She is the victim and not the perpetrator of a legacy of violence, which is both domestic and historical. Mala is also exonerated by the narrative that gradually reconstructs the scene of the crime from her perspective, on the one hand miming the fragmented remembering so typical of traumatized victims of incest,[13] and on the other adopting the discursive mode of magic realism, writing in the radical disjunctions and bewilderment about identity that characterizes the Caribbean postcolonial inheritance.[14] Briefly summarized, Mala's personal crisis occurs over her forbidden romance with her childhood playmate, Ambrose Mohanty ("also known as Boyie") when he returns from the Shivering Northern Wetlands transformed into an elegant but totally ineffectual "foreign educated fop."

Ambrose flees from the house when confronted by her father's murderous rage on discovering their love affair, though he manages accidentally
to stun Ramchandin by the blow from a slamming door as he dashes
away. Abandoned once again, Mala spits in her unconscious father's
face, then in desperation drags his inert body downstairs, and after locking him up in the sewing room she builds a barricade of furniture to
protect herself against him. Ramchandin never emerges and the reader
has to assume that he died of injuries and starvation. Mala is still so
terrified of her father that she takes up her residence on the verandah
and never sleeps inside the house again.

From the time of Ambrose's abandonment and her father's disappearance till the intrusion of Ambrose's son Otoh over twenty years
later, Mala leads a wild solitary existence alienated from the outside
world behind the high fences of the Ramchandin property, and increasingly alienated from herself. Known as the town's madwoman, she is
first teased and then forgotten by everybody except Ambrose. To him
she remains a mysterious object of desire, and he continues (from a safe
distance) to pay court to her, rousing himself from excessive lethargy
once a month to deliver gifts of food, a task that Otoh inherits as his
father grows older. Meantime Mala becomes a living ghost as she abandons language and leads a truly liminal existence, teetering on the
borderline between human and natural worlds as she sits in her rocking
chair on the verandah or under the mudra tree in her overgrown garden,
sometimes immersed in memory or daydream and sometimes
communing with the birds and the flowers. The garden itself is represented as a liminal space, for it exists in two different dimensions: it is a
real place where plants, animals, and insects are described in minute
physical detail, and it is also constructed as a space of imagination where
the natural world offers a radical alternative to the dark enclosed house
of patriarchal tyranny and incestuous abuse. Mala's garden, which was
originally her mother's, is a sheltered feminine space where the rhythms of
growth, decay, and death proceed uninterruptedly as she attunes herself
to a state of peaceful coexistence with nature. Like the wilderness landscape of much Canadian women's fiction, the garden functions as the
site of spiritual and emotional healing for a damaged female psyche.
Gradually Mala learns to inhabit her garden, not only looking at it but
also smelling it and listening to its sounds:

> She listened intently. With an ear pressed to the ground she heard ant
> communities building, transporting food and breeding. She listened to
> worms coiling arduously from place to place. She knelt on the ground

and whispered to the grass and other young plants, encouraging them to grow, and then she listened as they stretched up to her. (pp. 127–28)

Paying such close attention to the sounds and rhythms of nature, Mala turns away from the symbolic order of language, preferring to commune with the natural world through her body in a nonverbal language of intense sensation and emotion unmediated by the "unnecessary translation" of words: "The wings of a gull flapping through the air titillated her soul and awakened her toes and her knobby knees, the palms of her withered hands, deep inside her womb, her vagina, lungs, stomach and heart . . . Every fibre was sensitized in a way that words were unable to match or enhance" (p. 126). Words fall away as Mala learns another language of hearing, vision, and touch, imitating birdcalls and "harmonizing with whichever insects' shrills prevailed on a particular day" (p. 127). This is indeed the means of communication that she first uses in her negotiations with Tyler in the Alms House: "I would catch her watching me through the side of her eyes, as she did bird, cricket and frog calls as though she meant to entertain me" (p. 24).

The fascinating paradox here is that while Mala is able to exist outside language, Mootoo the novelist is still within it, writing Mala's nonverbal experience. How is it possible to give voice to a character who has slipped back into a prelinguistic world? Mootoo carefully frames Mala's subjective life within a narratorial account of her stages of language loss, which is later supplemented by Ambrose's "intoxicating sermon" on how "a world freed of nomenclature, syntax and lexical forms is experienced" (p. 211), before slipping into Mala's indirect interior monologue of heightened sensory perceptions. It is only by divesting herself of the limits of individual identity that Mala finds release from traumatic memory through her communion with nature. The emblem of her secret life of bliss is the night-blooming cereus, and it is with the lyrical intensity of that moonlit flowering that she is most intimately associated:

As night fell she dragged her rocking chair down the back stairs and into the yard under the fringes of the giant mudra tree. She sat upright like a concert director in front of the wall. As night unwound she witnessed the slow dance of huge, white cereus buds—she counted sixty-two—trembling as they unfolded against the wall, a choreography of petal and sepal opening together, sending dizzying scent high and wide into the air. The moonlight reflected off the blossoms' pure whiteness and cast a glow over the yard. Mala basked. (p. 134)

In her open-air theatre Mala sits for hours in such a state of rapture at the rhythms of the slowly opening fragrant flowers that she is totally overwhelmed by her synaesthetic experience and manages, at least momentarily, to enter into harmony with the organic life around her. Yet the image of Mala as concert director reminds the reader that she is still tenuously connected to culture. Though so sensitively attuned to nature, Mala remains in the position of spectator watching a spellbinding ballet performance that will come to its end like a dream, leaving the dreamer behind. All that is left in the morning are the ragged flowers hanging "limp, battered and bruised" from the assaults of moths and bats the previous night, like a horrible subliminal refiguring of Mala's own body memories of being battered and bruised by her father's sexual abuse. It would be wrong to identify Mala entirely with nature, for though she may coexist with it and sometimes lose herself in it, her garden is not a space outside time. On the contrary, it is a space haunted by times remembered where Mala as traumatized subject is liable to unpredictable fits of terror and panic attacks, just as it is a real place pervaded by the foul smell of bodily decomposition issuing from the locked room beneath the house. Her residence on the verandah is a sign of her in-between existence: she is still human, a woman who may speak the language of the animals but who wears clothes and sits on a chair in her garden. There she daydreams with her eyes closed, reliving and recreating new versions of her past: "She remembered a little and imagined a great deal" (p. 142), as the narrator's voice reminds us.

Mala is like a princess under a spell, and as all children know, spells have to be broken for the princess to be rescued. This story follows the traditional fairy tale pattern for when daylight comes and the cereus flowers have withered, Ambrose's son Otoh appears as if by magic in her garden. In reality Otoh is impelled not only by curiosity to see the woman whom his father has adored for so long but also by an obscure desire to rescue both Mala and his father from the mistakes of the past. What Otoh does not know is that in order to assume the heroic role of deliverer he must accompany Mala as she reenters the locked dark places of her private history. The strange episode of Otoh's visit flickers between realism and fantasy as the narrative shifts between Otoh's and Mala's perspectives, crossing from present to past and back again, with the result that neither of them is entirely sure what is real and what is imagined. When Otoh enters the garden he is also unknowingly breaking into the secret space of her fantasy life as she daydreams about Pohpoh, her abused childhood self, elaborately constructing an alternative story of rescue and escape for her. What he does know is that he is assailed by stinging nettles and a foul smell, "thick, like a miasma he had to wade through" (p. 153) before he can enter the garden, where he suddenly feels like a trespasser who has come upon an enchanted space in a lost jungle or a fallen paradise. This is the language of magic realism, offering a kind of suspension between two modes of apprehending the world, where neither realism nor magic is cancelled out. Magic realism is the narrative language of liminality, as Stephen Slemon phrases it: "A complete transference from one mode to the other never takes place, and the novel remains suspended between the two."[15] Otoh's first view of Mala offers an impressively visual figuring of the liminal, for as he stands on the edge of unfamiliar territory Mala's human form metamorphoses out of the landscape itself:

> Right there, directly in front of him, was the reason he had come. Mala Ramchandin. She sat in a rocking chair beside the tree, her eyes closed. Her figure was all but lost in the blueness of the mudra's trunk. She wore a petticoat, greens and browns and light blues, that blended into the background of leaves and gnarled, twisted limbs. Otoh's face burned. He stood and stared. (p. 155)

Mala's view of Otoh is no less hallucinatory, for when she opens her eyes it is only to shift from one fantasy to another. Daydreaming about Pohpoh, she wakens to the sound of Dixieland jazz on a gramophone and sees Otoh dressed up in the old suit of clothes that his father had worn whenever he visited her in the far-off days of their courtship: "We used to dance together. She and I. Did I ever tell you?" (p. 145). Mala and Otoh stand locked in each other's gaze like a pair of lovers but this is a very slippery vision, a case of mistaken identity and a blurring of times past and present. As they dance together in the garden Otoh is caught into the strange masquerade of being his own father in his youthful figuration, just as he feels himself drawn into Mala's dream world of romantic memory. However, the fairy tale twists into Gothic nightmare when she leads him into the house and down the dark stairs to the unspeakable secret hidden in the locked room: "He can't hurt you now, Ambrose. Come, come" (p. 161). When Otoh sees the decomposing body on the high wrought-iron bed, he collapses in terror and then like his father before him, he flees. Otoh's role may be that of rescuer but it is a traumatic deliverance, primarily for Mala as history repeats itself but also for him. He faints outside on the road, then blurts out the secret that destroys Mala's world: "A body, it have a body in she house" (p. 166). As his father wisely remarks, "Clearly you did not cause trouble. It seems that trouble was lurking like a diseased phantom, waiting to be revealed, and you had the misfortune to have come upon it" (p. 170).

Otoh's declaration is followed by the public invasion of Mala's house and garden, though she vainly attempts to resist this violation from the real world by returning to her rocking chair under the mudra tree, closing her eyes, and resuming her fantasy narrative about Pohpoh's adventures. By a curious process of repetition in a novel, which is haunted by uncanny returns of the repressed, the strategy Mala adopts is the same one she had practiced in her desperate bid for survival as the youthful victim of incest, where she had deliberately split herself in two in order to block out her father's abuse. The text itself is split between a realistic account of what is actually happening and blocks of Mala's interior monologue, though increasingly the borders blur as her present anxieties over the policemen's activities reshape her fantasy narrative: "She heard the voices of the police. She reconfigured what they said to match her story of how she saved Pohpoh that day" (p. 175). In her distress, Mala's identity fractures completely into a condition of schizophrenia where she is divided between the adult Mala and the child Pohpoh, caught in a time loop between present and past as she leads the police downstairs to her father's body. They all view the same decomposing corpse, but for Mala seeing through Pohpoh's eyes that dead body is still terrifyingly alive. As she continues to chatter to Pohpoh, the chief constable thinks that Mala has gone totally mad, though Mala is simply following her own emotional imperative to set Pohpoh free. She finally manages to fulfill her childhood fantasy of flying away: "Down below, her island was soon lost among others, all as shapeless as specks of dust adrift on a vast turquoise sea" (p. 186). Mala is taken into custody and the scandal of revelation is followed by the destruction of the Ramchandin house and garden by fire. With Mala's arrival at the Alms House the narrative switches back to its opening scene. Yet this account falsifies the novel—not the facts but the structure—for this is a very fractured narrative with its multiple voices, its temporal dislocations, and its hesitations between realism and fantasy, "with neither managing to subordinate or contain the other. This sustained opposition forestalls the possibility of interpretive closure through any act of naturalizing the text to an established system of representation."[16] Certainly it figures the complexities within reconstructions of the personal and historical past, but its rejection of a linear plot is also a deliberate strategy that creates the sensation of being caught in the middle of proliferating narrative versions where resolutions are promised but endlessly deferred. The protagonists' condition of always being "in-between" is mirrored in the reader's own experience of the text.

This disjunctive narrative language that foregrounds "in-betweenness" might also be seen as a language for figuring conditions of desire that relate not only to postcolonial identities but to sexual identities as well. While Mala's narrative as reconstructed by Tyler tells the story of one woman's social marginalization in Lantanamara, Tyler also manages to tell the story of another marginalized group—homosexuals on this Caribbean island. There is a painful realism in the account of his own social ostracism and his miserable state of mind: "Not a man and not ever able to be a woman, suspended nameless in the limbo state between existence and non-existence" (p. 77), just as there is the unfinished story of the gardener's brother Randolph ("He was kind of funny. He was like you," p. 73) who disappeared. It is from this "manacling" of nature that Mala rescues Tyler, by simply accepting him as he is, and their "shared queerness" opens the way to Tyler's own love story with "the alluring Otoh." As a handsome young man who began life as a girl, Otoh's sexual identity is so ambiguously represented that it borders on magic realism, and the romantic relationship between him and Tyler enacts a kind of liberation from conventional sexual identity categories as the old binaries are discarded. Through Otoh's identitary ambiguity, Mootoo like Tyler is pondering the "gender and sex roles available to people," though unlike Tyler she plays with the "rules that went with them" as she switches between the language of fantasy and seduction and Otoh's mother's down to earth practicality: "Now as I was saying, every village in this place have a handful of people like you. And is not easy to tell who is who. How many people here know about you, eh? I does watch out over the banister and wonder if *who* I see is really *what* I see" (p. 238). Such identity transgression is both jokey and serious in its defiance of conventional sex and gender categories, for Otoh possesses both masculine courage to act decisively and also feminine sensitivity. As we discover, it is he who has set fire to the old Ramchandin house to prevent its desecration and also to destroy the incriminating evidence against Mala, and it is he who presents her with the cereus clipping from her vanished garden, which flourishes in the garden of the Paradise Alms House.

The ending of the novel is filled with hope precariously balanced against loss as it is poised on the cusp between present and future, with everybody at the Alms House waiting for something to happen. Ambrose Mohanty sits beside his beloved Mala (who has just uttered her first public words) declaring "No time to waste," though nobody is sure what he is waiting for; Otoh and Tyler, now proudly holding his head high, are waiting for the opening of the pink cereus buds as the time to consummate their transgendered love affair; Mala is waiting to hear from Asha in Canada: "She expects you any day soon. You are, to her, the promise of a cereus-scented breeze on a Paradise night" (p. 249).

*Cereus* addresses multiple issues of liminality in a Caribbean context, but by looking beyond the home place toward Canada Mootoo is situating the immigrant's liminal position as a significant factor within Canada's multicultural agenda. Immigrant fictions do unsettle traditional discourses of nationhood, simply by introducing other stories and other histories that are supplementary to the dominant discourse, as postcolonial theorists and social policymakers are aware. Certainly *Cereus* rephrases definitions of Canadian identity based on territory or origins, and Margaret Atwood's question: "How do we know we are who we think we are... or thought we were a hundred years ago?"[17] would be answered very differently by a Caribbean immigrant speaking out of a colonial history that is other to that of nineteenth-century English Canada. The liminality of Mootoo's Indo-Caribbean-Canadian text is symptomatic of that "liminality within the nation-space,"[18] which is now being written into Canada's literary history by its minority writers.

There is a line in the title poem of Mootoo's recent collection, *The Predicament of Or*, which offers a different perspective on liminality as it is figured through a nomadic or immigrant consciousness. That line, marginalized as a parenthesis, is "(In-between *is* a place),"[19] and it carries the suggestion that liminality might be mapped through an imaginative cartography that traces the shifting positions of a Caribbean immigrant woman living in Canada. The poems speak in a very personal voice from "I" to "you," sometimes addressing a figure within the text but frequently speaking directly to the reader, who is positioned inside and not outside the poem. To cite Trinidad and Canada as the coordinates of Mootoo's poetic world would be to oversimplify into false binary structures, for the narrative moves restlessly through a series of geographical locations as far apart as Australia and New York State. These are travel poems filled with arrivals and departures, with cars, planes, and ships, and where boundaries between places are crossed and recrossed so frequently that geographical markers dissolve into landscapes of memory and desire. None of this should surprise Mootoo's readers, for *The Predicament of Or* is precisely that of being caught within a mobile present between past and future, which is not only a location of sorts but also a state of mind. If liminality is a "place" (or a space) that the subject occupies, then perhaps immigration is the most obviously liminal condition of all. So it is with the immigrant poems in the section entitled "The Quickened Diluvial Shore" that I am particularly concerned in this discussion of changing boundaries of identity.

However, the immigrant's position is only one of the possible liminal "places" as the four-part arrangement of the collection makes clear. The title poem occurs in the second section called "Or" (which precedes "Diluvial Shore") and it is a sequence of lesbian love poems about desire and loss and emotional indeterminacy, while the first section (entitled "The Way You Bounce Off a Pane of Glass") is pervaded by a strong sense of the narrator's Caribbean origins and lost locations, which are evoked as if in defiance of the erosions of time and memory: "The good thing about pen / and words: / The plan to ensnare and remember / is a true, a final, / a most perfect forgetting" ("Beach Composition III," *The Predicament of Or* (hereafter *PO*), p. 17). The short final section ("July Plum") returns to the intimately personal emotional dynamics of "Or" and ends with a poem called "Waiting," poised on the edge of the future and filled with an eager longing, which is strikingly similar to the ending of *Cereus*: "This time, I know you're coming / Only because, this time, / I'm ready, willing, waiting" (*PO*, p. 113). In many ways these erotic poems chart a similar emotional cartography to that of the poems about immigration with their narratives of desire and deferral, and perhaps most importantly with their search for a language adequate to describe that place "in-between," which itself unsettles accustomed idioms. Two examples from the title poem will illustrate: " 'But what of the future?' I said. 'Or...' / and left it there / (or was it here)?" (*PO*, p. 53) and "Then let us talk of home: / Does one *come* home / or / Does one *go* home?" (*PO*, p. 58).

That emotional and linguistic predicament is amplified in "Mantra for Migrants," which begins

> Always becoming, will never be
> Always arriving, must never land
> Between back home and home unfathomable, is me—
> By definition: immigrant (*PO*, p. 81)

This time the speaking "I" does manage to find an appropriate language to describe her sense of being caught in the shifting present where, trapped by the one-word definition of her identity as "immigrant," she watches her whole world destabilizing before her eyes. Words suddenly shift their meanings so that "always," "never," and "forever" are emptied of any promise of permanency and instead become signifiers of endless mobility, as the narrative voice ironically affirms: "Migrant immutable amazing unchangeable / Always becoming."[20]

The arrangement of this sequence highlights not only the immigrant's sense of alterity in the narrative poems illustrating different aspects of her experience but also her struggles to find her voice through a series of experimental language poems, like "All the Irish I Know" (*PO*, p. 95) and "All the Hindi I Know" (*PO*, p. 96). These poems may all be seen as explorations of the multiple dimensions of dislocation suffered by the immigrant subject. "A Recognition" sets up a dramatic encounter as the narrator addresses a fellow Caribbean with the words: "You're Trinidadian!...I recognize the accent!" (*PO*, p. 84) reaching for an identity frame based on shared recognition of origins. However, the sharp rejection of the reply: "I am Canadian" causes her to ponder the immigrant experience of reconstructing identities and the other person's unspoken reasons for choosing to escape from "always becoming" behind the label of an adopted nationality that masks ethnic and racial differences. The poem seems not to end but to pause, and the fact that there is no full stop leads the reader straight on to the next one entitled "The Edited." It is ostensibly about language and word deletions that leave a text incomplete: "hap-pens to deleted / words? th speed at which fall?" (*PO*, p. 86). This poem with its fractured words and syntax teeters on the edge of meaninglessness until the last two lines, when meanings suddenly shimmer into focus: "deletion is rare/ly convincingly abslute" (*PO*, p. 87). The poem makes its oblique criticism of the radical oversimplifications imposed both by textual editing and by subjective self-editing, where whatever is edited out has to be acknowledged through the traces it leaves behind.

Such suspensions of meaning might serve as prelude to the next pair of poems, "Game of Watch the Migrant Dream, #1 and #2," where the condition of liminality is represented not in realistic terms but through fantasy in the spectacle of a circus performance. The female immigrant figure stars not as rope dancer but as rope flinger, "Doing the migrant fling" (*PO*, p. 93). The "always arriving" migrant herself is suspended between "one side" and "the other side" while trapped in a dream that looks very like a nightmare. The reader too is in a state of suspension (suspense?) not only over the outcome but also forced to shift continually between the perspectives of the desiring subject and the crowd on the dock who are eagerly watching the performance. With mordant irony, the poems sketch two recurring dreams: in the first one the plane never takes off and in the second the ship never docks. The crossing over cannot be achieved, for there is always an "*abyss fissure chasm canyon crevasse crack*" (*PO*, p. 93). These images, eerily repeated from "Cracks and Crevasses," an earlier poem about the dynamics within a lesbian love relationship, carry the subtext of desire over into the immigrant's story, where her rope ladder always falls "a metre short, damn oh dear" (*PO*, p. 93). What is so alarming is the attitude of the crowd. People do not ignore the performance; indeed it is newsworthy and there are spectators, photographers, and "note takers abundant" but there are no helping hands, and finally the crowd subsides into indifference: "it's another migrant falling another migrant mauling for sure" (*PO*, p. 94). However, the reader cannot so easily block out the immigrant's plight, having become implicated in her desperate efforts to fling her ladder of dreams into what Bhabha has called "the Beyond." The immigrant says nothing (or perhaps the crowd cannot hear her) but the poem insists that the reader hears her by finding a language for the diasporic subject that is fractured by hope frustrated and desire deferred:

> She migrant this   migrant flinging
> dream   other side dreaming
> Inch by inch   hours of haul   hope as long as deep as
> *Abyss fissure chasm canyon crevasse crack* (*PO*, p. 93)

The poems about immigration end with one called "Point of Convergence," which presents an image of survival. This poem describes in detail the construction of a new transcultural Canadian identity for the narrative subject, yet it is a very ambivalent self-definition with the subject describing herself in terms of multiple cultural affiliations, which are both negated and acknowledged:

> union of back home
> way back then, and home
>
> where *I* depend neither
> on memory nor desire
> where *I* am neither
> mendhi, baigan, steelpan
>
> nor mindless of these (*PO*, p. 102)

As the poet declares, this is a definition of "hybridity," a popular term in postcolonial theory to describe the formation of mixed identities, opening a way to "conceptualizing an *inter* national culture."[21] With self-deprecating irony the narrator points out that the word has had a long history before its postcolonial refashioning, where it was framed by the discourses of biology and then of racism: "as in: 'offspring of tame sow and wild boar' / child of freeman and slave" (*PO*, p. 102) (with a footnote reference to "our" Oxford Dictionary so revered by Mrs. Ramsey in Mootoo's short story). Moreover, hybridity when subjectively experienced registers a sense of confusion as well as new possibilities, a realization mirrored in this poem by a babble of words out of which the voice of the "I" is struggling to emerge. She is framed by all the past selves of her heritage as well as by her official identity classifications, and

the poem ends not with a transcendent sense of selfhood but with the
subject still surrounded by a network of relationships and languages:

> where neither Nepalese great-grandmother
> nor mother, lover, government
> define *I*
>
> nor am
> *I*
> mindless of these. (*PO*, p. 103)

It is with an identity "always in process and always constituted
within, not outside representation" that I shall end this chapter, as
Mootoo situates the immigrant's liminal position in relation to
Canadian culture. Her work belongs within that growing body of diasporic writing, which is shifting boundaries of identity in a process that
has been described as "the gradual reinscription of Canada's social imaginary in ways that address the need to view minority Canadians not as
'interest groups' to be 'added on' to a preexisting nucleus but rather as
active, generative participants at the very core of a shared conflictual
history."[22]

# CHAPTER 8

## FIRST NATIONS: CROSS-CULTURAL ENCOUNTERS, HYBRIDIZED IDENTITIES

### WRITING ON THE BORDERS: GAIL ANDERSON-DARGATZ, *THE CURE FOR DEATH BY LIGHTNING*

My name is Beth Weeks. My story takes place in the midst of the Second World War, the year I turned fifteen, the year the world fell apart and began to come together again. Much of it will be hard to believe, I know.
(*The Cure for Death by Lightning*)[1]

Gail Anderson-Dargatz's first novel, *The Cure for Death by Lightning* shares many of the most traditional features of English-Canadian women's narratives. It is a white adolescent girl's story about growing up in a small rural community in the Rocky Mountains of British Columbia, told retrospectively when she has assumed her identity as a woman and a writer. It also belongs to the genre of pioneer women's narratives about the wilderness, stretching back in a line of descent from nineteenth-century texts like Catherine Parr Traill's *The Backwoods of Canada* (1836) and Susanna Moodie's *Roughing It in the Bush* (1852). This is certainly a novel that acknowledges female traditions, for Beth writes her memoir using her dead mother's scrapbook of country recipes and folk remedies as her model, though it is also a revision of tradition as she informs the reader right from the start: "The scrapbook was my mother's way of setting down the days so they wouldn't be forgotten. This story is my way" (*Cure*, p. 2). Writing in the late twentieth century, Beth not only rewrites her mother's version of a Canadian country-woman's life during World War II but also and most crucially she revises the white wilderness narrative through her postcolonial awareness of the significant presence of Aboriginal people and indigenous culture, marginalized but always there on the edges of the farming community around the small town called Promise.

Beth lives with her parents and elder brother on a dairy and flax farm beside the Turtle Creek Native Reserve; her father employs two Aboriginal youths as laborers, the matriarch of the reserve Bertha Moses and the women of her household are her mother's most frequent visitors, and Beth's two best friends Nora and Billy are Bertha's grandchildren, so that this is very much a story about cross-cultural relationships. Told by a girl whose imaginative life is influenced by stories from both white and Aboriginal traditions, the narrative offers an unsettling critique of European values and colonial beliefs in white superiority, just as it undermines concepts of otherness based on racial difference, which lead to the questioning of what constitutes a Canadian identity. Beth's acknowledgment of her pluralized cultural inheritance (like Anderson-Dargatz's thanks to "the First Nations Canadians and pioneer women" in her preface) does not change the traditional feminine storyline celebrating women's strength and survival in the wilderness, but it does introduce new perspectives into the genre at the same time as it shifts the emphasis away from realism toward fantasy and more magical interpretations of events. While this may be seen as symptomatic of a teenage girl's quest for identity where imagination struggles to come to terms with the new reality of being a woman, this oscillation between realism and fantasy also represents a textual strategy where white and Native ways of seeing are shown in conflict. In the end, Beth adopts a mediatory position where alternative ways of understanding the world are both contained though neither is privileged, within a magic realist mode of narrative discourse.

In this autobiographical fiction Beth is the center of her own story: she is chief victim, heroine, and survivor, and the challenge for her as for the reader is to map the different elements in her complex self-figuring as she seeks to understand who she is. Through what historical and cultural lenses might her identity as a white feminine subject become intelligible? Toward the end of her memoir when she is nearly sixteen, she confesses to an urge to make her own book and to "write everything down," for this is a version of the artist novel or *kunstlerroman*, where Beth finds her voice and vocation as a writer: "As Billy said, if you could only get things out of yourself—speak them, or write them down, or paste bits of them into a scrapbook—then you could sort things out" (*Cure*, p. 287). It is with Beth's sorting out process that this chapter is concerned. How does she find a language to write her story? What are the different discourses through which she represents the confusions and triumphs of the most traumatic year of her adolescence? And what is the relation between white and Native models of the feminine through which Beth negotiates her own evolving self-construction?

I emphasize the engendering of Beth's narrative for although her story is in important ways about cross-cultural and interracial relations, its dynamic is, I believe, primarily feminist and its main emphasis is on sexual politics.[2] (How does the adolescent narrator experience the emotional chaos and dangers of growing into womanhood?) Beth's narrative holds two or possibly three different kinds of female plot in sustained counterpoint. On the one hand there is the neurotic plot of wilderness Gothic where Beth is the beleaguered heroine under constant threat from a mysterious stalker in the bush and also the sexual victim of her mad incestuous father, while on the other there is the realistic plot of domestic fiction with its celebration of women's emotional and moral strengths, which sustain home and community, personified by her own mother and recorded in her scrapbook. There is also a third plot gradually taking shape under the guidance of Bertha, Beth's Aboriginal mentor, which is that of the female hero who repudiates the role of victim. With great courage she resists and defeats the misogynist representatives of patriarchy in a striking reversal of power relations between the sexes. Beth assumes that heroic role as a woman of action when she confronts first her stalker and then her father, but principally perhaps when she faces down her own terrified imagination. The novel ends with the rehabilitation of feminine values as Beth seeks to combine her mother's nurturing love and homemaking skills with Bertha's sturdily outspoken independence in her own version of writing in the feminine. Male violence is vanquished within Beth's local context, though in the wider world beyond Turtle Valley World War II still rages as a reminder that "such questions [and issues] persist, in spite of novels. It is a shock, when you have dealt so cunningly, powerfully, with reality, to come back and find it still there," as Alice Munro once so wisely remarked.[3]

Such unaccommodated remainders haunt this text, contributing to an overall impression of instability and indeterminacy as an older Beth struggles to reinvent the lost world of her adolescence. Through memory she reenters that borderline territory between childhood and adulthood where imaginary fears, dawning sexual desires, and real terrors create a world of such bewildering contradictions that fantasy and reality cannot easily be separated, even in retrospect. As Beth remarks at the beginning, challenging her readers' credulity: "No one can tell me these events didn't happen, or that it was all a girl's fantasy. The reminders are there, in that scrapbook, and I remember them all" (*Cure*, p. 2).

It is her mother's scrapbook that is central to Beth's autobiographical impulse, for this is a story about mothers and daughters and female inheritance as it traces Beth's relation with her mother and her mother's relation with her own dead English mother, just as it presents Bertha Moses's relation to all the women of Aboriginal and mixed race in her extended family of daughters and daughters' daughters. Beth's account is based as she claims on the documentary evidence provided by the scrapbook, which she has inherited as an heirloom: "I still have my mother's scrapbook. It sits inside the trunk that was her hope chest. I sometimes take out the scrapbook and sit with it at my kitchen table, by the stove that is electric and white" (*Cure*, p. 2). The scrapbook provides evidence of the solid substratum of a countrywoman's daily life to which Beth remains attached, though the decorums of domestic realism do not provide an adequate framework for Beth to speak about all the other dimensions of her emotional and imaginative experience, most specifically her sexual experience. While Nora's tinkling bell necklace provides a shimmering image for the seductions of adolescent female desire, Beth has to turn to Bertha's Aboriginal stories about Coyote to find a language for sexual trauma, where the Native Trickster figure becomes a metaphor for her recurring nightmare of incestuous abuse and panic fear of male violence. Beth's narrative braids together real and imagined sexual fears as part of her construction of femininity, but these are balanced against the solid evidence of women's strength and the healing power of adolescent love, which is promiscuously exploratory in its border crossings between races and sexes. Beth's writing in the feminine becomes a double-voiced discourse where realism and fantasy blend together in a subjective representation of her gendered identity.

The novel opens with a description of her mother's treasured scrapbook and its handwritten cure for death by lightning, which makes it look like a book of spells: "*Dunk the dead by lightning in a cold water bath for two hours and if still dead, add vinegar and soak for an hour more*" (*Cure*, p. 1). That initial entry like the novel's title seems to promise something magical and extraordinary, though beside it her mother has scribbled the derisive comment, "*Ha! Ha!*" Into that small textual conflict is coded the ambiguous relation between fact and fantasy, which characterizes Beth's narrative, though the impossible yearning to repair irreparable damage that is signaled here is evidently a feature of the mother's story as well. The folkloric remedy may be discredited by the rational mind, but having been written down it is not crossed out as it sits between the recipe for her father's favorite oatcakes and the pressed butterfly with a broken wing, the image of her mother's optimism and determination to survive against all odds. The scrapbook itself has all the charm of a handmade book where "every page was different" and it appears to have a mysterious life of its own as its pages proliferate with her mother's daily additions of recipes, cartoons, newspaper clippings of local events, and pressed flowers. This is her mother's secret chronicle of her life, always there in open view on her rocking chair but forbidden territory to the rest of the family. From one perspective it may be nothing more than one woman's fragmented record of "footnotes to the events of the day," but for her daughter it remains an object of fascination, as even after her mother's death she keeps finding new entries "as if my mother still sits each morning before I wake and copies a recipe" (*Cure*, p. 2). This is evidently a novel about Beth's longing for her lost mother and her scrapbook provides the most authentic means of assuaging a feeling very much like homesickness, where Beth sets out to reconstruct her mother's life and her own.

Beth gives the details for many of her mother's recipes—her Sally Lunn Teacake, Daffodil Cake, Bird's Nest Puddings—and the tastes and smells of country cooking permeate the novel, both in the mother's kitchen and in community celebrations like the Dominion Day Picnic or the annual Fowl Supper: "The food, though—you couldn't help getting distracted by the food" (*Cure*, p. 140). In this sense, the scrapbook contributes to the impression of a pioneer woman's narrative, where the regular domestic rhythms of farm work, women's gossip, and women's friendships are at the heart of social life. Everything that happens is jumbled together in the scrapbook, including unsettling events like the Swede's barn fire and the children gone missing on the reserve as well as the funeral notice of Beth's classmate Sarah Kemp who was killed by a bear. There is not much personal comment, though there is one notable exception where Beth finds her own name written in bold letters followed by an exclamation mark after the newspaper warning about bear attacks. Her mother's account conforms to the conventional limits of the feminine role, so that it is full of gaps and silences following a conscious strategy of editing out a great many unspeakable things that happen very close to home. The scrapbook shows the same quality of a woman's self-effacement that Misao Dean has described in her analysis of nineteenth-century pioneer narratives: "The ideology of the domestic woman held that her behaviour was governed by inner virtues such as modesty, frugality, devotion to duty, and self-control."[4] A woman's text becomes what Dean describes as "an ideological mending basket" which remakes the connections between the economic behavior demanded of female immigrants and their feminine inner selves. As Beth remarks while sitting in the kitchen watching her mother making raspberry buns "as if her life depended" on their fluffiness, that kitchen is a place of "warm, happy seduction" (*Cure*, p. 66), which covers over the enormous tensions that threaten to wreck this household.

Incest is the unspeakable secret that lurks in the gaps between the recipes and the pressed flowers, excluded from the discourse of dailiness but ever-present as unacknowledged threat and ready to spring out at any time like Freud's *unheimlich*, both familiar and alien. Though Beth lacks a language to speak of her father's sexual abuse, her traumatic experience is "spoken" through her body, translated into the pathological symptom of her "lightning arm," which seems to have an involuntary life of its own, sometimes going dead and sometimes swelling with an access of rage and power. A similar displacement is manifest in the fantastic imagery of nightmare, which pervades her narrative with its seemingly unlocalizable hysterical fears. For her mother, this repressed knowledge and her powerlessness to protect her daughter takes a different form of expression. She does find the words to say it, as rocking backwards and forwards in her chair, she gabbles to her dead mother in her secret language. From the fragments of those insane conversations with phrases like "Hell to pay," or "No, no, I can't do that" (*Cure*, p. 35), Beth knows that her mother is speaking about what her father is doing to her and that her mother is tempted to commit him to the lunatic asylum (which she finally does, though that event too is omitted from the scrapbook). Fascinatingly, the unspeakable knowledge is wordlessly coded into the scrapbook in the form of "a little square cut from a pair of nylons" (*Cure*, p. 219), though Beth only reveals this information much later on the night of the barn fire when her father is taken away. In the most detailed account that she gives of the scrapbook's contents Beth notes the tangible evidence of the disastrous nylons that her father had given her after one of his brutal assaults, and also something that she had not mentioned at the beginning: "On the space between the cure for death by lightning and the butterfly with its wing torn away... my mother had written my name and the date lightning had left my arm something close to useless" (*Cure*, p. 219). It is at precisely this point in Beth's narrative that Filthy Billy, Beth's loving protector and the closest figure to a holy fool, reminds Beth that she is trespassing into forbidden territory: "You should (shit) leave that alone" and "That's (fuck) your mother's private place" (*Cure*, pp. 219–20). Billy recognizes the uncanny when he sees it; after all, he has suffered all his life from Tourette's Syndrome and watched the onset of his epileptic fits, and he knows that the uncanny is "the name for everything that ought to have remained... secret and hidden but has come to light."[5] Billy insists on respect for the unexplained mysteries in other peoples' lives, arguing that the scrapbook is her mother's secret refuge where she is free to choose what to record and what to leave hidden in her own version of life writing. If Beth later uses the scrapbook as the basis for her memoir, all she has is "a collection of odds and ends" that she will use to tell her own very different version of a woman's life.

When the reader first meets Beth she is hiding in a hollow tree stump down beside the creek not far from her house, uncertain, afraid, and threatened by an unnameable "it" that is stalking her in the bush. The wilderness places in this novel are neither the empty spaces of white colonial myth nor are they the spaces of liberation "for women writers's exploration of female difference and a site of resistance to traditional structures of patriarchy and imperialism" as they have been figured in many contemporary Canadian women's fictions.[6] Anderson-Dargatz's bush territory is a dangerous place to be, situated on the borderlines between the haunted wilderness of Aboriginal legend and a frighteningly realistic terrain where children disappear and girls are sometimes raped and killed. Beth is sure that she is being followed, but is the stalker human or supernatural? The story is very ambiguous, for it is not entirely clear how much is real and how much is a figment of Beth's frightened imagination. Initially Beth's language for speaking about her fears is imprecise and inconsistent, for this is the voice of a bewildered adolescent traumatized by her own abuse and terrified by the various stories circulating around the murder of Sarah Kemp. While the white farmers declare that she was killed by a crazed bear, the Natives assert that she was killed by a man possessed by the spirit of Coyote. At the funeral Beth notices Coyote Jack, the town eccentric, creeping up to put a bunch of fading lilacs on Sarah Kemp's grave, and she records his appearances from time to time outside their kitchen window or standing beside the road watching her, though those pieces of information only sit on the margins of her life. At the storm center of Beth's narrative is her relationship with her father, though it is unclear at the beginning why she does not wish to be alone with him, or why when he suddenly appears beside the barn one night it "scares my heart into my throat" (*Cure*, p. 31). It is only when Bertha Moses and her daughters come to visit and Bertha starts talking about Coyote the Native Trickster figure who "keeps getting born, over and over" and who takes possession of a person "like them demons in the Bible" (*Cure*, p. 72), that Beth begins to find a figurative language through which to speak about the pain associated with her experience of sexual abuse. Even then, such language allows her to keep it in the dimensions of the nonrealistic and at one remove from conscious acknowledgment.

From one perspective this is a story about mothers and daughters, but there is a more threatening subtext here that concerns a father and his daughter and then radiates out into the wider territory of male violence. The novel pays a great deal of attention to female bodies. Beth's own adolescent body is the center of her story where she is lusted after, physically threatened, and sexually abused by a variety of men including her own father. There is also the murdered body of the white girl Sarah Kemp whose funeral happens early in the narrative and whose mysterious fate is referred to repeatedly, with warnings to Beth not to go wandering in the bush, especially at night. There are the stigmatized bodies of the Aboriginal women Bertha's daughters, all marked by physical peculiarities like their different colored eyes, webbed fingers or extra fingers, and even a newly born girl baby with purple-red patches on her face who looks like a puppy. In addition, the body of Beth's girl friend Nora is marked by self-abuse for Nora cuts herself, and her exit from the novel is marked in a trail of blood on the snow, which flows from the gashes she has made in her arms. Those signs of female victimization have their parallels in the nonhuman world as well, with the cow butchered by Beth's father in his mad attempt to remove her ovaries to make her fatten up for market, and the ewe savaged by a coyote whose blood like Nora's stains the snow as the coyote eats out her belly. Beth's narrative depicts a savagely misogynist world of male violence against the female species.

Yet this representation of malaise crosses gender boundaries, for the novel is full of damaged male bodies and psyches as well. Most of the men in Turtle Valley are disabled, eccentric, or mad, like Beth's father who was wounded in the head during World War I, or those born with congenital disabilities. These are the only males left in a community that has been depleted of young men who have gone off to the war in Europe: "A dispute over a strip of land half a world away had taken up all the young men and many of the young women besides" (*Cure*, p. 219). Beth inhabits a world pervaded by physical and moral madness that spreads like an infection through her home and out into the wilderness making them both unhomely places, and then across into the Native reserve, to disperse itself in the wider dimension of World War II.

It is Beth's attempt to find her own position in the damaged hostile world around her that leads to her white appropriation of the Coyote figure out of Aboriginal legend. Coyote, the shape-shifting Trickster, is a figure of enormous complexity in North American Native culture, a boundary crosser between animal and human, male and female, reality and fantasy, and the Coyote figure under any of his/her multiple names may be deployed across a huge range of positive and negative values. Coyote may operate as a powerful image for the survival of indigenous culture, while on the other hand Coyote may be taken as representative of anarchy and destructiveness.[7] In Beth's narrative Coyotes first appear as part of the realistic documentation of country life where they are predators who regularly attack chickens and sheep. Beth on several occasions sees animals savaged by coyotes, she and her brother regularly trap coyotes (Dan even has a recipe from Bertha for Coyote Scent, which appears on the back cover of the novel), and her bedroom is festooned with coyote skins stretched out to dry, where she can see "their dark eyeholes watching me" (*Cure*, p. 263). In the world of the white farmer coyotes are cunning predators but in Native legend they are invested with supernatural powers, and it is in this context that Coyote assumes his real significance in the novel. I say "he" because the figure here is definitely male and always associated with the destructive forces of madness and sexual violence.

It is Bertha Moses who first suggests to Beth's mother that her husband's increasingly violent bouts of insanity are due to Coyote: "I think what's got hold of Coyote Jack's got hold of your John" (*Cure*, p. 15), and her Coyote stories to Beth and Nora are all warnings against the dangers of wandering alone in the bush, now that "Coyote's back, sneaking around" (*Cure*, p. 108): "You be careful running around in the bush," said Bertha. "You'll end up like that Kemp girl. She's not the first to go like that...Coyote owns the bush. He always has" (*Cure*, p. 117). Bertha carefully chooses which Coyote stories to tell from a vast repertoire, for she tells the girls only the "scary ones" where Coyote is presented in a very negative light as a troublemaker, a thief, and a danger to women: "Coyote killed all his wives sooner or later" (*Cure*, p. 169) and "The things Coyote does, well, he does us women no good" (*Cure*, p. 241). Yet Bertha refuses to present this slippery figure so onedimensionally: "But that's too simple. He's not a bad guy exactly. No good guys and bad guys. The world doesn't work like that" (*Cure*, p. 170). Through her storytelling she tries to make Beth understand that Coyote is more like an anarchic concept closely bound up with the dynamic forces of creation and destruction, and she even gives Beth a glimpse of Coyote from the Aboriginal perspective on white colonization: "Did you know your ancestors, you white people, came from Coyote? You are his children." Actually Bertha's stories represent quite a complex figuring of Coyote as belonging to both culture and nature, an elemental force and an agent of history: "He gave us night and day, the seasons. Just like his children, you white people, he gave us good things and lots that weren't so good. In the stories, in the end, Coyote learns to feel sorry for what he done. Maybe some day his kids will learn to feel sorry for what they done. Maybe some day they'll come around" (*Cure*, p. 171). Bertha's stories are deliberately open-ended with no explicit moral: "It's just a story. You take what you want from it" (*Cure*, p. 170). Her oral storytelling method is a perfect illustration of the Native ethic of educating by "non-interference," as two Canadian Ojibwa cultural critics have recently described this principle: "You will often be told a story which seems to have nothing whatever to do with the question asked or the problem raised. You are given the autonomy to discover the relevance of the reply and hence to work out the problem for yourself. This is a sign of respect."[8]

What Beth chooses to take from Bertha's tales is a radically simplified version of Coyote as sexual predator, a fantasy figure on to which she can project all her sexual terrors as a victim of incest, for she uses Bertha's stories like her mother's scrapbook to figure out her own story. However, looked at from the perspective of race rather than gender, Beth's oversimplifications of Aboriginal legends might be interpreted a little differently. The questions Toni Morrison asks in her analysis of the significance of race in white American literature in *Playing in the Dark* might also be asked of this text in relation to Aboriginality, concerned as it is with the construction of a white Canadian girl's identity: "First, the Africanist character as surrogate and enabler. In what ways does the imaginative encounter with Africanism enable white writers to think about themselves?"[9] The answers in *Cure* are quite complex, for although Beth like her mother will have nothing to do with the racism that characterizes her father's attitude toward Aboriginal people and that of the white community generally (Beth is even called an "Indian lover" and a "squaw" by her classmates because of her friendship with Nora from the reserve, p. 89), she is still very aware of the separation between her home and the reserve, and the cultural gap between white and Native communities. She never goes far into the reserve nor into Native culture, for though she visits Bertha's house several times with Nora where she listens enthralled to Bertha's Coyote stories and enjoys being a guest in what seems like a safer alternative world, she does not learn a word of any Native language. She always remains a visitor, and it is Bertha who with great dignity never allows Beth to forget the distinction between Aboriginals and "you white people." Similarly, Bertha and her daughters are exotic visitors to Beth's mother's house, arriving like a parade of extravagant femininity and departing to the sound of birds and bells and singing: "Purple swallows zoomed around them. Bertha Moses and her daughters and her daughters' daughters sang hymns of praise all the way into town" (*Cure*, p. 15).

Beth and Nora develop a mutual fascination, bridging cultural and racial gaps through erotic desire as their friendship becomes an intense adolescent romantic love relationship. The two lonely girls, both victims of parental abuse and both socially ostracized, find comfort together in the realm of shared secrets and sexual play, and their meetings in the old Native winter house in the forest are among the most idyllic interludes in the novel. However, their relationship can only flourish in a wilderness space cut off from reality, and Nora's desire to escape with Beth to Vancouver, "We'll say we're sisters" (*Cure*, p. 272) only serves to remind Beth of the difference between romantic fantasy and real life. Finally Beth rejects Nora's love and the marginality that her lifestyle represents and instead she chooses to stay with the domestic obligations of her home life to which her primary loyalties are given, supported by the heterosexual love that Billy offers. Nora becomes an outcast figure as she vanishes down the road and out of the novel, watched by Beth and Billy and leaving behind her a trail of blood spots: " 'She'll get into some trouble,' said Billy" (*Cure*, p. 284).

Apparently race is not the crucial marker of difference here for Beth accepts Billy as her lover, and he like Nora is of mixed race. Brought up in the reserve by Bertha when his German-born mother left and his Native father committed suicide, he is regarded as Native throughout the novel. Billy embodies the pattern of racial hybridity that has a long history in the Turtle Valley community, though it is frequently marginalized under the category of "Indian" and banished to life on the reserve. Beth's choice of Billy dismantles this false racial binary, though questions of cultural identity are still to be resolved. Billy is represented at his gentlest and most caring in Beth's white home environment, sitting in her mother's kitchen or later assisting her invalid father when he returns home from the asylum, and all the wild behavior attributable to his epileptic fits (or what he would call his invasions by Coyote) takes place outdoors in wilderness territory. It is only when Billy is "transformed" that Beth really accepts his courtship, and she remains very doubtful about his Native beliefs. Beth seems to suffer from the "double temptation" of some white writers that Canadian American critic Arnold Davidson described, who on the one hand are fascinated by Aboriginal modes of relating to the world yet on the other hand desire to hold on to their own cultural certainties, so that they are constrained "to admit the romanticism at the heart of any desire to escape... The two temptations are inextricably linked, and the resonance between the two sounds persistently in the fictions of a complex artist."[10] This in-between position would seem to be dramatized here in Beth's story.

To return to Coyote as Beth's dark fantasy figure is to look again at her way of writing about sexual violation. Significantly, her father's incestuous abuse remains substantially outside verbal inscription in the text, and all Beth records are her panic fears of being left alone with him or his thunderous command, "Go to your room!" On the one occasion when she describes being raped, she writes as a split subject who dissociates herself completely from her body, as so many accounts by incest survivors confirm: "I removed myself into the forget-me-nots painted on the headboard of my bed, and watched from there, leaving all the fear and anger in my body. It was a moonless night" (*Cure*, p. 184). Beth retreats from physical sensation into a language of denial: "I felt nothing. I wasn't there. He didn't do that thing to me. That wisp of a black blanket under him wasn't me."[11] Beth cannot find words for this outrage though she does go outside and scream loudly, where "the sound was separate from me and had the power of many voices and made the sky expansive and huge." When she comes back into the house, her mother (who must have been awake all the time) asks her what happened, to which Beth replies "I don't know." Mother and daughter lack a language for speaking together about normal female sexuality let alone sexual abuse, and the gap of silence between them registers a shared trauma that is never healed. It marks the limits of her mother's power, just as it leaves Beth alone to devise a language and a strategy through which to resist the abuses of patriarchal domination. Only once are coyotes explicitly connected with Beth's subjective recognition of her father's assaults, and that is her nightmare on Christmas Eve when she dreams that like a sheep, she is being savaged by coyotes. Even then, the connection flickers as Beth resists her oneiric knowledge; the coyote skins on her bedroom wall come alive, swishing their wet tails between her legs and over her belly, pressing their claws over her mouth, before the climax of the dream when she finally sees the real monster plainly: "I hid my dream self in the darkest corner of my room and watched the shadows of the coyotes suck the breath from my body. When they had their fill, the shadows sighed deeply, came together, and took the form of my father" (*Cure*, p. 264).

When talking about Coyote Jack Beth comes closest to the Native magical interpretations that she has been hearing ever since the death of Sarah Kemp. She is sure that she is being stalked, for she hears a man's footsteps and swooshing noises in the grass behind her, just as once when she has been followed she turns to see a disembodied pair of hands clutching the boards of the home fence. Nora warns her that possibly Coyote Jack really is a coyote: "The bush makes you change shape, takes away your man-body, makes you into an animal" (Cure, p. 132). When finally her attacker materializes on Christmas night it is indeed Coyote Jack, though in her panic Beth believes that she sees the supernatural shapechanger (Cure, p. 272). In this crisis as Beth is thrown down in the snow and struggles for her life, her rational mind gives way to perceptions based on instinct alone and her vision distorts so that boundaries blur between the figure of the man and the savage force that he represents: "His body flitted back and forth between man and coyote, then the coyote dropped on all fours and cowered away from me. He bristled and growled. I stood slowly." Looking over to the side of the path, Beth sees Jack standing naked "covering his puckered genitals with one hand" (Cure, p. 272).

As normal vision returns Beth's terror changes to anger, and it is this pent-up fury, the accumulation of all her repressed revenge fantasies against her father, which gives her the courage to ride out with a gun and confront Jack in his own cabin in the hills. This is the first time that Beth finds her voice through which to challenge the brutality of male physical power: "You stay away from me," I said. "So help me God, I'll shoot you" (Cure, p. 274). Behind her defiance is Bertha's survival counsel empowering her in a way that her own mother, schooled in a gentler decorum of white feminine submission, could not manage to do: "You don't be scared. You be smart. If somebody hurts you, you hurt back until they stop" (Cure, p. 168). Exposed and shamed by Beth, Jack shrinks back to abjectly human dimensions as he covers his face with his hands and sobs; after she leaves, he hangs himself. That would be the rational reconstruction of events, though on Boxing Day—as if to challenge the limits of reason and to raise the possibility of the supernatural dimensions of this "haunting"—some extraordinary events occur. Billy announces that he is cured of his swearing and his fits and that Coyote has gone, "maybe for good" (Cure, p. 277), and when Jack's dead body is discovered, it shows unnatural signs of decay: "Frozen solid and rotting. Full of maggots this time of year. I never see the like" (Cure, p. 278).

Readers are confronted with a double perspective on the irrational as Beth's narrative teeters on the borderline between the supernatural and the psychological, which is the slippery realm of the fantastic. "The evidence for everything . . . is there" (Cure, p. 2), but Aboriginal myths and white medical science offer radically different interpretations.

Is Beth's father's madness caused by the piece of shrapnel embedded in his head? Is Billy affected by Tourette's Syndrome and epilepsy? Is Coyote Jack a psychopath and a serial killer? Are there pathological explanations, or are they all possessed by Coyote? These are the discourses of two totally incompatible belief systems, and Beth is caught in the space between:

> "You still don't believe any of this, do you?" said Billy. "After everything you seen."
> "I don't know," I said.
> "You see it with your own eyes and you don't believe it."
> "I'm not sure what I saw."
> "Well, I guess it don't matter much anymore." (*Cure*, p. 279)

Like the disjunctions of magic realism, the two opposed cultural discourses open up a space for speculation that resists explanation and defers certainty. As Beth retreats from explanations, so she disclaims any responsibility for the meaning of the Coyote stories that are after all Bertha's Native heritage and not her own. Beth's narrative brings together her mother's white discourse and Bertha's Native storytelling as she figures out her own identity in a mixture of the two. It is clear that both women offer very different models of female strength and female limits of power, and different constructions of what being a woman means in two different cultures that coexist in one Canadian province.

Beth's narrative ends with her release from emotional chaos and a new confidence in her identity as a young woman who is neither a victim nor a mere survivor but "a creative non-victim," to use Atwood's term from *Survival*. She is also in love with Billy whose gentleness and sweetness come close to traditional feminine values, dismantling the models of oppressive masculinity and male violence, which have so tormented Beth. The ending is like a late Shakespearean comedy with its transformations and promises of new beginnings, imaged here in the sudden coming of spring: "The world was shedding its skin and growing a new one so fast you could see it happening" (*Cure*, p. 286). Like a tragicomedy, there are unaccommodated remainders here too for not all damage is reparable, and Beth's narrative is realistic as well as magical: her father comes home a broken man and the last memory Beth recalls is of Nora disappearing forever down the road. Beth makes her independent choices as she begins to find a feminine language of her own, first making her scrapbook following her mother's recipe for paper but designing a different kind of book: "My scrapbook wouldn't be a collection of odds and ends as my mother's was. It would be a book of words, my words" (*Cure*, p. 287).

Beth defies her mother in her choice of Billy as she deliberately takes his hand when they are standing on Blood Road in full view of her parents, a choice that her mother acknowledges by turning her back on them. As the young and the old couples stand back to back looking in opposite directions, they take on an almost allegorical significance where Beth and Billy represent a new generation of Canadians just on the brink of adulthood at the end of World War II. Both of them are Canadian born and both are of mixed ancestry for their fathers were Canadians, one white and one Native, who fought in World War I, and their mothers were European war brides—Beth's mother from England and Billy's from Germany. These generational differences are a reminder that this is also a historical novel, and the future that Beth and Billy looked forward to is now the present time in which Beth is finally writing her memoir. The novel encourages the vision of a revised definition of Canadianness, which takes account of Canada's history in order to accommodate white immigrants and First Nations people and their descendants in a pluralized society. That vision is now encoded in Canada's Multiculturalism policy though the social transformation has not yet happened for the majority of Canada's indigenous peoples, as Eden Robinson's novel bears witness. There is also a tacit acknowledgment of unfinished process in Beth's own narrative with that curious temporal gap between the young Beth who tells her story and the older narrator who records it. The reader has no idea what choices Beth has made nor what happened in her relationship with Billy, only that years later after her mother is dead she writes her memoir with the aid of her mother's scrapbook, sitting beside her own "white" electric stove. What the narrative constructs is really a promise, where traditional power relations of gender and race are questioned at a crucial stage in the formation of a young white Canadian woman's identity and where Beth's change of heart in relation to Billy is registered as a change from blindness to clear vision. This would seem to have a resonance beyond the context of their adolescent romance, for it marks a necessary stage in a much wider process of social maturation, where white Canadians like Beth learn to accept individual differences across racial and cultural divides, and in this process of cross-cultural recognition find their own perspectives transformed: "Maybe it was I who had done the changing, like those lizards, got a fresh pair of eye skins to look through, so I could see him better" (*Cure*, p. 285).

# CHAPTER 9

# FIRST NATIONS: CROSS-CULTURAL
# ENCOUNTERS, HYBRIDIZED IDENTITIES

## WRITING IN ENGLISH, DREAMING IN HAISLA:
## EDEN ROBINSON, *MONKEY BEACH*

> Six crows sit in our greengage tree. Half-awake, I hear them speak to me in Haisla.
> *La'es*, they say, *La'es, la'es.*
> I push myself out of bed and go to the open window, but they launch themselves upward, cawing. Morning light slants over the mountains behind the reserve. A breeze coming down the channel makes my curtains flap limply. Ripples sparkle in the shallows as a seal bobs its dark head.
> *La'es*—Go down to the bottom of the ocean. The word means something else, but I can't remember what. I had too much coffee last night after the Coast Guard called with the news about Jimmy.
>
> (*Monkey Beach*)[1]

Dreaming in one language and writing in another, translating across cultures, negotiating a position from which to speak of difference and identity: these are the distinctive features of contemporary Native writing in Canada, where a new generation of young writers brought up in Aboriginal communities and educated in white Canadian schools and colleges are engaged in the creative process of refiguring Aboriginal identities and redefining contemporary indigenous culture. In the opening of her first novel, *Monkey Beach* quoted above, Eden Robinson, a young woman writer who belongs to the Haisla nation of British Columbia, sketches out the inevitably ambiguous location of this new writing where the narrator caught between waking and dream finds herself inhabiting two different worlds at once. Like Beth in *The Cure for Death by Lightning*, Robinson's narrator-protagonist Lisa Marie Michelle Hill has grown up under the dual influence of white and Aboriginal cultures, and her story of an adolescent girl's quest to find her identity is also a fluid narrative where borders blur between reality, fantasy, and the dream life. Yet the cultural balance is different in this novel, for nineteen-year-old Lisa is a young Aboriginal woman who writes out of an inheritance of oral storytelling and Native spirituality where the boundaries between the human and nonhuman (or more-than-human) worlds are drawn differently than in white culture. Beth's narrative mode of magic realism may have called in question rational assumptions and scientific explanations as the result of her contact with Aboriginal beliefs and her selective appropriation of Coyote stories, although she never quite accepts these alternative forms of knowledge. From Lisa's indigenous perspective the supernatural and the fantastic constitute another dimension of reality not separable from everyday experience, for "We acknowledge that the spirits of our ancestors are still with us, that they still walk the land, and are a very active part of our lives and our imaginations."[2] Lisa's narrative is full of ghosts and dreams and experiences on the threshold of consciousness, generating a multi-dimensional representation of reality rather than the disjunctive effects created by magic realism. Such cultural differences are important for a politics of writing and reading, for the emphases in the writing process fall differently for white and Aboriginal novelists. Unlike Anderson-Dargatz, Robinson is engaged in the double process of rehabilitating Native traditions for her indigenous readers and interpreting those traditions for a non-Native international readership. She faces the challenge of constructing—or reconstructing—contemporary Native identities through a narrative that both acknowledges and refigures the conventions of white literary genres while not erasing signs of Native difference.

   *Monkey Beach*, published by Alfred Knopf and nominated for two of Canada's major prizes, the Governor General's Award and the Giller Prize in 2000, has entered the mainstream of English-Canadian literature. Yet Robinson writes about a Canadian way of life and a cultural history that is outside the experience of the white Canadian majority, for this is writing from the margins in a different storytelling mode, which challenges and expands the imaginative limits of Canadian literature in new ways. Robinson is telling a different version of Canadian history and settlement as she rewrites Canadian history across generations, telling the story of European colonization and its disastrous consequences from a Native viewpoint, reconstructing the inevitably hybridized identities of Aboriginal people in the postcolonial present when so much of indigenous culture has been disrupted and destroyed by white cultural practices. Cultural identities are imbricated with history and ongoing historical processes, as postcolonial theorists like

Homi Bhabha and Stuart Hall or Aboriginal writers like Thomas King, Lee Maracle, and Jeannette Armstrong remind us. As Hall explains in relation to diasporic Caribbean identities in Britain: "Cultural identities come from somewhere, have histories, but like everything else which is historical, they undergo constant transformation. Far from being eternally fixed in some essentialized past, they are subject to the continuous play of history, culture, and power."[3]

Just as Hall refuses to believe in notions of authentic cultural identity that deny historical realities so does Robinson, who in an interview following the publication of her short-story collection *Traplines* (1996) declared: "I didn't want to start with native stories. Once you've been put in the box of being a native writer then it's hard to get out."[4] This resistance to being packaged as Native is evident in the lack of racial coding in several of these earlier stories, and though *Monkey Beach* is written from a specifically Haisla viewpoint, Robinson's narrative evades stereotypical representations of Native people with its complex analysis of generational conflicts and gender differences among the inhabitants on the Kitamaat Reserve community. Instead, like her fictional narrator, Robinson "sees things in double exposure" (*Monkey Beach* (hereafter *MB*), p. 265) because her storytelling imagination is embedded in her Native heritage of myths and cultural traditions but she is also distanced from that heritage by her English-Canadian education. (She has a Master's degree in Creative Writing from the University of Victoria and has worked on Native art projects at the British Columbia Museum of Anthropology.) Her novel is a striking example of a hybridized text where different cultural systems of representation with their different languages and narrative traditions are held together in tension. *Monkey Beach* is more than a girl's growing up novel or even a protest novel, for it is also a novel about spiritual quest where the protagonist seeks to move beyond personal loss and the damage inflicted on her Native culture toward a position of creative survival and a retrieval of her inheritance. The novel's visionary ending though fraught with ambiguity manages to celebrate Native spiritual healing, asserting the magical power of storytelling. This is a significant dimension of the cultural work that Native artists are doing in relation to their own communities and in the wider Canadian community from which they have been exiled for so long.

Just as Robinson is working across cultural and linguistic borders in her quest to extend the representation of Native identities, so outside readers who are neither Canadian nor Native are also engaged in an imaginative quest, learning to recognize and accept different cultural perspectives for apprehending the world. The challenge for outside readers is, as Helen Hoy aptly phrases it in the title of her recent study, *How Should I Read These?* How should an outsider read these texts so that we do not totally misunderstand and misrepresent their meanings? This is an ethical and social issue that involves cultural as well as aesthetic sensitivity and one of which critics have become increasingly aware since the debates over appropriation of voice in the early 1990s.[5] In fact, a similar sensibility is required when approaching any text written in the "New" Literatures in English or any other minority group's literature, for all these texts are sites of translation across cultural gaps. Perhaps the most vigorous statement by a white critic about the necessity for adopting a more open approach to reading beyond conventional literary parameters was made by the American Arnold Krupat in the introduction to his groundbreaking anthology of Native American literary criticism in 1993: "One cannot decently attend to the 'meaning and function' of song or story without also attending to the situation of the singer or storyteller, his or her existence not just as an artist, an informant, or a culture-bearer, but as a person enmeshed in the usual day-to-day social needs and relations—needs and relations that for Native Americans are both like and unlike those of other Americans."[6]

As a white non-Canadian reader, I have found the comments by Canadian Cree-Métis sociologist Kim Anderson on "reader response-ability" particularly clarifying in making me more sensitive not only to the texts but to my own readerly assumptions: "What is your ability to respond to literature written about (and by) Native women? What kind of education and experience do you bring to this text? . . . I would not ask that anyone suspend their own frame of reference. I merely caution readers to acknowledge their personal abilities to respond."[7]

I believe that as readers we have to work from what we are familiar with in regard to literary forms and storytelling codes when approaching a text like *Monkey Beach*, while paying close attention to its signs of difference and to the guidance that the writer gives us. Robinson is very aware that her novel occupies a border zone between cultures and she strives to establish an appropriate context for the reception of her work. At best we can only read provisionally, while noticing signs of cultural difference in the representation of human beings' interaction with the natural environment and in the dimensions of Native spirituality in this text, allowing ourselves to become sensitized into new ways of seeing the relationship between subject, object, and the nature of reality. Margaret Atwood's advice on ways of reading "new" texts is worth quoting here: "To lend support to an emerging literature does not mean that you have to silence yourself . . . the best thing you can do for a writer from a group in the process of finding its voices is to form part of a receptive climate. That is, *buy the book and read it*, as intelligently and sensitively as you can."[8]

*Monkey Beach* oscillates backwards and forwards between Haisla and white cultural traditions and narrative conventions, beginning with Lisa's dream before modulating into realism with the specific crisis of her brother's disappearance and her search for him. The novel opens a way of access to Western readers by adopting the familiar narrative genre of a quest. The quest pattern is a staple feature of mythological narratives across cultures, though that genre has gained a particular resonance in contemporary Canadian women's writing. As Barbara Godard observed: "One of the high canonical forms of Canadian fiction is the vision quest, or shamanic initiation, wherein the Native woman (or man) initiates a white woman into various Native religious practices through which she attains her creative and personal 'identity'... This has resulted in a vogue within [white] feminist circles for narratives of women's spiritual transformation."[9] Robinson's story of a journey made by a late twentieth-century female protagonist through a haunted wilderness into visionary territory in an underwater world may remind many readers of the narrative pattern in Margaret Atwood's *Surfacing* (1972). Indeed *Surfacing* might provide a way of access into *Monkey Beach*, for Robinson as Native storyteller is recontextualizing that visionary quest. Atwood represented the Canadian wilderness of white cultural myth as a mysterious trackless space full of secrets; thirty years later, Robinson leads readers into a different kind of Canadian wilderness where some of those secrets are named, revealing through her Haisla perspective on landscape the answers to questions raised in *Surfacing* where a sense of the sacred pervades the natural landscape. If Atwood in the 1970s presented Canadian literature as a map of the national psyche, then that wilderness territory is now being remapped through a different cultural lens.

Robinson does not refer to *Surfacing* though her novel might be read in dialogue with that earlier one, and she is certainly very self-conscious about the use of Native myths in a non-Native context. Her teenage protagonist comments on the way she has used the Native myth of T'Sonaqua, the wild woman of the woods, for a project at her English-speaking high school: "I pieced together three of her stories for the final English essay of the year . . . I had to modernize a myth by analyzing it and then comparing it with someone real, and had got as far as comparing her with Screwy Ruby" (*MB*, p. 337). Robinson carries the updating of mythic figures one stage further in a postmodern parodic mode where her wild man of the woods, the "elusive sasquatch" even has his own website at "www.sasquatch.com" (*MB*, p. 317), and Weegit the Raven, the shapechanging Trickster of Native mythology, has transformed himself into a successful stockbroker with "a comfortable condo downtown" whose "small sly smile reveals how much he enjoys pulling the wool over everyone else's eyes" (*MB*, pp. 295–96).[10]

As Robinson ranges eclectically across Native and white cultures, it is almost as if in order to survive as an artist she has become one of the shapeshifters out of Lisa's grandmother's mythic tales, just as her novel is distinguished by its border blur as it crosses boundaries between cultural traditions, time present and time past, reality and dream, bridging gaps between Native and non-Native readers. The novel makes it possible for outsiders to glimpse differences in its Aboriginal perceptions of the double nature of reality. Here is a worldview that resists definite boundaries, where that liminal creature the sasquatch hovering on the borders between the mythic and the real can also have his postmodern location at a website in yet another form of virtual reality. Robinson is telling old stories in new contexts, revisioning Native myths at the same time as refashioning white literary genres for her own purposes.

To theorize this process of the cross-cultural negotiation of identities a little further, I shall return to Hall's essay "Cultural Identity and Diaspora" where he outlines his paradigm of black Caribbean identity formation, for I believe it can be usefully adapted as a model to describe contemporary Canadian Aboriginal identities and artistic productions. Hall names three significant "cultural presences" in the identity equation: "*Présence Africaine*," which he calls the site of the repressed, "*Présence Européenne*" with its policies of colonialism, racism, and othering, and "*Présence Americaine*," the New World where many cultural tributaries meet.[11] (The fact that this pattern based on slave history may be applied with few revisions to Canada's First Nations is itself a devastating critique of colonial history.) In the Canadian context the crucial term to be revised is the first, where "*Présence Africaine*" becomes "*Présence Amerindienne*," referring to Native cultures and languages that were systematically discredited through colonial government policies, Christian missionaries, and residential schools, but which have survived albeit fragmentarily in Native communities. The second term "*Présence Européenne*" does not need revision for it bears the same negative colonial definitions of Native identity with all its damaging social consequences. "*Présence Americaine*" becomes "*Présence Canadienne*," the site of historical dispossession and present marginalization but which is paradoxically also the site of hope, for it represents the border zone between white and Native cultures, which is the only space available for the rehabilitation of Native identities. That is the territory being reclaimed by a Native writer like Robinson, though it is no small irony that Hall's concept of a diasporic identity should become an appropriate model for refiguring the identities of First Nations people whose experience of displacement has all happened on home territory.

Robinson recognizes the *"Présence Amerindienne"* in her use of Haisla words and her references to Haisla traditions and customs. The novel opens with Lisa's dream of crows speaking in Haisla and it ends with her vision of the family ghosts singing on Monkey Beach, where finally she believes she can understand their Haisla language. The Aboriginal language in this text might be seen as the sign of an almost forgotten Amerindian presence, where for a teenager like Lisa who has been brought up in English, Haisla is the language of her grandmother and the private language of her parents but not her own language. Though her grandmother offers to teach her a word a day, Lisa despairs of gaining any proficiency in a community where Haisla is no longer the common language of communication: "But, I thought dejectedly, even at one word a day, that was only 365 words a year, so I'd be an old woman by the time I could put sentences together" (*MB*, p. 211). Yet Haisla carries echoes of meaning from an indigenous cultural inheritance that disrupts Lisa's acculturation into white society. She is on the borderline, an ambiguous psychic space of anguish and vulnerability that Gaston Bachelard has described: "In this ambiguous space, the mind has lost its geometrical homeland and the spirit is drifting."[12] Lisa has unconsciously absorbed a very Aboriginal perspective on the world through being with her grandmother so much, listening to her stories about ghosts and shapeshifters, and going with her on fishing trips or excursions into the forest gathering berries and medicinal herbs, where she learns to see the spiritual within the material landscape, through the double vision that is such a distinctive feature of this novel. Native traditions are interwoven in Lisa's storytelling, just as they are to be found in Jeannette Armstrong's *Slash* (1985), or any of the stories in Thomas King's *All My Relations: An Anthology of Contemporary Canadian Native Fiction* (1990), or Lee Maracle's *Ravensong* (1993). These are signs that indigenous spiritual beliefs are still present in the subtext of the lives of Native people on reserves and in the cities, often preserved within living memory or in stories and religious practices surviving underneath the Christianity imposed by white missionaries and priests. Robinson is exploring how those beliefs might be rehabilitated as a source of psychic and spiritual survival for indigenous people while recognizing that they may be transformed in a contemporary context.

Though Lisa's perception of the spirit world is fragmented, the poetic structure of the novel provides a web of connections between the human and nonhuman worlds, which is figured through the language of dream and vision as she tries to bridge cultural gaps, reconnecting with ancient customs while being a modern teenager. Not only her dream experiences but also her lyric representations of the natural environment of the northwest coast bear witness to her relatedness to a wilderness that is awesome but more than merely terrifying, for it is her home place. When Lisa goes with her mother and Uncle Mick on a fishing trip to Kitlope Lake, her response to landscape is indicative with its multiple layering of realism and visionary experience as she stands at dawn looking over the lake to the mountains and watching a blue heron:

> A log, white with age, jutted out of the water. Balanced on top of the log was a long-legged bird staring out at the lake. At first, I thought it was a crane, but I couldn't remember cranes being blue. The bird's long thin beak pointed towards me as it rolled one yellow eye then the other, checking me out . . . I moved, wanting to run back to wake Mom and Mick but, startled, the bird launched itself over the lake, croaking, wings spread open, its neck bent back into a tight S. Later, when I looked it up in the library, I discovered it was a great blue heron, but while I watched it disappear in the distance I thought I was watching a pterodactyl straight from the Dinosaur Age. (*MB*, pp. 117–18)

That wilderness space where Aboriginal customs and beliefs are still practised provides the context where Lisa begins to see "with fresh eyes" as her uncle had advised her when her mother instructed her to wash her face in the Kitlope River: "You be polite and introduce yourself to the water," she had said. However, it is symptomatic of Lisa's liminal position that she should respond but not know how to describe what she feels or what she has seen until she has looked it up in a book at school. The blue heron and the singing ghost voices that she hears are all tied into Native myths that stretch beyond the history of her immediate family back into prehistory. Lisa stands on the edge of the lake here and on the beach at the end of the novel, just as she stands on the edge of a belief system that is almost lost but is still there. This is the visual image of a girl who hears faint echoes from traditions imperfectly understood but still resonating in the natural environment and which she gradually comes closer to deciphering as she negotiates her way through confusion to an awareness of her Aboriginal identity.

More disturbing are Lisa's sleepwalking episodes and her blurred visions of what she thinks she sees when she is standing in the ocean: "drifting hair of a corpse" (*MB*, p. 131), and "I saw one tiny grey corpse of what was once a kitten, or maybe a puppy" (p. 261), which recurs in another dream as "something in the water... drifting out with the tide" (p. 356). Though Lisa can neither explain nor control these psychic phenomena that actually belong to the subtext of someone else's story,[13] they are registered in the text and their effect is cumulative, so that the final visionary episode on Monkey Beach is filled with echoes of what has already been prefigured. Though it does not remove the ambiguity of the ending, the poetic structure locates this narrative of spiritual quest and revelation within a distinctively Amerindian framework.

As one of the heirs of the revivalist tradition within Canadian Native cultural and political life since the mid-1970s, Robinson shares the double vision that characterizes the "*Présence Canadienne*," caught between a desire to listen to voices from the past and a social commitment to represent the real lives of Aboriginal people in contemporary Canada. She establishes through her writing a context of situated knowledge that relates to specific geographical locations and one particular Native community. Though her novel does not chronicle in any systematic way the violent disruptions of colonial history, the deserted fishing villages and the crumbling moss-grown Native graveyard at Kemano that Lisa visits with her grandmother and Uncle Mick testify to the destruction of Aboriginal populations and cultures at the end of the nineteenth century with the coming of white settlement. Lisa's stories of her teenage friends and her own family trace the legacy of that history of violence in the present in interracial relations and most disastrously in the social problems she observes in her community.

Living on the reserve spells social marginalization but only partial separation from the white community, for many of the Native people like Lisa's father travel daily from the village to work in the Alcan aluminum plant in Kitimat, her brother goes to the nearby town of Terrace to train as a swimmer, and even her beloved Ma-ma-oo, that devoted guardian of Haisla beliefs and customs, is addicted to television soap operas like *Dynasty*, which she sees as another form of myth-making. Though her father makes fun of his mother, joking that "Your grandmother thinks the people on TV are real" (*MB*, p. 10), Lisa's own family life is a perfect illustration of the different degrees of cultural hybridization that characterize contemporary Native identities. Her parents have adopted the middle-class ambitions of the white world and deliberately suppressed their cultural background, though their lifestyle on the reserve mixes and tries to unite white and indigenous values, which lead to a profound instability of identity for both Lisa and her brother Jimmy. There are continual reminders that the Hill family is not white and a racialized awareness forms the subtext for all the Aboriginal identities here, from her grandparents' generation to her own in these stories without happy endings. Her father's experience of racism at work where he was passed over for promotion as an accountant and before that the memory of her grandfather who failed to secure a veteran's pension after losing a limb fighting in France during World War I, frames the social problems of Lisa's teenage friends with their failed aspirations, sexual abuse, suicides, and violent deaths. In order to survive, Lisa has to embrace a heritage of loss and to reassemble the fragments of a damaged culture, finding through that a renewed source of strength.

*Monkey Beach* may be read as the exploration of a young Native person's predicament in being caught between two cultures and her desperate need to transcend negative definitions of Native identity, "to find ways that help me make sense of tradition in a contemporary context."[14] Told from a feminine perspective through Lisa's first person narrative, there is a strong emphasis here on women's spiritual powers and the crucial importance of matriarchal figures as guides and preservers of tradition.[15] In her own community Lisa is an oddity and a misfit for she is prone to seeing ghosts and having dreams, talents that once used to be valued but now are regarded as signs of psychological disturbance. There are clear indications of conflicting views here, none more obviously than when her parents, eager to dismiss Haisla traditions and embrace modern secular values, take Lisa to visit a white female psychiatrist after one of her sleepwalking episodes to try to "normalize" her. When asked if she believes in ghosts, Lisa sits there trying not to focus on "the thing that was beside her, whispering in her ear. It had no flesh, just tight, thin skin over bones" (*MB*, p. 272). Robinson represents a strikingly similar drama of confrontation between white medical science and Native beliefs to the one in *Cure for Death by Lightning*, but this time the balance of credibility tips the other way. Lisa has the gift of second sight, inherited as her grandmother tells her through the female line of her family, for her great-grandmother was "a real medicine woman . . . If you wanted to talk to your dead, she was the one people went to . . . and she made beautiful songs" (*MB*, p. 154). All these are now forgotten and her own mother who also possessed the gift has suppressed it, but Lisa is encouraged by her grandmother to value these signs of her Aboriginal inheritance and to face the challenge of learning to develop her spiritual gift across the disruptions of history and her modern English-Canadian education:

> God knows what the crows are trying to say. La'es—Go down to the
> bottom of the ocean, to get snagged in the bottom, like a halibut hook
> stuck on the ocean floor . . . I used to think that if I could talk to the spirit
> world, I'd get some answers. Ha bloody ha. I wish the dead would just
> come out and say what they mean. (*MB*, p. 17)

This novel is specifically located in present place and time, for
Lisa gives a precise cartographic description of where her Haisla village
is and she describes in great detail the spectacular northwest British
Columbia terrain with its rocky inlets and tall forests, just as she very
clearly describes Monkey Beach. Yet a different concept of space-time
intervenes as realism is blurred by a visionary landscape, for the first
time she describes the beach it is in one of her dreams: "At least I didn't
tell them about the dream: the night *The Queen of the North* disappeared, I saw Jimmy at Monkey Beach. He stood at the edge of the sand,
where the beach disappeared into the trees. The fog and clouds smeared
the lines between land and sea and sky. He faded in and out of view as
the fog rolled by" (*MB*, pp. 6–7). Monkey Beach is represented as liminal territory: it is the geographical zone between land and sea hemmed
in by forests, and by the end it has become an imaginative sacred space
for negotiations between the living and the dead.

The place name codes in the most important Aboriginal legendary
figure in the novel, for the sasquatch or b'gwus, wild man of the woods,
occupies an analogous role here to Anderson-Dargatz's Coyote, as a
trope for wilderness and an image out of a discredited almost forgotten
culture. Sasquatch legends and stories of sasquatch sightings circulate in
both Native and white society, and Lisa's earliest memories are of her
father's sasquatch stories and his carved monkey mask inherited from his
father, which is used now to play scary childish games. The sasquatch
leads an ambiguous existence on the borders between reality and myth,
no longer believed in by the younger generation of indigenous people,
eluding the traps of white photographers, and yet still haunting the
periphery of awareness: "At night, very late and in remote parts of
British Columbia, if you listen long enough, you sometimes hear him.
His howl is not like a wolf's and not like a human's, but is something in
between" (*MB*, p. 318). Lisa twice thinks that she may have sighted a
sasquatch but she cannot be sure, for the image of a "tall man covered
in brown fur" (*MB*, p. 16) with "the sharply tilted forehead and the row
of pointed teeth" (*MB*, p. 315) vanished so quickly into the trees that she
wonders if she imagined it. Yet these sightings are for her a sign of her

Aboriginal inheritance: "As I drove away, I felt deeply comforted knowing that magical things were still living in the world" (*MB*, p. 316). In this context of Native storytelling the sasquatch's marginal existence "serves as a portal or channel for psychic energies, regulating a ghostly traffic between there and here, then and now," which is how a recent critic describes the role of African artifacts in ethnographic ghost stories.[16] The mediatory function is very similar in both cases, where the psychological resonance of the image blurs the rigid divisions between imagination and reality.

Throughout the narrative outlines become blurred as Lisa's memories, intuitions, and dreams connect in a subtext of meaning. This is where the non-Native reader is likely to feel most as an outsider. Accustomed to thinking of dreams in relation to Freud and the repressed (where a psychoanalytical reading suggests that dreams refigure a personal narrative of desire or loss that the dreamer cannot bring to consciousness) readers may be disconcerted to find that dreams here seem to figure the dimensions of an alternative reality that intertwines narratives of the self with the hidden narratives of others. Lisa's dreams are frequently not about her own life but about the lives (and deaths) of her brother or her grandmother. Lisa cannot interpret these dreams very well herself because much of her Native heritage is cut off from her and she does not understand Haisla very well even though her grandmother has tried to teach her: "to really understand the old stories, she said, you had to speak Haisla" (*MB*, p. 211). However she understands enough to heed the dream voices in the old language and the opening dream provides the key to the plot design, as if Lisa's real life only gradually catches up to her dream life. What the crows say at the beginning they repeat so urgently on the second morning after Jimmy's disappearance that she gets into her father's speedboat to go in search of him. Her quest ends at Monkey Beach, the goal figured in dream, where she hears the spirit voices and finally understands what they say to her. Like her foremothers, Lisa has learned to contact the dead and to listen to their secrets as she begins to reclaim her gift.

This story of a sister–brother relationship pays more attention to the girl's development. Indeed, Jimmy's academic success and his ambition as a swimmer with the potential to be an Olympic Gold Medallist seem to run in counterpoint to Lisa's pervasive sense of failure at school. The only times she is really happy are with her Uncle Mick, the Aboriginal activist and Elvis Presley fan, and with her grandmother, her beloved Ma-ma-oo. These two figures are loving mentors who lead the girl back into the forest or out onto the sea, telling her stories and teaching her the old ways of her ancestors. While Uncle Mick educates her political consciousness, proudly calling her "my little warrior," her grandmother nurtures her spiritual development, taking her to the graveyard to speak with the family dead and urging her not to be afraid: "You don't have to be scared of things you don't understand. They're just ghosts" (*MB*, p. 265). Yet Lisa's growing up is full of pain and loss, where the subjective resonance of events is figured almost subliminally through recurrent imagery of an anatomy of the heart, from her uncle's open-heart operation and her grandmother's heart attack to heart failure, heartbreak. Though apparently scattered at random, these images cluster around Lisa's anxieties about her brother as she speeds toward Monkey Beach, and around her memories of the deaths of Uncle Mick and her grandmother. Uncle Mick drowned and her grandmother died when her old house burned down, and in both cases Lisa believes that if she had heeded her spirit warnings she could have saved them. Instead, she is overwhelmed by guilt and wastes part of her grandmother's inheritance on a self-destructive course of alcoholism and drug abuse in Vancouver. Yet unlike so many of her schoolfellows, Lisa is saved through the generous intervention of her cousin Tab, a biker chick who cannot save herself.

Lisa returns home and goes back to school, where her development seems to follow an opposite pattern to her brother's, for it is he who now feels a failure. Having abandoned his hope of becoming an Olympic swimmer after an accident to his shoulder, he is tormented by a lack of confidence and self-worth, and the tragedy of Jimmy's life forms a kind of shadow narrative to her own. Lisa tries to rescue her brother by taking him to their favorite childhood place Monkey Beach, but things are more complicated than she imagines and all she can do is to win a partial victory over circumstances. Out at sea Jimmy is granted one moment of ecstatic freedom when he swims with the killer whales, like them at home in a parallel nonhuman world: "I hold him there in my memory, smiling, excited, telling me how they moved like submarines, and how the water looked so much more magical when they were swimming in it" (*MB*, pp. 353–54). But Jimmy is doomed. Even his romantic dream is shattered when he discovers that his beloved girlfriend Karaoke has been sexually abused by her uncle Josh, and Jimmy goes off in the salmon boat with him, "to make things right" (*MB*, p. 39). Jimmy disappears along with Josh and the fishing boat, and he is the absent presence who focuses the direction of Lisa's quest when she sets out in the speedboat. That boat ride is her meditation on longing and loss, with its mixture of realistic descriptions of tides and weather, her narrative of memory, and the eerie refrain, "Contacting the dead," which blurs the boundaries between human and spirit worlds. The final visionary section set on Monkey Beach is called "The Land of the Dead." This marks Lisa's spiritual crisis and the end of her quest, when out of longing for her lost brother she calls on the hungry ghosts, offering her own blood in a ritual gesture of propitiation. In return she is given the dream knowledge that Jimmy murdered Karaoke's abuser and sank his boat, but that Jimmy also drowned. In her own near-drowning experience when she goes down to the bottom of the sea (following a shamanic ritual that has its parallel in Atwood's *Surfacing*),[17] Lisa believes that she meets Jimmy in the watery underworld: "Jimmy stands beside me and holds his hand out for me. The moment I touch it, warmth spreads down my arm" (*MB*, p. 372). However, he pushes her vigorously upwards and disappears, while the ghosts of Ma-ma-oo and Uncle Mick encourage her to return to life. Saved by her family ghosts, Lisa finds herself back on Monkey Beach; it is here that she has her vision of the ghost dance and suddenly understands the words the ghosts are singing, "even though they are in Haisla and it's a farewell song" (*MB*, p. 374). The novel ends elegiacally with Lisa left alone on the deserted beach at evening, listening to the mingled sounds of a voice "not quite human, not quite wolf," and "in the distance, I hear the sound of a speedboat" (*MB*, p. 374). My reading is that Lisa has survived and is now ready to face the future with a new sense of her Native identity and growing confidence in her own spiritual powers.

Lisa's survival is closely connected with what I perceive to be the function of storytelling for a contemporary Native writer like Robinson, whose narrative opens a way to cultural memory and psychic healing. It also seems to me that, perhaps paradoxically, storytelling functions here in a traditionally Aboriginal manner as a kind of magic that blurs the borders between material and spirit worlds as it does between past and present. Robinson constructs a complex figuring of identity for her Aboriginal protagonists, all of whom are split subjects oscillating between the values and traditions of two cultures. Any singular identity is not possible when one identity is always shadowed by the other, and the Aboriginal subject may be in danger of psychic fragmentation or nervous breakdown. Robinson registers these possibilities in her carefully balanced representations of survival and loss within Lisa's family and community, though this visionary ending does serve to relocate Lisa within a context of Native spirituality. Though it would not be possible to read the ending of *Monkey Beach* as the assertion of an essentialist Native identity, given the intricate cross-cultural negotiations conducted through the double vision of its main protagonist, the novel seems to affirm the importance of the spiritual dimension in any redefinition of what being Native might mean.

Like *The Cure for Death by Lightning*, this novel ends with deferrals of certainty and a resistance to closure, though perhaps for different reasons. One reason might be that stories about the redefinition of Aboriginal identities in Canada as elsewhere are far from finished in real life or in fiction, for these are identities always in process. Another reason that pays more attention to narrative art would suggest that just as a novel like this shifts the boundaries of white literary conventions to accommodate different myths and ways of apprehending reality, so the ending breaks up closure in order to open the way for a recognition that Canadian wilderness quest narratives have always contained echoes of Native myths. Atwood intimated as much when discussing the visionary episodes in *Surfacing*, one of the defining texts in contemporary Canadian women's writing: "There was some Indian influence on *Surfacing* at that point."[18] Yet another reason for the open-endedness of *Monkey Beach* might focus on the fact that Lisa is still on the margins, though with a renewed sense of her Aboriginal inheritance within a contemporary context. If one of the major functions of storytelling is to negotiate a position from which to speak of difference and identity, then storytelling like this can make a vital contribution to the ongoing process of rehabilitating the position of First Nations people. This process involves an imaginative effort to see "with fresh eyes" for Native and non-Native readers alike, in an acknowledgment of "what has always been there. It comes through the acceptance of the stories, people, and histories that have filled our Canadian experiences."[19]

# CONCLUSION

This matters, the remaking of an untenable world through the nib of a pen; it matters so much I can't stop doing it.

(Carol Shields, *Unless*)[1]

It seems appropriate, after my investigations into the multiple ways in which identities are being refigured in contemporary English-Canadian women's fiction, to end with the words of an American-born Canadian writer who has never subscribed to a Canadian cultural nationalist agenda and whose novels constitute a radical critique of any foundational fictions of identity, either national or personal. Yet those matters are almost peripheral to the assertions in this statement that is focused on the importance of the writing activity itself. Yes, fiction is a response to the real often "untenable" world in which the writer finds herself, but it is also an act of transformation where telling stories reinterprets the world from different angles, reclaiming secrets from the past or hidden within personal histories, reshaping and enlarging the dimensions of imaginative possibility through which readers, like writers, inhabit their worlds. Carol Shields emphasizes both the urgency and the compulsiveness of fiction writing with its double dimension of aesthetics and social morality, for the novelist's activity as she conceives it is an act of hope or at least a gesture toward psychological survival. This attitude toward fiction is shared by all the writers whom I have been discussing, though expressed in a variety of ways. For Margaret Atwood and Ann-Marie MacDonald this "remaking" takes the form of historical fictions that question the heritage myths of white Anglo-Canadian history, prising open "the locked box of our inheritance" or refiguring the family tree by unburying secrets hidden in its tangled roots underground, in order to construct more legitimate representations of family, local, or national history through revelations of illegitimacy. History itself provides the ground for optimism in these Gothic tales where identities can only be refigured when the determining power of the past over the present is destroyed. The novels of Kerri Sakamoto and Eden Robinson also engage with Canadian history via two of its deliberately forgotten tragic subplots, though the terms of engagement spell their disengagement from the negative othering that history has imposed. Sakamoto, who declared that "writing is a hopeful act,"[2] has to perform a violent narrative act of exorcism in order to free her protagonist from the psychological damage of the past, while Robinson employs an opposite maneuver. Her young narrator seeks to retrieve her lost Aboriginal inheritance through the magic of storytelling as a form of psycho-spiritual empowerment, where contemporary and traditional worlds may be allowed to coexist in the same imaginative dimension of space-time. Writing from a parallel position of liminality—that of the immigrant—Shani Mootoo figures a different narrative of desire with its doubled hopes of transformation in a time (and possibly a place) beyond the present, as well as the restitution of loss. All this is to be accomplished through the printed word, broadcast to a wide anonymous readership but actually addressed to one ideal reader who will understand the confusion and longing encoded there: "By setting this story down, I, Tyler...am placing trust in the power of the printed word to reach many people. It is my ardent hope...that Asha Ramchandin...will chance upon this book."[3] The "book" in Gail Anderson-Dargatz's novel represents writing as a transformative act where the past is both recalled and transcended by a teller who locates herself at a distance from the crises of her youth fifty years earlier in the middle of World War II. Her adolescent urge "to write everything down, set it down so I wouldn't lose it"[4] is amplified through her adult retrospective narrative that records the dismantling of outmoded fictions of identity and the promise of a transformation in social attitudes toward Aboriginal people, though the narrator remains curiously silent about the realization of those hopes. For Alice Munro worlds are remade through narrative shifts of emphasis that record the secret transformations and reinventions of identity occurring in the subjective lives of her female protagonists over the space-time of many years. Perhaps it is the "hope of accuracy," of getting in "every last thing" (though such a task is acknowledged to be "crazy, heartbreaking")[5] that acts as the writer's compulsion: "Every story is an investigation for me. And sometimes I'm a little surprised by what I'm thinking about it, and I see how it's going to turn out and I think 'Oh, is that what happens?'"[6]

All these fictions are situated at what Atwood once described as "the interface between language and what we choose to call reality, although even that is a very malleable substance."[7] Reality becomes even more malleable when the time frame of narration is extended backwards into the past and the Grand Narratives of national history and heritage are challenged by these female storytellers who insist on writing in what has been left out of the official written record. Reconstructing the past may mean deconstructing the past, casting doubt on historical certainties by uncovering hidden histories, many of which exist only in fragments that need to be deciphered, reassembled, or even translated. It is this process of re-membering what is frequently a suppressed maternal inheritance that constitutes the narrative dynamic in many of these stories, as history is reinvented and heritage renegotiated. Though the inheritors may never be free to "reinvent themselves at will" and some of the damage of history cannot be repaired, yet radical reassessments of identity become possible through different lenses of perception. "Something that should never have been dismantled in the first place" is put back together, or to borrow MacDonald's feminine image for this process of narrative reconstruction, "Something's going to be born. Something's going to come together."[8] From another point of view these reconstructions of history might be seen as ways of negotiating with the dead, tracking back through the subjective time of memory while seeking to unbury all that has become unspeakable through repression or deliberate forgetting. So, fiction becomes a legitimate practice for resurrecting the dead. This Gothic mode would seem to characterize not only the genealogical narratives of Atwood and MacDonald but also those of Sakamoto and Mootoo, writing out of her Caribbean colonial heritage. "Gothic," a very European term to describe manifestations of the uncanny and the return of the repressed, would be the wrong word to describe the Shamanistic dimensions of Robinson's novel, for she draws on Aboriginal spiritual traditions that blur the boundaries between human and nonhuman worlds. Her narrative offers detailed though enigmatic instructions for "contacting the dead" in three easy lessons in a spiritual quest that culminates in the narrator's dream vision of the ghost dance, carrying her back across the disruptions of white settlement history to the precolonial indigenous culture that is the inheritance she is seeking to repossess.

It will have become evident that the identity motif is a basic figure in all these fictions, even if it disappears at times into the subtext of a complex plot. It will be equally evident that the identities of these female protagonists exceed any socially scripted boundaries of nationality, gender, or race as their subjective lives are remade "through the nib of a pen"—which may be their own pens or that of the author.[9] What is perhaps less obvious are the ways in which all these narratives, encode women's resistance to literary and cultural traditions that would seek to keep them in their place; instead, through their refashioning of traditional genres like the fictive autobiography, the historical novel, quest narratives, or even pioneer women's wilderness narratives, they "throw the storyline open to question," or as Munro describes these narrative innovations in spatial terms, they "throw the windows open on inappropriate unforgettable scenery."[10] The fictional protagonists may not be nomadic subjects—indeed, very few of them are, athough many are imprisoned either literally in a gaol like Grace Marks or within their homes—yet they all devise ways of slipping out of the "ugly oversized dress" of their identities. These stories are full of disguises, split selves, dark doubles, and shifting subjective locations, all of which demonstrate "the illusory stability of fixed identities" that is Braidotti's way of characterizing the "nomadic aesthetics" of the polyglot writer.[11] These escape mechanisms may be entirely subjective and invisible to others, but they are no less significant as strategies for eluding the imprisonment of fixed representation—and identities, as Stuart Hall reminds us, "are always constituted within, not outside, representation."[12]

To return to the representation of national identity in these fictions is to come face to face again with Barbara Godard's question of how to define "Canadian" in literary discourse. Are we any closer to answering that question over ten years after her essay was published?[13] Yes, I think we are, if we take her comments on the "conflictual social relations" that in the early 1990s threatened to disrupt the assumptions of Canadian literary nationalism, not merely as predictions but as the new agenda for Canadian literature. While several of these writers like Atwood, MacDonald, and Anderson-Dargatz engage explicitly with the question of what being Canadian might mean, Munro and Shields from their very different perspectives do not raise it as an issue for argument at all, while Sakamoto, Mootoo, and Robinson (all writers from visible minorities) negotiate the question obliquely from marginalized positions of otherness.

How to interpret the significance of such a literary profile? Godard's challenging claims about feminism, antiracism, and anti-imperialism are obviously relevant factors, but so is the visibility of this very diverse ethnocultural and multiracial representation of English-Canadian literature at home and on the international literary scene. It would not be a sufficient explanation to say that evidently there is no dominant paradigm or defining cluster of themes and images that characterize Canadian literature, nor that definitions of Canadian identity have been historically unstable—"Not British, not American"—nor that Canadians for a long time engaged in a kind of negative self-othering that has been amplified into an identity crisis through the current celebration of diversity within multiculturalism. Though each of these "explanations" may code in a partial truth (or even a historical half-truth) none of them can begin to account for the dynamics that impel so many women into "the remaking of an untenable world through the nib of a pen." Untenable worlds may be wider than the nation-space or much more localized and personal, though the need to reinvent reality so that it conforms more closely to narratives of desire is a strong imaginative imperative, as well as an act of optimism: "If you don't believe that change can come about, you won't write."[14] These women's fictions refigure identities first of all in the subjective spaces of individual characters' lives, but also in the wider relational context of social spaces in which they live as embodied subjects. And what are the bonds, if any, between subjective identities and Canadian national identity? This is the question that all these writers are negotiating directly or indirectly, and it is to this project of reimagining Canadianness beyond the boundaries of an outmoded cultural nationalism that I believe fiction writers make their most significant contribution. If national identity is being superceded or eroded by other identificatory markers, then it is time to refashion that "ugly oversized dress" into more appropriate dimensions, though not the time to throw it away and go naked.

"Remaking," "refiguring," "refashioning" are all words to describe the same process of transforming the discourse of Canadian national identity in order to accommodate the heterogeneous identities of the nation's inhabitants. Perhaps the question should be rephrased: How to give the rhetoric of "multicultural Canada" a meaningful content as experiential reality, as social policy, as self-image at home and internationally? What readers all need to know is how a nation in the contemporary globalized context might manage to transform perceptions of "dominant" and "other," and novels would seem to offer one kind of model, providing a textual theater where complex negotiations across the barriers of Us and Them (whoever "we" are) are enacted. Not that women's novels offer solutions, but they do present a more honest recognition of the differences and multiple affiliations within individual identities that need to be negotiated by politicians and social policymakers as well as by individual citizens. The diversity of voices in contemporary women's fiction both echo and revise Canada's national motto, "A mari usque ad mare," and my aim in this book has been to search beneath that traditional nineteenth-century Anglo-Canadian masculine rhetoric, to see instead the patterns that are emerging in the nation-space as women's fiction opens up textual spaces for more heterogeneous narratives of identity in contemporary multicultural Canada.

# NOTES

## Introduction

1. The Multiculturalism Act of 1988 and the Multicultural Program of Canadian Heritage, designed in response to immigration policies, does not include Canada's Aboriginal peoples, the First Nations. Increasingly however, as multiculturalism has become "multicolorism," so the terminology of the latest Annual Report on the Act refers to people of "Aboriginal or visible minority origins" while the Report contains a summary of Indian and Northern Affairs social and educational programs.

2. For the francophone dimension, I refer anglophone readers to Marie Vautier, *New World Myth: Postmodernism and Postcolonialism in Canadian Fiction* (Montreal: McGill-Queens, 1998) and Milena Santoro, "Recent Approaches to Feminist Criticism: Research in and on Quebec," *International Journal of Canadian Studies* 23 (Spring 2001): 189–94.

3. Stuart Hall, "Cultural Identity and Diaspora," in *Colonial Discourse and Post-Colonial Theory*, ed. P. Williams and L. Chrisman (New York and London: Harvester-Wheatsheaf, 1993), 392–403.

4. Carl E. James and Adrienne Shadd, eds., *Talking about Identity: Encounters in Race, Ethnicity and Language* (Toronto: Between the Lines, 2001), 174.

5. Margaret Atwood, *In Search of Alias Grace* (Ottawa: University of Ottawa Press, 1997), 4.

6. Smaro Kamboureli, *Scandalous Bodies: Diasporic Literature in English Canada* (Toronto: Oxford University Press, 2000), 101.

7. Katrin Schwenk, "Introduction: Thinking about Pure Pluralism," in *Cultural Difference and the Literary Text: Pluralism and the Limits of Authenticity*, ed. W. Siemerling and K. Schwenk (Iowa: University of Iowa Press, 1996), 1–9.

8. Homi K. Bhabha, *Nation and Narration* (London and New York: Routledge, 1990), 292.

9. Barbara Godard, "Canadian? Literary? Theory?" in *Open Letter*, 8th Series, Number 3 (Spring 1992): 9.

10. Robert Wright, *Hip and Trivial: Youth Culture, Book Publishing, and the Greying of Canadian Nationalism* (Toronto: Canadian Scholars' Press, 2001), 218.

11. Margaret Atwood, *Good Bones* (Toronto: Coach House Press, 1992), 19.

12. Atwood, *In Search of Alias Grace*, 19.

13. Carol Shields, "Arriving Late, Starting Over," in *How Stories Mean*, ed. J. Metcalf and J.R. (Tim) Struthers (Erin, Ontario: Porcupine's Quill, 1993), 244–51.

## Chapter 1   Refiguring Identities

1. Margaret Atwood, *The Blind Assassin* (London: Virago, 2001), 627.
2. Ann-Marie MacDonald, *Fall on Your Knees* (London: Vintage, 1997), 559.
3. Arun Mukherjee, "The 'Race Consciousness' of a South Asian (Canadian, of course) Female Academic," in *Talking about Identity: Encounters in Race, Ethnicity, and Language*, ed. Carl E. James and Adrienne Shadd (Toronto: Between the Lines, 2001), 213.
4. *Canadian Multiculturalism Act*, assented to July 21, 1988: 3 (1) (a).
5. Canadian multiculturalism is a hotly contested issue, and there is voluminous literature relating to the meaning of the term and the evolution of its social and political agendas. For a recent summary of the debates, see Stephen E. Nancoo, ed., *21st Century Canadian Diversity* (Mississauga Ontario: Canadian Educators' Press, 2000).
6. Robert Bernasconi, "'Stuck Inside of Mobile with the Memphis Blues Again': Interculturalism and the Conversation of Races," in *Theorizing Multiculturalism: A Guide to the Current Debate*, ed. Cynthia Willett (Massachusetts and Oxford: Blackwells, 1998), 276–98.
7. Arun Mukherjee, *Postcolonialism: My Living* (Toronto: TSAR, 1998), 73. This essay was first published in *Essays in Canadian Writing* 56 (Fall 1995): 78–95.
8. For a historical discussion of ethnic minority writing in Canada, see Smaro Kamboureli, *Scandalous Bodies: Diasporic Literature in English Canada* (Toronto: Oxford University Press, 2000), 131–74. On Aboriginal writing, see Daniel David Moses and Terry Goldie, eds., *Anthology of Canadian Native Literature in English* (Toronto: Oxford University Press, 1992) and S. Kamboureli, ed., *Making a Difference: Canadian Multicultural Literature* (Toronto and Oxford: Oxford University Press, 1996).
9. This tradition is outlined in Donald Creighton, *The Road to Confederation. The Emergence of Canada: 1864–67* (Toronto: Macmillan, 1964), 423–24. It is also referred to by Ged Martin, *Britain and the Origins of Canadian Confederation 1837–67* (London: Macmillan, 1995), 282.
10. Gerald Lynch, *The One and the Many: English-Canadian Short Story Cycles* (Toronto: University of Toronto Press, 2001), 190. The British North America Act of 1867 created the Dominion of Canada out of four provinces: Ontario, Quebec, Nova Scotia, and New Brunswick, with Sir John A. MacDonald as Canada's first prime minister. The process of confederation was not completed till 1949 when Newfoundland joined, a historical event commemorated/reconstructed in Wayne Johnston's novel *The Colony of Unrequited Dreams* (1999). With the Repatriation of the Constitution in 1982, Canada formally severed its last colonial ties with Britain, though it remains a member of the British Commonwealth.

11. Internal pressures include competing claims to nationhood within Canada from Quebec and the First Nations, while externally the NAFTA Agreement, multinational capitalism, and globalization are seen as threats to Canada's unity and independence. There is an enormous literature by historians and cultural theorists in this area: Ramsay Cook, *The Maple Leaf Forever: Essays on Nationalism and Politics in Canada* (Toronto: Macmillan, 1977) and *Canada, Quebec and the Uses of Nationalism*. New edition (Toronto: Macmillan, 1995); Ken McRoberts, *Misconceiving Canada: The Struggle for National Unity* (London: Oxford University Press, 1997); John Ralston Saul, *Reflections of a Siamese Twin: Canada at the End of the Twentieth Century* (New York: Viking Penguin, 1997); Stephane Dion, "Federalism and Diversity: The Canadian Experience" and "Unity as Diversity: The Canadian Way," in *21st Century Canadian Diversity*, ed. Stephen E. Nancoo (Mississauga, Ontario: Canadian Educators Press, 2000), 87–101.

12. Homi K. Bhabha, ed., *Nation and Narration* (London and New York: Routledge, 1990), 3.

13. Margaret Atwood, *The Robber Bride* (London: Virago, 1993), 4.

14. I borrow the term "fractious politics" from the classic essay by D. Stasiulis and R. Jhappan, "The Fractious Politics of a Settler Society: Canada," in *Unsettling Settler Societies: Articulations of Gender, Race, Ethnicity and Class*, ed. D. Stasiulis and N. Yuval-Davis (London: Sage, 1995), 95–131.

15. Barbara Godard, "Canadian? Literary? Theory?," *Open Letter*, 8th Series, Number 3 (Spring 1992): 5–27.

16. Frank Davey, *Post-National Arguments: The Politics of the Anglophone-Canadian Novel since 1967* (Toronto: University of Toronto Press, 1993).

17. Lynette Hunter, *Outsider Notes: Feminist Approaches to Nation State Ideology, Writers/Readers and Publishing* (Vancouver: Talonbooks, 1996).

18. W.H. New, *Land Sliding: Imagining Space, Presence and Power in Canadian Writing* (Toronto: University of Toronto Press, 1997) and Jonathan Kertzer, *Worrying the Nation: Imagining a National Literature in English Canada* (Toronto: University of Toronto Press, 1998).

19. Margaret Atwood, *Wilderness Tips* (London: Virago, 1992), 221.

20. Neil Bissoondath, *Selling Illusions: The Cult of Multiculturalism in Canada* (Toronto: Penguin, 1994). See also Will Kymlicka, *Finding Our Way: Rethinking Ethnocultural Relations in Canada* (Toronto: Oxford University Press, 1998).

21. Arun Mukherjee, *Postcolonialism: My Living* (Toronto: TSAR, 1998).

22. Smaro Kamboureli, *Scandalous Bodies: Diasporic Literature in English Canada* (Toronto: Oxford University Press, 2000) and Himani Bannerji, *The Dark Side of the Nation: Essays on Multiculturalism, Nationalism and Gender* (Toronto: Canadian Scholars' Press, 2000).

23. Helen Hoy, *How Should I Read These? Native Women Writers in Canada* (Toronto, Buffalo, London: University of Toronto Press, 2001) and Robert Wright, *Hip and Trivial: Youth Culture, Book Publishing, and the Greying of Canadian Nationalism* (Toronto: Canadian Scholars' Press, 2001).

24. Nothing comes out of the blue. See Thomas King, Cheryl Calver, and Helen Hoy, eds., *The Native in Literature: Canadian and Comparative Perspectives* (Toronto: ECW Press, 1987) and Barbara Godard, "The Politics of Representation: Some Native Canadian Women Writers," in *Native Writers and Canadian Writing*, ed. W.H. New (Vancouver: University of British Columbia Press, 1990), 183–225.

25. Wright's study was commissioned as a report by the Book Publishing Industry Development Program of the Department of Heritage: "Reading Canadian: Youth, Book Publishing and the National Question" (Ottawa: Department of Heritage, 2000).

26. For a more skeptical critical assessment of the possible effects of globalization on the literary representation of Canadianness, see Stephen Henighan, *When Words Deny the World: The Reshaping of Canadian Writing* (Erin, Ontario: Porcupine's Quill, 2002).

27. Atwood et al., *Story of a Nation: Defining Moments in our History* (Mississauga, Ontario: Doubleday Canada, 2001).

28. *Tenth Annual Report on the Operation of the Canadian Multiculturalism Act, 1998–99* (Ottawa: Department of Canadian Heritage, 2000), iii.

29. Thomas King, "Contributor's Note: Why I Wrote about the Indian Act," in *Story of a Nation: Defining Moments in Our History*, 273–74.

30. D. Stasiulis and R. Jhappan, "The Fractious Politics of a Settler Society: Canada," in *Unsettling Settler Societies*, 118.

31. The latest Canadian census was taken in 2001. In January 2003, the ethno-cultural statistics on this census will be released.

32. Stuart Hall, "Cultural Identity and Diaspora," in *Colonial Discourse and Post-Colonial Theory*, ed. P. Williams and L. Chrisman (New York and London: Harvester-Wheatsheaf, 1993), 392–403.

33. Bernasconi, "Stuck Inside of Mobile," 283.

34. Bhabha, *Nation and Narration*, 4.

Chapter 2   "Don't ever ask for the true story": Margaret Atwood,
*Alias Grace*, and *The Blind Assassin*

1. Margaret Atwood's Charles R. Bronfman Lecture in Canadian Studies, delivered at University of Ottawa in November 1996 was published as *In Search of Alias Grace* (Ottawa: University of Ottawa Press, 1997), 8–9. All further page references to this will be included in the text.

2. Anne Williams, *Art of Darkness: A Poetics of Gothic* (Chicago: University of Chicago Press, 1995), 171.

3. Margaret Atwood, *The Blind Assassin* (London: Virago, 2001), 621. All further page references to this paperback edition will be included in the text.

4. Homi K. Bhabha, ed., *Nation and Narration* (London and New York: Routledge, 1990), 292.

5. Margaret Atwood, *Cat's Eye* (London: Virago, 1990), 3.

6. Hayden White, "The Historical Text as Literary Artifact," in *The Writing of History: Literary Form and Historical Understanding*, ed. R.H. Canary and H. Kosicki (Madison: University of Wisconsin Press, 1978), 43.

7. Ania Loomba, *Colonialism/Postcolonialism* (London and New York: Routledge, 1998), 216.
8. Margaret Atwood, *The Robber Bride* (London: Virago, 1994), 3.
9. Margaret Atwood, *Morning in the Burned House* (London: Virago, 1996), 51.
10. Sigmund Freud, "The Uncanny," in *Art and Literature*, Penguin Freud Library, vol. 14 (London: Penguin, 1990), 335–76.
11. Bhabha, *Nation and Narration* (London and New York: Routledge, 1990), 4.
12. Linda Hutcheon, *The Canadian Postmodern: A Study of Contemporary English-Canadian Fiction* (Toronto: Oxford University Press, 1988), 146.
13. Margaret Atwood, *Alias Grace* (London: Virago, 1997), 537. All further page references to this paperback edition will be included in the text.
14. In this discussion of nineteenth-century psychiatric discourse I am especially indebted to Jenny Bourne Taylor, "Obscure Recesses: Locating the Victorian Unconscious," in *Writing and Victorianism*, ed. B. Bullen (London and New York: Longman, 1997), 137–79.
15. See Martha Noel Evans, *Fits and Starts: A Genealogy of Hysteria in Modern France* (Ithaca and London: Cornell University Press, 1991), chapter I "Charcot and the Heyday of Hysteria".
16. Eve Kosofsky Sedgwick, *The Coherence of Gothic Conventions* (New York and London: Methuen, 1986), 12–13.
17. M. Rogerson, "Reading the Patchworks in *Alias Grace*," *JCL* 33.1 (1998): 5–22; Coomi S. Vevaina, "Quilting Selves: Interpreting Margaret Atwood's *Alias Grace*," in *Margaret Atwood: The Shape-Shifter*, ed. C.S. Vevaina and C.A. Howells (New Delhi: Creative Books, 1998), 64–74.
18. Bhabha, *Nation and Narration*, 310–11.
19. Ibid., 11.
20. Hayden White, "The Historical Text as Literary Artifact," 51.
21. Paul De Man, "Autobiograpy as De-facement," *MLN* 94 (1979): 931–35. For further discussion of De Man on autobiography, see C.A. Howells, *Margaret Atwood*, 151–53.
22. De Man, "Autobiography as Defacement," 936.
23. See C.A. Howells, *Margaret Atwood* (London: Macmillan, 1996), 151–53.
24. Freud, "The Uncanny," 372.
25. Ibid., 356.
26. Marina Warner, "Eyes Wide Open: *The Blind Assassin*," *Globe and Mail* (September 2, 2000): D8–D9.
27. Margaret Atwood, *Good Bones* (Toronto: Coach House Press, 1992), 48.
28. Margaret Atwood, *Negotiating with the Dead: A Writer on Writing* (Cambridge: Cambridge University Press, 2002).
29. Margaret Atwood, *Wilderness Tips* (London: Virago, 1992), 221.
30. Diana Brydon, "It's Time for a New Set of Questions," *Essays on Canadian Writing* 71 (Fall 2000): 14–25.

## Chapter 3    Intimate Dislocations: Alice Munro,
*Hateship, Friendship, Courtship, Loveship, Marriage*

1. Alice Munro, *Hateship, Friendship, Courtship, Loveship, Marriage* (Toronto: McClelland & Stewart, 2001). All further page references to the stories in this volume will be included in the text.
2. Peter Gzowski, "You're the same person at 19 that you are at 60: Interview with Alice Munro," *The Globe and Mail* (September 29, 2001), Focus F4–F5.
3. Robert Thacker, "Introduction: Alice Munro, Writing 'Home': 'Seeing This Trickle in Time,'" *Essays on Canadian Writing* 66 (Winter 1998): 1–20.
4. Alice Munro, *Something I've Been Meaning to Tell You* (1974) (Harmondsworth: Penguin, 1985), 13.
5. Alice Munro, "What Is Remembered," *Hateship, Friendship, Courtship, Loveship, Marriage*, 230.
6. Catherine Sheldrick Ross, "'At Least Part Legend': The Fiction of Alice Munro," in *Probable Fictions*, ed. Louis B. MacKendrick (Toronto: ECW Press, 1983), 112–36.
7. Gerald Lynch, *The One and the Many: English-Canadian Short Story Cycles* (Toronto, Buffalo, London: University of Toronto Press, 2001), 160. *Who Do You Think You Are?* is the Canadian title for the collection published in the United States and Britain as *The Beggar Maid*, obliterating this radical questioning of identity in its title.
8. Henri Lefebvre, *The Production of Space*. Translated by Donald Nicholson-Smith (Oxford, U.K. and Cambridge, U.S.A.: Blackwell, 2001). For a fuller exposition of Lefebvre's approach and methodology see 1–67. Other useful analyses of relations between geographical and psychological space may be found in K. Kirby, *Indifferent Boundaries: Spatial Concepts of Human Subjectivity* (London and New York: Guildford Press, 1996), 1–36, and C.A. Howells, *Alice Munro* (Manchester: Manchester University Press, 1998), 4–12.
9. Gzowski interview, F4.
10. P. Boyce and R. Smith, "A National Treasure: Interview with Alice Munro," *Meanjin* 54, 2 (1995): 222–32.
11. Stuart Hall, "Cultural Identity and Diaspora," in *Colonial Discourse and Post-Colonial Theory*, ed. P. Williams and L. Chrisman (New York and London: Harvester-Wheatsheaf, 1993), 392–403.
12. Gzowski interview, F4.
13. The phrase is Luce Irigaray's in *This Sex Which Is Not One*, trans. Catherine Porter (Ithaca and New York: Cornell University Press, 1985), 164.
14. My reference here is to the first two books of critical essays published on Munro in the early 1980s: Judith Miller, ed., *The Art of Alice Munro: Saying the Unsayable* (Waterloo, Ontario: University of Waterloo Press, 1984), and Louis MacKendrick, ed., *Probable Fictions: Alice Munro's Narrative Acts* (Toronto: ECW Press, 1983).
15. Dennis Duffy, "'A Dark Sort of Mirror': 'The Love of a Good Woman' as Pauline Poetic," *Essays on Canadian Writing* 66 (Winter 1998): 169–90.

16. Munro has been charting such glimpses of uncharted territory from the beginning. This phrase occurs at the end of the first story in her first collection, *Dance of the Happy Shades* (Harmondsworth: Penguin, 1983), 18.
17. Jean Baudrillard, *Seduction*, trans. Brian Singer (London: Macmillan, 1990), 90.
18. Though only *Lives of Girls and Women* (which was published as a novel) and *Who Do You Think You Are?* are true story cycles, many of Munro's collections are structured as sequences. See my chapter on *The Moons of Jupiter* in *Alice Munro* (Manchester: Manchester University Press, 1998), 67–74, and Natalie Foy, " 'Darkness Collecting': Reading 'Vandals' as a Coda to *Open Secrets*," *Essays on Canadian Writing* 66 (Winter 1998): 147–68.
19. M. Redekop, *Mothers and Other Clowns: The Stories of Alice Munro* (London and New York: Routledge, 1992), 25–34.
20. Alice Munro, *Lives of Girls and Women* (Harmondsworth: Penguin, 1982), 250.
21. Carol Shields, "In Ontario: Review of *Friend of My Youth*," *London Review of Books* (February 7, 1991), 22–23.
22. Adrienne Rich, "Women and Honor: Some Notes on Lying" (1975), in *On Lies, Secrets, and Silence: Selected Critical Prose 1966–1978* (London: Virago, 1980), 185–94.
23. Alice Munro, "Author's Commentary," in *Sixteen by Twelve: Short Stories by Canadian Writers*, ed. J. Metcalf (Toronto: Ryerson, 1970). Quoted by Catherine Sheldrick Ross, *Alice Munro: A Double Life* (Toronto: ECW Press, 1992), 45.
24. Natalie Foy, "Darkness Collecting: Reading 'Vandals' as a Coda to *Open Secrets*," 149.
25. "Oranges and Apples" in *Friend of My Youth* (London: Vintage, 1991), 106–36, and "What Do You Want to Know For?" in *Writing Away: The PEN Canada Travel Anthology* (Toronto: McClelland and Stewart, 1994), 203–20.
26. Gzowski interview, F4.
27. Sigmund Freud, *Jokes and Their Relation to the Unconscious*. Penguin Freud Library, vol. 6 (London: Penguin, 1991), 137.
28. Ibid., 194.
29. Munro, *Friend of My Youth*, 216.
30. Helene Cixous, "Sorties," in *New French Feminisms*, ed. E. Marks and I. de Courtivron (New York and London: Harvester-Wheatsheaf, 1981), 90–98.
31. "Women Writers and the Prairie: Spies in an Indifferent Landscape," in Aritha van Herk, *A Frozen Tongue* (Sydney: Dangaroo, 1992), 140.
32. Duffy, "A Dark Sort of Mirror," 170.
33. Alice Munro, *The Moons of Jupiter* (Harmondsworth: Penguin, 1984), 111.
34. Munro, *Hateship, Friendship, Courtship, Loveship, Marriage*, 6.
35. Gzowski interview, F4.
36. Ibid., F4.
37. This feminist critique of a nineteenth-century male plot bears interesting similarities to Aritha van Herk's critique of Tolstoy's *Anna Karenina*, in *Places Far from Ellesmere* (Alberta: Red Deer College Press, 1990), 131–39.

38. As if to underline the ongoing revisionary process of Meriel's romantic fantasy, Munro changed the ending of the story in this collection from its original published version in *The New Yorker* (February 19, 2001), 196–207, totally altering the emphasis of the final paragraph: "She wondered if he'd stayed that way, or if some other role had been waiting for him, up ahead."
39. H. Lefebvre, *The Production of Space*, 85.
40. Ajay Heble, *The Tumble of Reason: Alice Munro's Discourse of Absence* (Toronto: University of Toronto Press, 1994), 20.
41. Alice Munro, "The Peace of Utrecht," *Dance of the Happy Shades* (Harmondsworth: Penguin, 1983), 209.
42. Sigmund Freud, *New Introductory Lectures on Psychoanalysis*, Penguin Freud Library, vol. 2 (Harmondsworth: Penguin, 1977), 37.
43. What did the bear discover? "The other side of the mountain" is the enigmatic answer in the rhyme.
44. P. Boyce and R. Smith, "A National Treasure: Interview with Alice Munro," *Meanjin* 54, 2 (1995): 222–32.

Chapter 4    Identities Cut in Freestone: Carol Shields,
*The Stone Diaries*, and *Larry's Party*

1. Carol Shields, *The Republic of Love* (London: Fourth Estate, 1993), 154.
2. This term "foundational fictions of identity" is a modification of Judith Butler's "foundational illusions of identity" in *Gender Trouble: Feminism and the Subversion of Identity* (New York and London: Routledge, 1990), 34. Though I am much indebted to Butler's discussions of sexuality and gender, I have altered her terminology slightly to indicate my concerns with wider social and national issues as well.
3. Carol Shields, "Arriving Late: Starting Over," in *How Stories Mean*, ed. J. Metcalf and J.R. (Tim) Struthers (Erin, Ontario: Porcupine's Quill, 1993), 244–51.
4. Ibid., 247.
5. Anne Denoon, "Playing with Convention," *Books in Canada* 22, 9 (December 1993): 8–12.
6. Carol Shields, *Small Ceremonies* (London: Fourth Estate, 1995), 154.
7. Faye Hammill, "Carol Shields's Native Genre and the Figure of the Canadian Author," *Journal of Commonwealth Literature* 31.2 (1996): 87–100.
8. In a lighthearted and nontheoretical way, Shields is referring to current debates over the emergence of a new continental North American identity, which would coexist with specific national citizenship. As Quebec critic Don Cuccioletta explains this concept in relation to Mexican immigrants to the United States: "The recognition of this common duality of *americanité* adds not only to the understanding of our individual cultural identities but also provides important linkages across each of our national boundaries as dictated by our respective nation states," in *Le grand récit des Amériques: polyphonie des identités culturelles dans le context de la continentalisation* (Montreal: Presses de l'Université Laval, 1991), 41–50. For a more hostile

criticism of Shields's novels as "Free Trade Fiction" see Stephen Henighan, *When Words Deny the World* (Erin, Ontario: Porcupine's Quill, 2002), 81–85.

9. Judith Butler, *Gender Trouble: Feminism and the Subversion of Identity* (New York and London: Routledge, 1990), 6.

10. Marjorie Anderson, "Interview with Carol Shields," *Prairie Fire* 16.1 (Spring 1995): 139–50.

11. Virginia Woolf, "A Sketch of the Past," in *Moments of Being*, ed. J. Schulkind (London: Panther, 1978), 78–164.

12. Denoon, *Books in Canada*, 10.

13. Butler, *Gender Trouble*, 16.

14. Carol Shields, *The Stone Diaries* (London: Fourth Estate, 1994), 124. All further references to this novel will be included in the text.

15. Carol Shields, *Larry's Party* (London: Fourth Estate, 1998), 165. All further references to this novel will be included in the text.

16. Paul De Man, "Autobiography as Defacement," *Modern Language Notes* 94 (1979): 931–55.

17. Denoon, *Books in Canada*, 10.

18. Hans Bak, "Between the Flower and the Stone: The Novel as Biography/The Biography as Novel—Carol Shields's *The Stone Diaries*," in *European Perspectives on English-Canadian Literature*, ed. C. Forceville and H. van't Land (Amsterdam: Free University Press, 1995), 11–22. *The Stone Diaries* is not strictly speaking a diary fiction any more than it is strictly speaking an autobiography. It does not follow a diurnal chronology, and as if to underline the point, Daisy loses her diary on the train to Ottawa and gives up on the practice of keeping a private journal (*SD*, p. 156).

19. Denoon, *Books in Canada*, 10.

20. Simone Vauthier likens this central absence of the mother to a "strange attractor" in her fascinating reading of this novel through the lens of Chaos theory in "Ruptures in Carol Shields's *The Stone Diaries*," *Anglophonia: French Journal of English Studies* 1 (1997): 177–92.

21. Helene Cixous, "The Laugh of the Medusa," in *New French Feminisms*, ed. E. Marks and I. de Courtivron (New York and London: Harvester-Wheatsheaf, 1981), 252.

22. Julia Kristeva, "Stabat Mater," in *The Kristeva Reader*, ed. Toril Moi (Oxford: Blackwell, 1986), 178.

23. De Man, "Autobiography as Defacement," 925.

24. Anderson, "Interview with Carol Shields," 142.

25. Butler, *Gender Trouble*, 17.

26. Denoon, *Books in Canada*, 12.

27. Anderson, "Interview," 142.

28. Shields, "Arriving Late," 248.

29. Ibid., 249.

30. Shields, "The Same Ticking Clock," in *How Stories Mean*, 87–90.

31. Butler, *Gender Trouble*, 141.

32. Ibid., 33.

33. Judith Butler, *Bodies that Matter: On the Discursive Limits of Sex* (New York and London: Routledge, 1993), 106.
34. Mark Honigsbaum, "Goddess of Small Things," *Guardian*, Saturday Review (May 23, 1998): 6–7.
35. Sigmund Freud, "Psychological Consequences of the Anatomical Distinction between the Sexes," *Complete Psychological Works*, vol. 19, 257–58.
36. Butler, *Bodies that Matter*, 126.
37. Carol Shields, *Unless* (London: Fourth Estate, 2002), 314.
38. Adriana Trozzi, *Carol Shields' Magic Wand: Turning the Ordinary into the Extraordinary* (Rome: Bulzoni, 2001), 330–36.
39. Denoon, *Books in Canada*, 12.
40. Shields, "Ticking Clock," 88.
41. Shields, "Arriving Late: Starting Over," 247.
42. Shields, "Ticking Clock," 88.

Chapter 5    "How do we know we are who we think we are?":
Ann-Marie MacDonald, *Fall on Your Knees*

1. Ann-Marie MacDonald, *Fall on Your Knees* (London: Vintage, 1997). All page references will be to this edition and are included in the text.
2. "Jane Eyre in a Cape Breton Attic: Eve Tihanyi speaks with Ann-Marie MacDonald," *Books in Canada* 26, 8 (1996): 21–23.
3. "Jane Eyre in a Cape Breton Attic," 22.
4. "Ann-Marie MacDonald," in *Writers on Writing*, ed. James Roberts, Barry Mitchell, and R. Zubrinich (Victoria: Penguin Australia, 2002), 203–04.
5. Ibid., 202.
6. "Jane Eyre in a Cape Breton Attic," 22.
7. Melanie A. Stevenson, "Othello, Darwin, and the Evolution of Race in Ann-Marie MacDonald's Work," *Canadian Literature* 168 (Spring 2001): 34–56.
8. I am indebted to Marta Belaguer Benito, member of my postgraduate seminar at the Universita Autonoma de Madrid in 2001, for so generously bringing this very significant allusion to my attention.
9. See Suzanne Becker, *Gothic Forms of Feminine Fictions* (Manchester: Manchester University Press, 1999), 66–76, who explores this concept, first used by Barbara Godard in "Heirs of the Living Body: Alice Munro and the Question of a Female Aesthetic" in *The Art of Alice Munro: Saying the Unsayable*, ed. J. Miller (Waterloo: University of Waterloo Press, 1984), 43–71.
10. "Jane Eyre in a Cape Breton Attic," 21.
11. Becker, *Gothic Forms of Feminine Fictions*, 111.
12. Anne Williams, *Art of Darkness: A Poetics of Gothic* (Chicago: University of Chicago Press, 1995), 171.
13. Becker, *Gothic Forms of Feminine Fictions*, 21–40.
14. Eve Sedgwick, *The Coherence of Gothic Conventions* (New York and Ithaca: Methuen, 1986), 4–5.

15. Sigmund Freud, "The Uncanny," Penguin Freud Library, vol. 14 (London: Penguin, 1990), 335–76.
16. See Becker, 104–06 and Homi K. Bhabha, *The Location of Culture*, 9–18.
17. Melanie A. Stevenson's "Othello, Darwin, and the Evolution of Race in Ann-Marie MacDonald's Work," *Canadian Literature* 168 (Spring 2001): 34–56, demonstrates how problems of race and fears of miscegenation are unstable social constructions that shift to fit different circumstances. In this novel race is not a problem in business or professional relations but only where sexual relations are concerned.
18. Katarzyna Rukszto, "Out of Bounds: Perverse Longings, Transgressive Desire and the Limits of Multiculturalism: A Reading of *Fall on Your Knees*," *International Journal of Canadian Studies* 21 (Spring 2000): 17–34.
19. "Jane Eyre in a Cape Breton Attic," 22.
20. Gaston Bachelard, *The Poetics of Space* (Boston: Beacon Books, 1969), 26.
21. Sigmund Freud, "The Uncanny," 372.
22. For this exploration of the old French mine I am indebted to my former Reading postgraduate student, Linda Jones, and it was she who first pointed out to me the significance of the "Name of the Rose."
23. Stuart Hall, "Cultural Identity and Diaspora," in *Colonial Discourse and Post-Colonial Theory: A Reader*, ed. P. Williams and L. Chrisman (London and New York: Harvester-Wheatsheaf, 1993), 392.
24. M. Atwood, *In Search of Alias Grace*, 19.
25. "Jane Eyre in a Cape Breton Attic," 23.

Chapter 6    Monsters and Monstrosity: Kerri Sakamoto, *The Electrical Field*

1. Kerri Sakamoto, *The Electrical Field* (Toronto: Vintage Canada, 1998), 135. All further references to this novel will be included in the text.
2. Eva Tihanyi, "A Sequel to Internment: Eva Tihanyi speaks with Kerri Sakamoto," *Books in Canada* 27.6 (September 1998): 2–3.
3. In 1942 after the Japanese attack on Pearl Harbor, the 21,000 Japanese Canadians (either Canadian born or naturalized citizens) living in British Columbia west of a line drawn a hundred miles inland from the Pacific Coast were evacuated to camps and detention centers in the interior of the province or sent to work as laborers in the sugar beet fields of Alberta and Manitoba. Their property was confiscated and after the war they were given the choice of being deported to Japan or moved east to the prairie provinces, Ontario or Quebec, but were not allowed to return to British Columbia. "Only in 1988 were they granted Redress by the Canadian government in the form of an official acknowledgement of the injustice, an individual cash settlement to 14,000 internees still living, and a monetary award to the Japanese Canadian community." I am indebted for this information to John Herd Thompson's *Ethnic Minorities during Two World Wars*, Canada's Ethnic Groups 19 (Ottawa: Canadian Historical Association with the Support of the Multiculturalism Program, Government of Canada, 1991). See also Ken Adachi, *The Enemy that Never Was: A History of the Japanese Canadians* (Toronto: McClelland and Stewart, 1976. Reprinted 1991);

Tomako Makabe, *The Canadian Sansei* (Toronto: University of Toronto Press, 1998).
4. Robert C. Christopher, *The Japanese Mind: The Goliath Explained* (Tokyo: Charles E. Tuttle Company, 1988), 184.
5. Guy Beauregard, "The Emergence of 'Asian Canadian Literature': Can Lit's Obscene Supplement?" *Essays in Canadian Writing* 76 (Spring 1999): 53–75.
6. Rosi Braidotti, *Nomadic Subjects: Embodiment and Sexual Difference in Contemporary Feminist Theory* (New York: Columbia University Press, 1994), 78.
7. Ibid., 80.
8. Guy Beauregard, "The Emergence of 'Asian Canadian Literature,'" 62.
9. Tihanyi Sakamoto interview, 2.
10. Ibid., 3.
11. Ibid., 3.
12. Sigmund Freud, "The Uncanny," in *Art and Literature*, Penguin Freud Library, vol. 14 (Harmondsworth: Penguin, 1990), 345.
13. For further discussion of the vocabulary of racism and the racialization process, see Smaro Kamoureli, *Scandalous Bodies: Diasporic Literature in English Canada* (Toronto: Oxford University Press, 2000), 175–221, from which the Adachi reference is taken. See also M. Vautier, *New World Myth: Postmodernism and Postcolonialism in Canadian Fiction* (Montreal and Kingston: McGill-Queen's University Press, 1998), 195–98, on the question of racist language in *Obasan*.
14. Joy Kogawa, *Obasan* (Harmondsworth: Penguin, 1983), 83.
15. Ruth Benedict, *The Chrysanthemum and the Sword: Patterns of Japanese Culture* (Boston: Houghton Mifflin Company, 1989), 24. See also Albert Axell, *The Kamikaze* (London: Pearson Education Ltd., 2002), a translation of the manual that Kamikaze pilots carried in their cockpits for inspiration.
16. Braidotti, *Nomadic Subjects*, 83.
17. See Benedict, *The Chrysanthemum and the Sword*, 43–55, for a fuller discussion of traditional Japanese cultural patterns within the family.
18. Christopher, *The Japanese Mind*, 185.
19. It is significant that Chisako's affair transgresses racial and sexual codes, and in a different discussion one would highlight her agenda as a recent Japanese immigrant in love with white Western values.
20. See Christopher, *The Japanese Mind* for his discussion of this topic, which he calls the "gaijin complex," 170–90.
21. My thanks to Claire Uchida for explaining this concept to me and for the reference to *The Japanese Mind*, 185–87.
22. Tihanyi, "A Sequel to Internment," 2.
23. Benedict, *The Chrysanthemum and the Sword*, 145.
24. Tihanyi, "A Sequel to Internment," 2.

Chapter 7    Changing the Boundaries of Identity: Shani Mootoo,
*Cereus Blooms at Night*

1. Smaro Kamboureli, *Making a Difference: Canadian Multicultural Literature* (Toronto and New York: Oxford University Press, 1996), 12.

2. Shani Mootoo, "Sushila's Bhakti," in *Out on Main Street* (Vancouver: Press Gang Publishers, 1993), 60.
3. Homi K. Bhabha, "DissemiNation," in *Nation and Narration* (London and New York: Routledge, 1990), 292.
4. Stuart Hall, "Cultural Identity and Diaspora," in *Colonial Discourses and Post-Colonial Theory: A Reader*, ed. P. Williams and L. Chrisman (New York and London: Harvester-Wheatsheaf, 1993), 392.
5. Bhabha, "DissemiNation," 299.
6. Shani Mootoo, *Cereus Blooms at Night* (Vancouver: Press Gang Publishers, 1996), 238. All further page references to this novel will be included in the text.
7. Homi K. Bhabha, *The Location of Culture* (London and New York: Routledge, 1994), 4.
8. Bhabha, *The Location of Culture*, 11.
9. As a supplementary note, "Queerness" offers another alternative discourse within Canadian fiction, signaling the presence of differences not only of culture and race but of sexuality as well. Gay theorist Peter Dickinson, arguing for the need to accommodate queer sexualities within the Canadian literary canon, which he sees as masculinist and heterosexual, asserts that "a nation's narrative does not tell the stories of all its citizens" (*Here Is Queer*, 148). Mootoo's novel may be seen as part of the same enterprise of deconstructing "the inside(r)/outside(r) binary of national, sexual and therefore cultural authenticity," 7.
10. See Frank Birbalsingh, ed., *Indenture and Exile: Indo-Caribbean Experience* (Toronto: TSAR, 1989), and David Dabydeen and Brinsley Samaroo, eds., *Across the Dark Waters: Ethnicity and Indian Identity in the Caribbean* (London: Macmillan, 1996).
11. Bhabha, *The Location of Culture*, 45.
12. Ibid., 9.
13. For a theoretical discussion of this topic, see Cathy Caruth, ed., *Trauma: Explorations in Memory* (Baltimore: Johns Hopkins University Press, 1995) and Jodi Lundgren, "Writing 'in Sparkler Script': Incest and the Construction of Subjectivity in Contemporary Canadian Women's Autobiographical Texts," *Essays on Canadian Writing* 65 (Fall 1998): 233–47.
14. See Stephen Slemon, "Magic Realism as Post-Colonial Discourse," *Canadian Literature* 116 (Spring 1988): 9–24.
15. Slemon, "Magic Realism," 11.
16. Slemon, "Magic Realism," 12.
17. Atwood, *In Search of Alias Grace*, 8.
18. Bhabha, *The Location of Culture*, 301.
19. Shani Mootoo, "The Predicament of Or," in *The Predicament of Or* (Vancouver: Polestar Book Publishers, 2001), 53. All further references to poems will be included in the text as *PO* plus the page reference.
20. Mootoo's poem offers a fascinating parallel to Smaro Kamboureli's theorizing of the diasporic experience of "othering" in a Canadian context, in *Scandalous Bodies: Diasporic Literature in English Canada* (Toronto: Oxford University Press, 2000), 138–40.

21. Bill Ashcroft et al., *Key Concepts in Post-Colonial Studies* (London and New York: Routledge, 1998), 118–19.
22. Kamboureli, *Scandalous Bodies: Diasporic Literature in English Canada*, 162.

Chapter 8    First Nations: Cross-Cultural Encounters, Hybridized Identities: Writing on the Borders: Gail Anderson-Dargatz, *The Cure for Death by Lightning*

1. Gail Anderson-Dargatz, *The Cure for Death by Lightning* (London: Virago, 1997), 2. All further references to this novel will be included in the text.
2. My thanks to Heidi Slettedahl Macpherson for sharing with me her conference paper, "Coyote as Culprit: Her-story and the Feminist Fantastic in Gail Anderson-Dargatz's *The Cure for Death by Lightning*," forthcoming in *British Journal of Canadian Studies*. I am indebted to her discussion of how the subject of incest is written here, though I have tried to develop this topic in an explicitly feminist context for I disagree with her that this is a postfeminist novel.
3. Alice Munro, *Lives of Girls and Women* (Harmondsworth: Penguin, 1984), 247.
4. Misao Dean, *Practising Femininity: Domestic Realism and the Performance of Gender in Early Canadian Fiction* (Toronto: University of Toronto Press, 1998), 13.
5. Freud, "The Uncanny," 345.
6. Coral Ann Howells, *Private and Fictional Words: Canadian Women Novelists of the 1970s and 80s* (London: Routledge, 1987), 106.
7. The classic reference text is Paul Radin, *The Trickster: A Study in American Mythology* (New York: Schocken Books, 1956). For discussions of Coyote in Canadian fiction, see Arnold E. Davidson, *Coyote Country: Fictions of the Canadian West* (Durham and London: Duke University Press, 1994) and Mark Shackleton, "Native Myth Meets Western Culture: The Plays of Tomson Highway," in *Migration, Preservation, and Change*, ed. J. Kaplan, M. Shackleton, and M. Toivonen (Helsinki: Renvall Institute, 1999), 47–51, and Shackleton, "Whose Myth Is It Anyway? Coyote in the Poetry of Gary Snyder and Simon J. Ortiz," in *American Mythology: New Essays on Contemporary Literature*, ed. W. Blazek and M.K. Glenday (Liverpool: University of Liverpool Press) forthcoming 2003.
8. D.H. McPherson and J.D. Rabb, "Indigeneity in Canada: Spirituality, the Sacred and Survival," *International Journal of Canadian Studies* 23 (Spring 2001): 57–80.
9. Toni Morrison, *Playing in the Dark: Whiteness and the Literary Imagination* (London: Picador, 1993), 51.
10. Davidson, *Coyote Country*, 22.
11. See Jodi Lundgren, "Writing 'in Sparkler Script': Incest and the Construction of Subjectivity in Contemporary Canadian Women's Autobiographical Texts," *Essays on Canadian Writing* 65 (Fall 1998): 233–47.

Chapter 9    First Nations: Cross-Cultural Encounters, Hybridized
Identities: Writing in English, Dreaming in Haisla:
Eden Robinson, *Monkey Beach*

1. Eden Robinson, *Monkey Beach* (London: Abacus, 2000), 1–2. All further
   page references to this novel will be included in the text.
2. Tomson Highway, Cree playwright and novelist, who described his own
   creative process as "writing in English, dreaming in Cree," made this
   comment about Native spirituality after the publication of *Kiss of the Fur
   Queen* in an interview with Heather Hodgson, *Books in Canada* 28.1
   (1999): 2–5.
3. Stuart Hall, "Cultural identity and Diaspora," in *Colonial Discourse and
   Post-Colonial Theory*, ed. P. Williams and L. Chrisman (New York and
   London: Harvester-Wheatsheaf, 1993), 394.
4. Quoted by Helen Hoy in *How Should I Read These? Native Women Writers
   in Canada* (Toronto, Buffalo, New York: University of Toronto Press,
   2001), 153.
5. See Hoy, *How Should I Read These?* 2–31, and Lynette Hunter, *Literary
   Value/Cultural Power: Verbal Arts in the Twenty-First Century* (Manchester
   and New York: Manchester University Press, 2001), 49–64.
6. Arnold Krupat, ed., *New Voices in Native American Literary Criticism*
   (Washington and London: Smithsonian Institution, 1993), xxi.
7. Kim Anderson, *A Recognition of Being: Reconstructing Native Womanhood*
   (Toronto: Second Story, 2000), 49–51.
8. Margaret Atwood, "If You Can't Say Something Nice, Don't Say Anything
   at All," *Saturday Night* (January 6, 2001), 27–33.
9. Barbara Godard, "The Politics of Representation: Some Native Canadian
   Women Writers," in *Native Writers and Canadian Writing*, ed. W.H. New
   (Vancouver: University of British Columbia Press, 1990), 189–90.
10. The sasquatch figure has a significant role in this novel as a cross-cultural
    shifter between Native myth and white technology, though the sasquatch
    website address is one of Robinson's jokes. This address does exist, but it is
    an internet service provider in California and the logo features a large
    footprint and a very hairy man sitting at his computer terminal.
11. Hall, "Cultural Identity and Diaspora," 398–402.
12. Gaston Bachelard, *The Poetics of Space* (Boston: Beacon Books, 1969), 218.
13. These fragmented images all coalesce around the story of her brother's girl-
    friend Karaoke, who has been sexually abused by her uncle and has had an
    abortion. That story remains unspeakable in this novel till near the end,
    though it has already been told in "Queen of the North" in Robinson's earlier
    collection, *Traplines*. They provide a crucial piece of evidence for Jimmy's
    disappearance, which is finally uncovered in Lisa's visions at the end.
14. Anderson, *A Recognition of Being*, 253.
15. See Hoy, *How Should I Read These?* 40; Anderson, *A Recognition of Being*,
    118–21; Lee Maracle and Sandra Lalonde, eds., *My Home As I Remember*
    (Toronto: Natural Heritage Books, 2000), 35–36 and 140–42.

16. Anthony Purdy, "'Like People You See in a Dream': Penelope Lively and the Ethnographic Ghost Story," *Mosaic* 35, 1 (March 2002): 35–52.

17. See Kathryn Van Spanckeren, "Shamanism in the Works of Margaret Atwood," in *Margaret Atwood: Vision and Forms*, ed. K. Van Spanckeren and Jan Garden Castro (Carbondale and Edwardsville: Southern Illinois University Press, 1988), 183–204.

18. Earl Ingersoll, *Margaret Atwood: Conversations* (London: Virago, 1992), 114.

19. Howard Ramos, "It Was Always There?" in *Talking about Identity: Encounters in Race, Ethnicity, and Language*, ed. Carl E. James and Adrienne Shadd (Toronto: Between the Lines, 2001), 114.

Conclusion

1. Carol Shields, *Unless* (Toronto: Random House Canada, 2002), 208.

2. "Eve Tihanyi speaks with Kerri Sakamoto," *Books in Canada* 26.6 (September 1998): 2.

3. Shani Mootoo, *Cereus Blooms at Night* (Vancouver: Press Gang Publishers, 1996), 3.

4. Gail Anderson-Dargatz, *The Cure for Death by Lightning* (London: Virago, 1997), 287.

5. Alice Munro, *Lives of Girls and Women* (Harmondsworth: Penguin, 1984), 249.

6. Peter Gzowski, "Interview with Alice Munro," *The Globe and Mail* (September 29, 2001): Focus F4.

7. Earl E. Ingersoll, ed., *Margaret Atwood: Conversations* (London: Virago, 1992), 246.

8. "Jane Eyre in a Cape Breton Attic: Eve Tihanyi speaks with Ann-Marie MacDonald," *Books in Canada* 26.8 (1996): 23.

9. *Larry's Party* and *Cereus Blooms at Night* feature male protagonists who share many of these characteristics, opening up new directions in the debate around gender identities as normative social definitions that may be nothing more than socially convenient lies.

10. Alice Munro, *The Beggar Maid: Stories of Flo and Rose* (Harmondsworth: Penguin, 1979), 177.

11. Rosi Braidotti, *Nomadic Subjects: Embodiment and Sexual Difference in Contemporary Feminist Theory* (New York: Columbia University Press, 1994), 15.

12. Stuart Hall, "Cultural Identity and Diaspora," in *Colonial Discourse and Post-Colonial Theory*, ed. P. Williams and L. Chrisman (New York and London: Harvester-Wheatsheaf, 1993), 394.

13. Barbara Godard, "Canadian? Literary? Theory?" in *Open Letter*, 8th Series, Number 3 (Spring 1992): 5–27.

14. "Eve Tihanyi speaks with Kerri Sakamoto," *Books in Canada* 27.6 (September 1998): 2.

# WORKS CITED

Anderson, Kim. *A Recognition of Being: Reconstructing Native Womanhood.* Toronto: Second Story Press, 2000.

Anderson, Marjorie. "Interview with Carol Shields." *Prairie Fire* 16.1 (Spring 1995): 139–50.

Anderson-Dargatz, Gail. *The Cure for Death by Lightning.* London: Virago, 1997.

Andrews, Jennifer. "Rethinking the Relevance of Magic Realism for English-Canadian Literature: Reading Ann-Marie MacDonald's *Fall on Your Knees.*" *Studies in Canadian Literature* 24.1 (1999): 1–19.

Ashcroft, Bill, Gareth Griffiths, and Helen Tiffin. *Key Concepts in Post-Colonial Studies.* London and New York: Routledge, 1998.

Atwood, Margaret. *Surfacing.* London: Virago, 1979.

———. *Good Bones.* Toronto: Coach House Press, 1992.

———. *Cat's Eye.* London: Virago, 1994.

———. *Alias Grace.* London: Virago, 1997.

———. *In Search of Alias Grace* (Charles R. Bronfman Lecture in Canadian Studies). Ottawa: University of Ottawa Press, 1997.

———. "Survival, Then and Now." *Maclean's* (July 1999): 54–58.

———. *The Blind Assassin.* London: Virago, 2001.

———. "If You Can't Say Something Nice, Don't Say Anything at All." *Saturday Night* (January 6, 2001): 27–33.

———. *Negotiating with the Dead: A Writer on Writing.* Cambridge: Cambridge University Press, 2002.

Atwood et al. *Story of a Nation: Defining Moments in Our History.* Mississauga, Ontario: Doubleday Canada, 2001.

Bachelard, Gaston. *The Poetics of Space.* Trans. Maria Jolas. Boston: Beacon Books, 1969.

Bak, Hans. "Between the Flower and the Stone: The Novel as Biography/The Biography as Novel. Carol Shields's *The Stone Diaries.*" In *European Perspectives on English-Canadian Literature,* ed. C. Forceville and H. van't Land, 11–22. Amsterdam: Free University Press, 1995.

Bannerji, Himani. *The Dark Side of the Nation: Essays on Multiculturalism, Nationalism and Gender.* Toronto: Canadian Scholars' Press, 2000.

Baudrillard, Jean. *Seduction.* Trans. Brian Singer. London: Macmillan, 1990.

Beauregard, Guy. "The Emergence of 'Asian Canadian Literature': Can Lit's Obscene Supplement?" *Essays on Canadian Writing* 67 (Spring 1999): 53–75.

Becker, Susanne. *Gothic Forms of Feminine Fictions*. Manchester and New York: Manchester University Press, 1999.

Benedict, Ruth. *The Chrysanthemum and the Sword: Patterns of Japanese Culture*. Boston: Houghton Mifflin, 1989.

Bhabha, Homi, ed. *Nation and Narration*. London and New York: Routledge, 1990.

———. *The Location of Culture*. London and New York: Routledge, 1994.

Braidotti, Rosi. *Nomadic Subjects: Embodiment and Sexual Difference in Contemporary Feminist Theory*. New York: Columbia University Press, 1994.

Brydon, Diana. "It's Time for a New Set of Questions." *Essays on Canadian Writing* 71 (Fall 2000): 14–25.

Butler, Judith. *Gender Trouble: Feminism and the Subversion of Identity*. New York and London: Routledge, 1990.

———. *Bodies That Matter: On the Discursive Limits of Sex*. New York and London: Routledge, 1993.

Caruth, Cathy. "Unreclaimed Experience: Trauma and the Possibility of History." *Yale French Studies* 79 (1991): 181–92.

Christopher, Robert C. *The Japanese Mind: The Goliath Explained*. Tokyo: Charles E. Tuttle Company, 1988.

Cuccioletta, Donald. "Pan-American Integration, Multiple Identities, Transculturalism and Americanité: Towards a Citizenship for the Americas." In *Le grand récit des Amériques: Polyphonie des identités culturelles dans le contexte de la continentalisation*, ed. C. Cuccioletta, J-F. Coté and F. Lesemann, 41–50. Saint-Nicholas, Quebec: Les Presses de L'Université Laval, 2001.

Davey, Frank. *Post-National Arguments: The Politics of the Anglophone-Canadian Novel since 1967*. Toronto: University of Toronto Press, 1993.

Davidson, Arnold E. *Coyote Country: Fictions of the Canadian West*. Durham and London: Duke University Press, 1994.

Davis, R.G. and R. Baena, eds. *Tricks with a Glass: Writing Ethnicity in Canada*. Amsterdam and Atlanta: Rodopi, 2000.

Dean, Misao. *Practising Femininity: Domestic Realism and the Performance of Gender in Early Canadian Fiction*. Toronto, Buffalo, London: University of Toronto Press, 1998.

Denoon, Anne. "Playing with Convention." *Books in Canada* 22.9 (December 1993): 8–12.

Dickinson, Peter. *Here is Queer: Nationalisms, Sexualities, and the Literatures of Canada*. Toronto, Buffalo, London: University of Toronto Press, 1999.

Duffy, Dennis. "'A Dark Sort of Mirror': 'The Love of a Good Woman' as Pauline Poetic." *Essays on Canadian Writing* 66 (Winter 1998): 169–90.

Evans, Martha Noel. *Fits and Starts: A Genealogy of Hysteria in Modern France*. Ithaca and London: Cornell University Press, 1991.

Foy, Natalie. "'Darkness Collecting': Reading 'Vandals' as a Coda to *Open Secrets*." *Essays on Canadian Writing* 66 (Winter 1998): 147–68.

Freud, Sigmund. "The Uncanny." Penguin Freud Library. Vol. 14, 335–76. London: Penguin, 1990.

——. *Jokes and Their Relation to the Unconscious.* Penguin Freud Library. Vol. 6. London: Penguin, 1991.

——. "Some Psychological Consequences of the Anatomical Distinction between the Sexes." *Complete Psychological Works.* Vol. 19, 257–58. London: Hogarth Press and Institute of Psychoanalysis, 1953–1974.

Godard, Barbara. "The Politics of Representation: Some Native Canadian Women Writers." In *Native Writers and Canadian Writing,* ed. W.H. New, 183–225. Vancouver: University of British Columbia Press, 1990.

——. "Canadian? Literary? Theory?" *Open Letter.* 8th Series, Number 3 (Spring 1992): 5–27.

Gzowski, Peter. " 'You're the same person at 19 that you are at 60:' Interview with Alice Munro." *Globe and Mail* (September 29, 2001): Focus F4–F5.

Hall, Stuart. "Cultural Identity and Diaspora." In *Colonial Discourse and Post-Colonial Theory: A Reader,* ed. P. Williams and L. Chrisman, 392–403. New York and London: Harvester-Wheatsheaf, 1993.

Hammil, Faye. "Carol Shields's Native Genre and the Figure of the Canadian Author." *Journal of Commonwealth Literature* 31.2 (1996): 87–100.

Heble, Ajay. *The Tumble of Reason: Alice Munro's Discourse of Absence.* Toronto: University of Toronto Press, 1994.

Henighan, Stephen. *When Words Deny the World: The Reshaping of Canadian Writing.* Erin, Ontario: Porcupine's Quill, 2002.

Honigsbaum, Mark. "Goddess of Small Things." *Guardian Saturday Review* (May 23, 1998): 6–7.

Hoy, Helen. *How Should I Read These? Native Women Writers in Canada.* Toronto, Buffalo, London: University of Toronto Press, 2001.

Hunter, Lynette. *Outsider Notes: Feminist Approaches to Nation State Ideology, Writers/Readers and Publishing.* Vancouver: Talonbooks, 1996.

——. *Literary Value/ Cultural Power: Verbal Arts in the Twenty-First Century.* Manchester and New York: Manchester University Press, 2001.

Hutcheon, Linda. *The Canadian Postmodern: A Study of Contemporary English-Canadian Fiction.* Toronto: Oxford University Press, 1988.

Ingersoll, Earl G. *Margaret Atwood: Conversations.* London: Virago, 1992.

Irigaray, Luce. *This Sex Which Is Not One.* Trans. Catherine Porter. Ithaca, New York: Cornell University Press, 1985.

James, Carl E. and Adrienne Shadd, eds. *Talking about Identity: Encounters in Race, Ethnicity, and Language.* Toronto: Between the Lines, 2001.

Kamboureli, Smaro, ed. *Making a Difference: Canadian Multicultural Literature.* Toronto and New York: Oxford University Press, 1996.

——. *Scandalous Bodies: Diasporic Literature in English Canada.* Toronto and New York: Oxford University Press, 2000.

Kertzer, Jonathan. *Worrying the Nation: Imagining a National Literature in English Canada.* Toronto, Buffalo, London: University of Toronto Press, 1998.

Kogawa, Joy. *Obasan.* Harmondsworth: Penguin, 1983.

Krupat, Arnold, ed. *New Voices in Native American Literary Criticism.* Washington and London: Smithsonian Institution, 1993.

Lefebvre, Henri. *The Production of Space.* Trans. Donald Nicholson-Smith. Oxford and Massachusetts: Blackwell, 2001.

Lundgren, Jodi. "'Writing in Sparkler Script': Incest and the Construction of Subjectivity in Contemporary Canadian Women's Autobiographical Texts." *Essays on Canadian Writing* 65 (Fall 1998): 233–47.

Lynch, Gerald. *The One and the Many: English-Canadian Short Story Cycles.* Toronto, Buffalo, London: University of Toronto Press, 2001.

MacDonald, Ann-Marie. *Fall on Your Knees.* London: Vintage, 1997.

McPherson, Dennis H. and J. Douglas Rabb, "Indigeneity in Canada: Spirituality, the Sacred and Survival." *International Journal of Canadian Studies* 23 (Spring 2001): 57–80.

Mann, Paul de. "Autobiography as Defacement." *Modern Language Notes* 94 (1979): 931–55.

Maracle, Lee. *Ravensong.* Vancouver: Press Gang Publishers, 1993.

Marks, E. and Isabelle de Courtivon, eds. *New French Feminisms.* New York and London: Harvester-Wheatsheaf, 1981.

Masschelein, Anneleen. "The Concept as Ghost: Conceptualization of the Uncanny in Late Twentieth-Century Theory." *Mosaic* 35 (March 2002): 53–68.

Mootoo, Shani. *Out on Main Street.* Vancouver: Press Gang Publishers, 1993.

——. *Cereus Blooms at Night.* Vancouver: Press Gang Publishers, 1996.

——. *The Predicament of Or.* Vancouver: Polestar, 2001.

Morrison, Toni. *Playing in the Dark: Whiteness and the Literary Imagination.* London: Picador, 1993.

Mukherjee, Arun. *Postcolonialism: My Living.* Toronto: TSAR, 1998.

Munro, Alice. *Lives of Girls and Women.* Harmondsworth: Penguin, 1982.

——. *Dance of the Happy Shades.* Harmondsworth: Penguin, 1983.

——. *Something I've Been Meaning to Tell You.* Harmondsworth: Penguin, 1985.

——. *Who Do You Think You Are?* Harmondsworth: Penguin, 1985.

——. *The Progress of Love.* London: Flamingo, 1988.

——. *Friend of My Youth.* London: Vintage, 1991.

——. "What Do You Want to Know For?" In *Writing Away: The PEN Canada Travel Anthology,* ed. Constance Rooke, 203–20. Toronto: McClelland and Stewart, 1994.

——. *Open Secrets.* London: Vintage, 1995.

——. *Hateship, Friendship, Courtship, Loveship, Marriage.* Toronto: McClelland and Stewart, 2001.

Nancoo, Stephen E. *21st Century Canadian Diversity.* Mississauga, Ontario: Canadian Educators' Press, 2000.

New, W.H. *Land Sliding: Imagining Space, Presence and Power in Canadian Writing.* Toronto, Buffalo, London: University of Toronto Press, 1997.

Purdy, Anthony. "'Like People You See in a Dream': Penelope Lively and the Ethnographic Ghost Story." *Mosaic* 35.1 (March 2002): 35–52.

Redekop, Magdalene. *Mothers and Other Clowns: The Stories of Alice Munro.* London and New York: Routledge, 1992.

Rich, Adrienne. "Women and Honor: Some Notes on Lying." In *On Lies, Secrets and Silence: Selected Critical Prose 1966–1978,* 185–94. London: Virago, 1980.

Roberts, James, Barry Mitchell, and Roger Zubrinich, eds. *Writers on Writing.* Victoria: Penguin Books Australia, 2002.

Robinson, Eden. *Monkey Beach*. London: Abacus, 2000.

Rogerson, Margaret. "Reading the Patchworks in *Alias Grace*." *Journal of Commonwealth Literature* 33.1 (1998): 5–22.

Rukszto, Katarzyna. "Out of Bounds: Perverse Longings, Transgressive Desire and the Limits of Multiculturalism: A Reading of *Fall on Your Knees*." *International Journal of Canadian Studies* 21 (Spring 2000): 17–34.

Sakamoto, Kerri. *The Electrical Field*. Toronto: Vintage Canada, 1998.

Schwenk, Katrin. "Introduction: Thinking about Pure Pluralism." In *Cultural Difference and the Literary Text: Pluralism and the Limits of Authenticity in North American Literatures*, ed. W. Siemerling and K. Schwenk, 1–9. Iowa City: University of Iowa Press, 1996.

Sedgwick, Eve Kosofsky. *The Coherence of Gothic Conventions*. New York and London: Methuen, 1986.

Shackleton, Mark. "Native Myth Meets Western Culture: The Plays of Tomson Highway." In *Migration, Preservation and Change*, ed. J. Kaplan, M. Shackleton and M. Toivonen, 47–58. Helsinki: Renvall Institute, 1999.

Shields, Carol. "In Ontario: Review of *Friend of My Youth*." *London Review of Books* (February 7, 1991): 22–23.

———. *The Republic of Love*. London: Flamingo, 1992.

———. "The Same Ticking Clock" and "Arriving Late: Starting Over." In *How Stories Mean*, ed. J. Metcalf and J.R. (Tim) Struthers, 87–90 and 244–51. Erin, Ontario: Porcupine's Quill, 1993.

———. *The Stone Diaries*. London: Fourth Estate, 1994.

———. *Small Ceremonies*. London: Fourth Estate, 1995.

———. *Larry's Party*. London: Fourth Estate, 1998.

———. *Unless*. London: Fourth Estate, 2002.

Slemon, Stephen. "Magic Realism as Post-Colonial Discourse." *Canadian Literature* 116 (1988): 2–24.

Stasiulis, Daiva and Rhada Jhappan. "The Fractious Politics of a Settler Society: Canada." In *Unsettling Settler Societies: Articulations of Gender, Race, Ethnicity and Class*, ed. D. Stasiulis and N. Yuval Davis, 95–131. London: Sage, 1995.

Stevenson, Melanie A. "Othello, Darwin, and the Evolution of Race in Ann-Marie MacDonald's Work." *Canadian Literature* 168 (Spring 2001): 34–56.

Taylor, Jenny Bourne. "Obscure Recesses: Locating the Victorian Unconscious." In *Writing and Victorianism*, ed. J.B. Bullen, 137–79. London and New York: Longman, 1997.

Thacker, Robert. "Introduction: Alice Munro, Writing 'Home': 'Seeing This Trickle in Time.'" *Essays on Canadian Writing* 66 (Winter 1998): 1–20.

Thomas, Clara. "Carol Shields: *The Republic of Love* and *The Stone Diaries*: 'Swerves of Destiny' and 'Rings of Light.'" In *Unity in Partition: Essays in Honour of Jeanne Delbaere*, ed. G. Debeussher and M. Maufort, 153–60. Liège: University of Liège Press, 1997.

Tihanyi, Eve. "Jane Eyre in a Cape Breton Attic: Eva Tihanyi Speaks with Ann-Marie MacDonald." *Books in Canada* 26.8 (November 1996): 21–23.

———. "A Sequel to Internment: Eve Tihanyi Speaks with Kerri Sakamoto." *Books in Canada* 27.6 (September 1998): 2–3.

Trozzi, Adriana. *Carol Shields' Magic Wand: Turning the Ordinary into the Extraordinary*. Rome: Bulzoni, 2001.

Van Herk, Aritha. *A Frozen Tongue*. Sydney: Dangaroo, 1992.

Van Spanckeren, Kathryn. "Shamanism in the Works of Margaret Atwood." In *Margaret Atwood: Vision and Forms*, ed. K. Van Spanckeren and J. Garden Castro, 183–204. Carbondale and Edwardsville: Southern Illinois University Press, 1988.

Vautier, Marie. *New World Myth: Postmodernism and Postcolonialism in Canadian Fiction*. Montreal, Kingston, London, Buffalo: McGill-Queen's University Press, 1998.

Vevaina, Coomi S. and C.A. Howells, eds. *Margaret Atwood: The Shape-Shifter*. New Delhi: Creative Books, 1998.

Warner, Marina. "Eyes Wide Open: *The Blind Assassin*." *Globe and Mail* (September 2, 2000): D8–D9.

White, Hayden. "The Historical Text as Literary Artifact." In *The Writing of History: Literary Form and Historical Understanding*, ed. R.H. Canary and K. Kozicki, 41–62. Madison: University of Wisconsin Press, 1978.

Willett, Cynthia, ed. *Theorizing Multiculturalism: A Guide to the Current Debate*. Malden, Massachusetts and Oxford: Blackwell, 1998.

Williams, Anne. *Art of Darkness: A Poetics of Gothic*. Chicago: University of Chicago Press, 1995.

Woolf, Virginia. "A Sketch of the Past." In *Moments of Being*, ed. J. Schulkind, 78–164. London: Panther, 1978.

Wright, Robert. *Hip and Trivial: Youth Culture, Book Publishing, and the Greying of Canadian Nationalism*. Toronto: Canadian Scholars' Press, 2001.

# INDEX